D1715240

'In *Strong and Hard Women*, Tanya Bunsell has delivered an outstanding ethnography of female bodybuilding. The book is a rich portrait of becoming, being, and having a muscular female body. By investigating the question of whether female bodybuilding can be an empowering transgression of hegemonic standards of feminine embodiment, Bunsell offers an important book that deserves to be widely read and debated.'

Brett Smith, Editor of *Qualitative Research in Sport, Exercise and Health* and Senior Lecturer at Loughborough University, UK.

'As one of the first sustained ethnographic studies of the subculture of female bodybuilding, Bunsell's energetic thesis focuses on the *lived* experience of female bodybuilding and the actual process of building and sculpting muscles during all those hours of dedication to the gym. This book will be an essential read for researchers of sport, exercise and the body, scholars of feminism and gender politics and anyone who has ever known the lure of the gym, its clang of metal weights and the exquisite pain of pumped muscles.'

Niall Richardson, Senior Lecturer in Media and Film, University of Sussex, UK.

'This remarkably insightful ethnography examines the women who inhabit the subculture of bodybuilding, an activity which she presents as both transgressive and troubling. Bunsell's approach is made all the more poignant by showcasing the lived experiences of not only the female bodybuilders whom she interviews, but also herself, hence offering an unusually intimate investigation of both research and researcher.'

Adam Locks, Programme Co-ordinator of Media and Cultural Studies, University of Chichester, UK.

WITHDRAWN

MARK & HELEN OSTERLIN LIBRARY
NORTHWESTERN MICHIGAN COLLEGE
TRAVERSE CITY, MICHIGAN 49686-3061

Strong and Hard Women

Females with large muscles evoke strong reactions from men and women, often involving disgust, discomfort, anger and threat. The controversial nature of female bodybuilding has caused significant rupture on feminist ground. Whilst proponents claim that female bodybuilding is a way of empowering and liberating women, others see it as a form of corporeal entrapment. This book investigates the controversy. Do women who pump iron resist physical restrictions of imposed femininity, or are they engaged in an ultimately oppressive quest for 'perfect bodies'?

In an original two-year ethnographic study based in the South of England, Tanya Bunsell immersed herself in the world of female bodybuilders. By mapping these extraordinary women's lives, the research illuminates the pivotal spaces and essential lived experiences that make up the female bodybuilder. Whilst the women appear to be embarking on an 'empowering' radical body project for themselves, the consequences of their activity remain culturally ambivalent. This research exposes the 'Janus-faced' nature of female bodybuilding, exploring the ways in which the women negotiate, accommodate and resist pressures to engage in more orthodox and feminine activities and appearances.

This book will be of interest to academics and students in the fields of gender studies, the sociology of sport, the body and research methodology.

Tanya Bunsell is a Lecturer in Sport Sociology at St Mary's University College, Twickenham. She has been teaching since 2003 and was awarded her PhD in Sociology from the University of Kent in 2010.

Routledge Advances in Ethnography
Edited by Dick Hobbs
University of Essex
and
Geoffrey Pearson
Goldsmiths College, University of London

Ethnography is a celebrated, if contested, research methodology that offers unprecedented access to people's intimate lives, their often hidden social worlds and the meanings they attach to these. The intensity of ethnographic fieldwork often makes considerable personal and emotional demands on the researcher, while the final product is a vivid human document with personal resonance impossible to recreate by the application of any other social science methodology. This series aims to highlight the best, most innovative ethnographic work available from both new and established scholars.

Strong and Hard Women

An ethnography of female bodybuilding

Tanya Bunsell

Routledge
Taylor & Francis Group

LONDON AND NEW YORK

First published 2013
by Routledge
2 Park Square, Milton Park, Abingdon, Oxon, OX14 4RN

Simultaneously published in the USA and Canada
by Routledge
711 Third Avenue, New York, NY 10017

*Routledge is an imprint of the Taylor & Francis Group, an informa
business*

© 2013 Tanya Bunsell

The right of Tanya Bunsell to be identified as author of this work has been
asserted by her in accordance with sections 77 and 78 of the Copyright,
Designs and Patents Act 1988.

All rights reserved. No part of this book may be reprinted or reproduced or
utilised in any form or by any electronic, mechanical, or other means, now
known or hereafter invented, including photocopying and recording, or in
any information storage or retrieval system, without permission in writing
from the publishers.

British Library Cataloguing in Publication Data
A catalogue record for this book is available from the British Library

Library of Congress Cataloging-in-Publication Data
Bunsell, Tanya.
Strong and hard women: an ethnography of female bodybuilding /
Tanya Bunsell.
  pages cm. – (Routledge advances in ethnography)
  1. Bodybuilding for women. 2. Bodybuilding for women–Social
aspects. 3. Femininity. 4. Self-perception in women. I. Title.
  GV546.6.W64B86 2013
  796.41082–dc23
  2012040233

ISBN: 978-0-415-62441-1 (hbk)
ISBN: 978-0-415-82437-8 (pbk)
ISBN: 978-0-203-10475-0 (ebk)

Typeset in Times New Roman
by Sunrise Setting Ltd, Paignton, UK

Contents

Acknowledgements

My most important debt of gratitude goes to Professor Chris Shilling. I have been blessed by his enthusiasm, encouragement, knowledge and inspiration.

My thanks go to all those who participated in this study, especially the female bodybuilders who gave so willingly in terms of their time, commitment and friendship.

I also wish to thank those people who supported me in the writing of this book – you know who you are.

Preface

Alice down the rabbit hole: my research journey through the fascinating world of female bodybuilders

> A journey entails endings and beginnings, loss and retrieval. It offers a chance of change and renewal, but also a risk of disorientation and displacement. Researchers as voyagers, travel from familiar inner and outer landscapes into unknown territories with new horizons…The 'voyage' tenders experimental possibilities for alternative understandings of who they are, who they could be and what they know. It opens up transitional spaces for the formation of a new sense of identity.
>
> (Batchelor and Di Napoli 2006:13).

The idea that research may be described as a 'journey' usefully highlights how events and relationships unfold during fieldwork in a manner that can change both the field under scrutiny and the individual researcher. The metaphor also evokes a sense of personal growth and perpetual waves of transformation that can occur as the adventurer negotiates their surroundings in a pursuit to position themselves and make sense of the world around them. Within this book lies multiple narratives, stories and journeys – not only of the muscular women themselves who embark on their own 'heroic' travels, but of my own journey of discovery which has undoubtedly changed my viewpoint on the world. Indeed I am not the same person who I was when I began this research journey. In Chapter 2, I detail the ways in which I am (ontologically and epistemologically) inextricably entwined in the research project and how this inevitably impacted upon the findings and presentation of this book. However, it is only now, as this project draws to a close that I can reflect back and see just how far I have personally travelled; thus demonstrating just how momentous and life changing the research experience really is.

It has been argued that researchers develop a new habitus as a result of their work, and I would suggest that this is especially relevant to the corporeal ethnographic undertakings of researching female bodybuilders. As I became physically and emotionally immersed in the field and 'moved' through the research process, my interpretations of the world have evolved and transformed. My ways of 'looking' at what was occurring around me were thus changed by my shifting ways of 'being in the world'. My body became 'an instrument of research' (Patton 2002:45), in which lived experiences mediated my initial theoretical commitments. These 'practical lessons in the interaction between theory and experience' led me to question my starting assumptions (Blaxter 2009:765). By 'acting as my own informant' (Rapport 1995:269), I have become drawn to and aware of a more complex and contradictory understanding of women's empowerment and 'reclaimative' discourse than I had previously anticipated. Indeed my ethnographic analysis of the life world of the female bodybuilder revealed a picture of complexity and subjective difference beyond what I ever expected to discover. Subsequently, my narratives (of self and research thesis), driven by continual moments of interpretive recursivity, have changed as they have given way to new perspectives and new ways of seeing the world. This has not being a straightforward linear process, but one of unease, struggle, vulnerability and insecurity, as I fluctuated between certainty and uncertainty, trying to piece together conflicting evidence in relation to my ideological beliefs and my findings.

Throughout this work, I invite the reader to glimpse some of the rich and complex detail that makes up the lives and experiences of female bodybuilders, but I ask that you remain aware of my own 'shadow' presence as a researcher as I present these women in and through my writing. In so doing, you will not just be following the lives of these female bodybuilders, but my own walk through the fascinating subculture of female bodybuilding. Before the reader's journey through the book begins, I kindly request you to participate in this reflexive voyage of discovery – to question and interrogate your own understanding of female bodybuilders and to be open to other possible pathways of interpretation.

1 Introduction

As Gelsthorpe and Morris (1990: 88) argue, 'one of the essential ingredients of feminist approaches is that theorizing has to *begin* with the researcher's own experiences. There is no other knowable place to begin'. For this reason, my introduction begins by providing some biographical details in order to illustrate some of the influences and processes that have informed this study.

Storying myself

There are multiple motivations that propel interest into particular research areas. The very beginning of my research into female bodybuilders had its roots in my childhood. Indeed, 'seeds' of thought around the subject matter were planted through defining moments and epiphanies. These ideas and perspectives on the world grew and developed as they were nourished by academic studies. Thus the idea to embark on research into this area evolved through numerous experiences embedded within my own biography. In this section of the chapter, I try to utilize the 'sociological imagination' (Mills 1959) by investigating how memories of my encounters with social norms and social scripts in the past influenced my self-identity and have consequently impacted on the construction of the book (Douglas 2009). This is commensurate with Cain's (1990: 139) suggestion that '[t]he theory we produce should account for our own knowledge as well as that of those we investigate… [This] does not imply a smooth or continuous theoretical totalization but… allows for contradictions and discontinuities'.

'Unveiling' the self can, of course, be an uncomfortable experience that leaves me, the researcher, open and vulnerable to criticism. However, as feminists argue, I believe there needs to be transparency in our research, and that the 'personal' is indeed the 'political'. It should be noted here, before I 'story myself' (Douglas 2009), that all biographies are partial, complex and fragmented. Nevertheless, I have tried to account for some of the personal motivations that led me to explore this fascinating research area. According to Gordon (2008), all sociologists are storytellers, so this is my story:

> **My first encounter with a female bodybuilder** (scenario 1, aged 8)
> I wanted to learn to dance and act, so here I was, at Hilda Barrett's School of Dancing (set in the incongruous location of an Old People's home) having

an elocution lesson. 'A, E, I, O, U', I pronounced out a loud – as slowly as I could, trying to clearly articulate the vowels. 'No, no, no', the old, retired dancer shouted at me, waving her walking stick in the air. 'It's 'I', not 'I' – push the letter forward through to the front of your mouth'. I tried again a few times and failed to win her approval. She sighed and turned her attention to the pupil standing next to me. My mind began to drift. I looked up and saw a woman doing a gymnastic routine on the muted television screen. I watched her do the splits, one armed press-ups and even a back flip. I was awestruck, not so much by the routine, but by the combination of her skills and her appearance. I had never seen a woman look like that before. She was wearing a shiny bikini, displaying her tanned, muscular body. She had lots of make-up on and styled 'big' hair. She looked so happy, independent, strong and carefree.

I know now that the woman performing the routine was a 'Fitness competitor' (see Chapter 3). Unlike the majority of people, who immediately react with repulsion at the mere sight of a muscular woman, I immediately found her appearance, demeanour and capabilities appealing. Even at that young age I was drawn to and fascinated by a woman so apparently possessed of herself.

Gendered sports (scenario 2, aged 10)
We didn't have playing fields at my primary school. So every week, during games lessons, we boarded a coach that took us to a local secondary school to use their facilities. As usual, the girls, wearing their short, pleated, blue PE skirts, got off the coach and headed over to the netball courts, whilst the boys, in shorts or tracksuit bottoms, ran over to the far field to play football. I turned to my female PE teacher and questioned: 'But why? Why can't I play football with the boys?'

I had grown up as a 'tomboy' – a word rarely used now, but defined by the American Heritage dictionary (Morris 2009) as 'a girl considered boyish or masculine in behaviour or manner... who acts or dresses in a boyish way, liking rough outdoor activities'. From a very young age I didn't understand why females and males were treated so differently. I couldn't understand why gender was so important, nor why it prevented me from joining in boys' activities and sports.

Body image (scenario 3, aged 18)
I swam far out to sea, embracing the coolness of the water after the heat of the scorching sun. I stopped to catch my breath, keeping myself buoyant with my legs and the occasional swish of my hands under the water. I turned to look back at the beach, situated on the Grecian island of Samos. I could immediately locate my best friend. Unlike the other bronzed bodies stretched out on the beach, she was sitting by herself, covered from head to toe in dark baggy clothes. Not because she feared the damage the sun might do but because she despised her body so much.

During my secondary school years, I had three close female friends, and two of them had severe body image issues. One went through a short period of anorexia, another through a longer period of bulimia. Only one of my friends remained unaffected; the rest of us had low self-esteem which we, at least at the time, attributed to our imperfect bodies.

Injury and the obsession with weights (scenario 4, aged 18)
It hurt so much. I couldn't move without a pain shooting down my neck, trapezius and upper back. Just breathing was painful. I felt sick. I was in hospital being checked over for any spinal injuries. The doctor did a series of tests, checking that my body was fully functioning and that my bodily sensations were responding normally. The X-ray had shown that my neck (the seventh cervical) was broken and that my trapezius (traps) were badly damaged. To the fascination of the medical staff, my injury was the result of performing squats with a 100kg barbell. My muscles had adapted quickly to my new, intense heavy training regime, but unfortunately my bones had not. My traps had literally torn the bone apart under the pressure of the weight.

The doctor told me that I was incredibly lucky and that with plenty of rest and time I would heal. He said I must be very careful in the future and I would have to wear a neck-brace for the next few weeks.

'When can I get back to work?' I asked. I knew if I wanted to train, I had to get back to my job as a fitness instructor. I was already desperate, knowing that I had only a window of ten days before my muscles (which were not visible at the time) would begin to decrease.

My debut as a serious weight-trainer was over almost before it had begun. I recall the immense pain of the incident (which caused problems for several years afterwards), but equally I can remember the overwhelming frustration of not being able to train and the consequent realization that I had become 'addicted' to exercise. This incident made me question both the power and the restrictions of this lifestyle. Although I continued to work and train in gyms, it was not until I began this research project that I once more began to use heavy weights.

My interest in weight training began around my fifteenth birthday, when I asked for a set of dumbbells. The following year, on my sixteenth birthday, I was given membership of a local gym. I remember the feelings of excitement and anticipation as I entered this underground gym – with dimmed lights and loud music, reminiscent of a nightclub atmosphere. It became my home, my refuge, my release. I embraced the endorphin highs and enjoyed the workouts, which consisted of a variety of activities such as using cardiovascular machines, running, aerobics, boxercise and circuits, as well as resistance weights and limited free weights exercises. It was not until I left college at 18 and became a full-time, qualified gym instructor that I became more involved in weight training rather than 'keep-fit', encouraged by two women who regularly trained with weights. I loved how I felt in the gym – both the atmosphere and the experience of the workouts themselves. I also wanted to embody traits of power, independence and a controversial beauty.

These social moments are just a selection of those that helped shape and define my identity and influenced the way in which I now see and interpret the world. Perhaps, in light of my enjoyment of physical sports and weight training, my questioning of natural gender roles and my peer group's poor body image, it is not so surprising that I came to study female bodybuilders. I wanted to discover whether an alternate body project and way of being could provide a body of 'content', 'substance' and existential solidity in today's society. These 'experiential episodes' also serve to introduce the key themes of this book: sports and gender, gendered space, gendered attitudes (feminism), weight training, exercise, obsession, pain, injury, self-identity, body image and self-esteem.

The context

My desire to sculpt (using weights) a body symbolic of my desired self-identity was not as unique as I may have believed at the time. Indeed, over the past 30 years there has been a propensity to treat the body as a self-reflexive entity, a 'project which should be worked at and accomplished as part of an individual's self-identity' (Shilling 1993: 5). Bodies, in this sense, are viewed as 'corporeal surfaces on which the engraving inscription or "graffiti" are etched' (Grosz 1994: 63), as canvases that reflect the 'soul'. Individual 'body projects' are situated within the context of an increasingly 'body-focused' and 'body-conscious' Western society. Every day we are relentlessly bombarded with information about our bodies through the media, consumer culture, government, science and new technologies. Evidence for this is provided by the plethora of advertisements and articles in magazines, newspapers and television programmes concerned with the health, shape, size and appearance of the body and by the invention of an ever-increasing array of products and technologies designed to modify the body. In addition, there has been an unprecedented visibility of the body both in and outside of consumer culture.

This unabashed display of the body has occurred for several reasons, such as changing social attitudes to the body, the type of clothing worn, the environment (central heating/leisurewear), advertising, Hollywood, television and other modes of visual display (Featherstone 1991). Furthermore, self-reflexive 'body projects' have flourished at a fragile time in history in 'post-modernity'; an era characterized by uncertainty, a fragmentation of social life and a volatile economic environment. In this way, body projects can be seen as a form of control in an 'unstable' world. As Roseneil and Seymour (1999: 4) suggest, they can be seen as an attempt to 'anchor our sense of self in this maelstrom of social life, to create ontological security in a world of rapid social change'.

At the same time as this new-found emphasis on the individualization of the body, social theorists have pointed out that unprecedented societal value has been placed 'on the youthful, trim and sensual body' (Shilling 1993: 3). This is demonstrated by Foucault's (1980: 57) statement about bodily freedom: 'get undressed, but be slimmed, good-looking, tanned!' In this way, the physical appearance of the body, including its size and shape, has not only become increasingly important to an individual's sense of self, but has also come under increasing scrutiny from others. More than ever, people's bodies have become central to judgements associated with their social identity, sexual worth and even moral standing. Indeed, there is now wide consensus in sociological literature that the pressures to 'look good' have never been so strong (see for example Bordo 2004; Grogan 2004; Cash 2004; Brace-Govan 2002; Featherstone 1991; Jeffreys 2005; Shilling 2003; Rodin 1992; Sullivan 2004; Arthurs and Grimshaw 1999). Under this societal pressure of bodily conformity, individuals are required to participate in habitual body maintenance regimes to 'improve' their appearance and health. Thus, according to Featherstone (1991: 187), in contemporary consumer society there is an emergence of a 'performing self' – one which focuses upon the display and appearance of the body and impression management. This new emphasis on the body has been associated with a number of cultural phenomena, including an increase in cosmetic surgery and a surge in eating disorders. More commonly still, it has informed the unprecedented numbers of people in the affluent West who now 'work out' on and with their bodies in one way or another. In this respect, American ideals of 'trim, taut and terrific' bodies, incorporating within their very flesh the appearance of efficiency and hard work so prized within social and corporate life, have become increasingly popular in Europe over the past few decades.

Consumer society's obsession with 'working on the body' to attain hegemonic beauty norms and maintain social standing has not gone uncontested, however. Indeed, critical commentators are quick to point out that 'body projects' perpetuate social inequalities: not everyone has access to the resources (such as time, finance, physical capabilities) necessary for participation in 're-moulding' the body. Feminists, furthermore, argue that women are under more pressure to conform to beauty norms and maintain an attractive appearance than are their male counterparts. As Shilling (1993: 8) explains, the body projects engaged with by some women 'appear to be more reflective of male designs and fantasies than an expression of individuality'.

Although the majority of 'body projects' conform to contemporary norms of appearance, there are some 'alternative' body modifications that seem to oppose and resist the unblemished, smooth, pristine ideal of the body's surface. Indeed, there has been a rapid growth in non-mainstream body modification practices, including heavy tattooing, multiple piercings, bodybuilding, branding and binding. Curry (1993: 76) believes that these represent 'a revolution in claiming freedom to explore one's own body and claim the territory discovered as one's own'. Such unconventional forms of body modification have been met with revulsion, disgust, pathology, horror and abject fascination by mainstream society and also by some feminists (Pitts 2003). Others, however, have celebrated these 'hardcore' modes of body modification on the basis of their potential to effect a rebellion against Western hegemonic norms of beauty. In this book, however, I argue that we do not yet have enough evidence to assess whether these new practices are empowering, and that there is a distinct need for more empirical research to be conducted in this area. This research needs to go beyond notions of the body as a 'text' in order to ascertain the actual processes and experiences associated with such modifications. This is not to downplay the importance of textual analysis, but rather to emphasize that this method alone is insufficient to analyse whether body modifications have the potential to empower women. As Budgeon (2003: 42) argues, the experiential dimensions associated with the processes and practices 'through which the self and the body become meaningful' have often been left unexplored and untheorized. Against this background, I argue that it is essential to engage in the phenomenology of the 'lived' body in order to evaluate women's body modification practices more fully. This involves focusing on the experience of the body (including pain and pleasure), on the materiality of embodiment and on the interconnections and interactions made by bodies, in order to explore how the self and identity are transformed and re-created. In this way, as Budgeon (2003: 50) posits:

> Bodies then can be thought of not as objects, upon which culture writes meanings, but as events that are continually in the process of becoming – as multiplicities that are never just found but are made and remade... Changing shift from asking 'what do bodies mean' to what do bodies do?

This brief overview has highlighted the importance of the body in relation to understanding the world we live in, both in terms of individual self-identity and in terms of the issues of social reproduction, control and social order. It has also illustrated the complexity and enigmas surrounding body projects. I now turn to the specific body project engaged in by female bodybuilders.

Female bodybuilders: the scope and aims of the research

One of the most interesting and culturally significant examples of shaping and sculpting of the body is the recent growth in women's bodybuilding – a phenomenon that at once appears closely associated with the current focus on the body, yet also deviant in relation to conventional norms of femininity. Female bodybuilders, indeed, are engaged in the pursuit of a visual ideal long viewed as the *antithesis of femininity.* Weight lifting has a long history, stretching back to ancient Greece and Egypt, whilst the early years of bodybuilding are generally located in the period 1880–1930 (Dutton 1995) – but this is a *male* history. Eugene Sandow was one of the first exponents of bodybuilding – engaging in public performances of 'muscular display' and promoting the 'Grecian ideal' of symmetry and mass as a model of male physicality – but bodybuilding was widely viewed as an exclusively male phenomenon. The apparently inherent maleness of this activity has meant that it is not just the *appearance* of female bodybuilders that transgresses gendered norms, but also the choices, actions, experiences and patterns of consumption characteristic of these 'abnormal' women.

Females with large muscles evoke strong reactions from men and women, often involving disgust, discomfort, anger and threat. As a consequence Bartky (1988), a Foucauldian feminist, was one of the first to herald female bodybuilders as resisting hegemonic norms by creating 'new styles of the flesh'. Feminists such as Frueh (2001) also celebrate hypermuscular women as creating aesthetic/erotic projects for *themselves* and not for the pleasure of men. However, not all feminists share this view. Bordo (1993) argues that female bodybuilding lies on the same axis as anorexia in terms of control and hatred of the body. This disagreement over the potentially liberatory capacity of female bodybuilding continues within feminist discourse. Do women who pump iron resist physical restrictions of imposed femininity, or are they engaged in an ultimately oppressive quest for 'perfect bodies'? What is striking about the debate over women bodybuilders is that no suitable empirical work exists that would allow us to begin to properly adjudicate between these views. Furthermore, the current theories imply that female bodybuilders either resist norms of femininity or are oppressed – as if it is simply a choice of one or the other, rather than a more complex situation that may require us to go beyond this binary opposition.

Over the past 20 years there has been a small but growing research tradition in this area. However, much of this literature – including St Martin and Gavey (1996), Aoki (1996) and Mansfield and McGinn (1993) – has focused on the *textual symbolism* of what this flesh represents. Little attention, in contrast, has been devoted to phenomenological issues involving the *experience* of the lived body. Frequently, the muscular body is referred to as a costume, or a 'coat of muscles' (Ian 1995: 75), but this neglects the actual sweat, effort and pain of the bodybuilding process. In order to assess whether female bodybuilding can be seen as resistant, transgressive or empowering, there needs to be in-depth research into the actual processes of bodily activity (Bartky 1988; Lloyd 1996: 91; Bordo 1992: 16). In other words, there needs to be an exploration into the 'carnal realities of the sporting body'; research that focuses on women's phenomenological, sensual experiences and those processes involved in the corporeal transformations that take place as they train in the gym (Sparkes 2009: 27). The subculture of male bodybuilders has been documented in some detail (by Klein (1993) in the US and Monaghan (2001) in the UK), but no comprehensive ethnographical study has yet taken place exploring how female bodybuilders construct their identities in this male-dominated environment. In order to assess the liberatory potential of female bodybuilding, more in-depth research is needed into the daily lifestyles, identities, interactions (inside the gym and outside the subculture) and phenomenological experiences associated with this activity. Against this background, this ethnography is a contribution to the 'filling in' and 'fleshing out' of this lacunae.

The aim of the study and the problem of 'empowerment'

The aim of this research is to investigate whether female bodybuilding can be seen as an emancipatory and empowering transgression from hegemonic standards of femininity. Although the concept of 'empowerment' is pivotal to this research, it is extremely difficult to operationalize. Indeed, as will become clear throughout this book, feminists interpret the term in different ways depending on their beliefs and the context in which it is used. Furthermore, in the same way that explicit definitions of empowerment are rare (Gilroy 1989), indicators measuring progress towards empowerment remain even more elusive. Nevertheless, a useful definition of women's empowerment is offered by Mosedale (2005: 252): 'the process by which women redefine and extend what is possible for them to be and do in situations where they have been restricted, compared to men, from being and doing'. Others agree with this approach but argue for a more pro-active definition that affects gendered social roles and structures. For example, Women Win, a charity aimed at empowering girls and women worldwide through sport, suggests in its online mission statement that empowerment must effect an improvement in women's possibilities for 'being and doing' through an enhancement in 'opportunities for girls and women to gain awareness of their rights and capabilities, the courage and ability to make life-changing decisions, and access to resources, leadership possibilities and public structures'. Similarly, Kate Young (1993: 157) claims that discussions surrounding empowerment must include a 'transformatory potential' that takes into account the need to bring about permanent changes to women's political and social position in society. Thus, whilst some feminists believe that a practice can be considered 'empowering' even if it has a very small effect on an individual and personal level, others argue that 'empowerment' must have a profound impact on social relations and gender inequality.

Moving to the dimension of this issue most relevant to my research, whilst there are variants in the definitions provided by sports feminists advocating 'bodily empowerment', the following interpretation has been popular in feminist literature:

> Bodily empowerment lies in women's abilities to forge an identity that is not bound by traditional definitions of what it 'means to be female', and to work for a new femininity that is not defined by normative beauty or body ideals, but rather by the qualities attained through athleticism (such as skill, strength, power, self-expression).
>
> (Hesse-Biber 1996: 127; see also Hall 1990; Lang 1998)

This can be broken down into two related but distinct aspects:

1. Individual empowerment. This could comprise a number of elements, such as gaining a sense of self-definition through taking control of the body (both by manipulating the body's appearance and through bodily practices and processes), body self-possession, bodily self-respect, bodily satisfaction, physical presence, skills and bodily competences (self-strength, autonomy, self-power), own choice and a life of dignity in accordance with one's values (McDermott *et al.* 1996; Gilroy 1997; Willis 1990).
2. Social empowerment. This could include challenging the objectification of women's bodies and re-defining gender roles by resisting the cultural processes which tend to define or control the female body (Hall 1990; Gilroy 1989; McDermott *et al.* 1996; Willis 1990).

The purpose is not to provide an all-encompassing definition, but rather to advocate the multiplicities of 'empowerment' which will be considered during this study. Furthermore, empowerment must be viewed as complex, sometimes contradictory, and a multi-dimensional concept that can be understood as a process (involving minimally individual and social dimensions) rather than simply an event.

Chapter outlines

Chapter 2 sets out to explore the underpinning theoretical and methodological issues of my research. There are two main purposes of this chapter. The first is to describe how the research was conducted and to justify the methodological tools employed. The second is to discuss the epistemological and ontological concerns of the investigation using a reflective approach as, ultimately, the shape and nature of 'what' is known is inevitably entwined and intimately connected with 'how' it is known (Stanley 1990). In Chapter 3, I outline the neglected history of female bodybuilding, before moving on to review the small but increasing corpus of literature on this subject in Chapter 4. Much of this work comes from feminists who have had strongly divided reactions to this relatively new but growing phenomena. Chapters 5, 6, 7, 8 and 9 draw upon my empirical data. Chapter 5 focuses on the identity, experiences and lifestyle of the female bodybuilder outside the gym environment. As the first substantive empirical chapter, it also introduces the recurring and prominent theme of the 'Janus-face' of female bodybuilding. In Chapter 6 I continue this theme by turning to the most deviant aspect of female bodybuilding – muscle worship and steroid use. In Chapter 7, I explore the 'life-world' (Husserl 1971 [1936]) of the female bodybuilder in the gym. Here, I argue that female bodybuilders perceive the gym as 'home' – as a hospitable sanctuary that, at least in part, shelters them from the negative interactions of wider society. Chapter 8 investigates the actual phenomenological experiences of the female bodybuilders as they train in the gym, looking at how the women's subjectivities are expressed, lived and created through their bodies. In Chapter 9, I turn to the most important part of the life of the female bodybuilder – the competition: an event that deals with the culmination of their ambitions and 'sets the seal' on these women's identities. In addition, this chapter follows the journey of 'Michelle' (a bodybuilder of five years and my key informant) from the start of her preparation to competition, to that moment of climax. In the concluding chapter I return to my main research aim and use my findings to assess whether female bodybuilding can indeed be an emancipatory and empowering transgression from hegemonic standards of feminine embodiment.

This book explores the lives and experiences of the fascinating world of female bodybuilders. It explores the double-edged sword and 'Janus-face' of muscular female body projects by looking at the positive and negative processes, practices and interactions associated with this lifestyle.

2 Researching female bodybuilders

It feels like there's a black hole, a vacuum pulling me towards it, one minute I'm running towards it and the next I'm trying to pull back. But the lure is there. The obsession. It's all-encompassing. Bodybuilding haunts and comforts my dreams and waking hours. Maybe it's the hardest place to be – sitting on the fence. Feeling the power, the draw, but still being unable to commit. Sometimes I delight in it, but other times it feels like a weight, a burden. The religion of 'muscle'. Today I feel overwhelmed. My brain and body both hurt. Ethnography was not the easy option. I'm both hooked and fascinated – yet want to run away. The bizarre world of bodybuilding is taking over.

(Field diary entry, 4 September 2007)

Welcome to my world, or what was my world. As I am opening myself up yet again, by reliving the events which consumed my being for several years, I stand on that fault line and recall my vulnerability, my confusion, my dedication, excitement and passion as I became engulfed by the domain of the female bodybuilder. As Anne Bolin (2009) persuasively argues, reflexive ethnography must encompass embodied knowledge, which can only be procured through somatic engagement. Hence ethnography is an experiential and emotional affair which turns the life of the researcher inside out. The aim of this chapter is not only to explain the methods which were employed during the research, but also to explore the intimate relationship between the ethnographer and the case study under investigation – thus illustrating how the particular methods and techniques chosen and used when conducting research have a profound impact on both the research process and the substantive findings.

Fleshing out the theory

The overriding aim of the research was to facilitate a rich portrait of the values, practices, norms and, above all, lived experiences of female bodybuilders. With this aim in mind, my research approach sought not only to analyse the wider milieu in which female bodybuilding occurs, but also to explore via ethnography and interview the interactions and phenomenological experiences associated with this activity. Phenomenology is a very broad term that encompasses a range of diverse academic theories. Simply put, the origins of phenomenological thought focused on 'lived' experiences as understood from the first-person perspective. Throughout this book I use the term to refer to the school of philosophy associated with the work of Maurice Merleau-Ponty, who describes this technique as 'a manner or style of thinking' without any prior formal experience or education (Merleau-Ponty 1962: viii). As Wertz (2009: 3) notes, 'in focusing on the person's ways of being-in-the-world, phenomenology descriptively elaborates structures of the I ("ego" or "self"), various kinds of intentionality (experience), and the constitution of the experienced world'. Like others within the phenomenological tradition, such as Heidegger and Sartre, Merleau-Ponty postulated that the body, as a mode-of-being in the world, was always embedded within the social and contextual fabric of society. The search for a 'pure' form of transcendental bodily essence would consequently be a futile endeavour. However, these phenomenologists adeptly argued that as all experience is embodied – the body is a living, breathing and moving phenomenon that actively interprets and interacts with the world – nothing can be done or understood without the medium of the body. Merleau-Ponty took this theoretical approach one step further, postulating that consciousness itself is embodied, and consequently 'we are our body' (1962: 206).

Feminists have criticised traditional phenomenology and the work of Merleau-Ponty for overlooking women's experience and omitting any gender-specific analysis. This neglect, however, has been rectified – at least in part – by the pioneering work of Iris Marion Young in the late 1970s and the explosion of research into female embodiment in the late 1980s by feminist scholars such as Sandra Bartky, Christine Battersby, Susan Bordo, Judith Butler and Elizabeth Grosz. Young (2005) argues that the increasing popularity and significance of 'the lived body' in women's studies is understandable, given that much feminist thought has focused on the ways in which women's bodily differences have been used to justify structural inequalities. Furthermore, feminists such as Kruks, Marshall, Grimshaw and, increasingly, Grosz have joined Young in advocating the importance of phenomenological descriptions of the lived body experience to feminist theory and practice. It was Iris Marion Young's 1990 paper 'Throwing like a Girl' which initially drew me to this theoretical approach. By reworking Merleau-Ponty's *Phenomenology of Perception* this essay seeks to explore the ways in which women's movement and motility are restricted. Young suggests that 'it is the ordinary purposive orientation of the body as a whole towards things and its environment that initially defines the relation of a subject to its world' (1990: 134). However, she also argues (drawing on Simone de Beauvoir's work on immanence and transcendence) that women's bodily movement is experienced and inhabited in a different way to males'. Taking this difference as the starting point for her own feminist analysis, Young suggests that there are three commonalities of female embodiment in relation to action/movement. Her first point is that women tend to live their lives in 'ambiguous transcendence' (2005: 35), refraining from throwing their whole bodies into movement and viewing their bodies as a 'fragile encumbrance' (2005: 34). Secondly, the female body suffers from 'inhibited intentionality' (2005: 35): instead of believing in their bodies and physical capacities, women limit themselves by thinking 'I cannot' (2005: 36). Last of all, Young identifies a 'discontinuous unity' (2005: 38) between women and their bodies, as well as between their bodies and their environment, including the space that surrounds them. Young's work on female bodily experience and space provides a useful tool to aid the investigation of female bodybuilders and 'empowerment', helping us explore how these women use their bodies, feel about their bodies and experience their bodies – not with the belief that a 'pure' embodied experience can be identified, but as a unique and useful contribution to the analysis of female bodies. As Grosz (1994: 236) convincingly points out, phenomenology remains essential, as 'without some acknowledgement of the formative role of embodied experience in the establishment of knowledge, feminism has no grounds from which to dispute patriarchal norms'.

Despite recent work on embodiment carried out by feminists, phenomenological theorists have been criticized for their lack of engagement with empirical data (Kerry and Armour 2000). In this context, Sparkes (2009) and Hockey and Allen-Collinson (2007: 117) have called for insights from other critical perspectives in order to 'flesh out' the analyses. Research into 'body pedagogics' using ethnographic work, alongside interviews, may potentially bridge this gap and provide a more holistic, grounded and empirical account incorporating the carnal realities of the lived body. Shilling (2007: 13) defines the analysis of body pedagogics as involving the study of

> the central pedagogic *means* through which a culture seeks to transmit its main corporeal techniques, skills and dispositions, the embodied *experiences* associated with acquiring or failing to acquire these attributes, and the actual embodied *changes* resulting from this process.

Thus body pedagogics involves 'deploying the body as a tool of inquiry and vector of knowledge' (Wacquant 2004: viii). If, then, as Bourdieu (2000 [1997]: 41) declares, humans 'learn by the body', it is imperative that researchers become immersed in the culture being investigated and 'strive to acquire the appetites and the competencies that make the diligent agent in the universe under consideration' (Wacquant 2004: viii). In this context, body pedagogical accounts not only fit in well with and complement ethnographic approaches of research, but are also vital in unfurling the knowledge, values and beliefs embedded in athletes' bodily experiences (Bolin 2011: 22). In summary, an underlying theme of my investigation was an attempt to explore the 'body pedagogics', or corporeally relevant aspects of education and socialization (Shilling 2007, 2008b; Shilling and Mellor 2007), involved in becoming and being a female bodybuilder.

Why ethnography?

Ethnography 'seeks to capture, interpret and explain how a group, organization or community live, experience and make sense of their lives and their world'

(Robson 2000: 89). The captivating nature of ethnographic work 'rests in its ability to offer rich and detailed knowledge of a group's distinctive way of life' (Lowe 1998: 670). As Ferrell and Hamm (1998: 225) note, the participant observation and immersion in the life of a group central to ethnography provides a way of 'getting inside the skin of one's subjects' by gaining empathy with, and to an extent sharing the lived experiences of, those 'emotions, sentiments, and physical/ mental states that shape their responses to this world'. Habitual presence in the researched environment, combined with observation and supplemented by interviews that can range from casual conversations to more structured dialogue, can build trust and enable the researcher to develop a layered and nuanced picture of the cultural milieu and its occupants (Krane and Baird 2005: 94; see also Creswell 1998). Ethnographic research methods, in short, provide a means by which it is possible to understand the 'culture of a group from the perspective of group members' (Krane and Baird 2005: 87). Furthermore, the sympathetic and experiential methods utilized and endorsed by ethnography, which complement phenomenological insights, appear ideally compliant with feminist research (Klein 1983; Reinharz 1983; Mies 1983; Stanley and Wise 1983). Both approach 'knowledge' as contextual and interpersonal, citing the importance of respect, connection and empathy between the researcher and participant. For these reasons, there has been a growth of 'feminist ethnographers' in recent years, emphasizing the quality of relationships within the research and 'the quality of the understanding that emerges from those relationships' (Reinharz 1983: 185).[1]

Overview of the study: research sites, access, sample, interviews, profile of the women

My two-year ethnographic study took place in the South of England from 2006 to 2008 (although further studies continued until 2012). The majority of the ethnographic study focused on one site, a gym located in a large city that formed part of the biggest health and fitness club group in the world.[2] Once initial contacts were established in this gym, the study spread to other sites and eventually covered a total of six gyms in the region, as well as involving my attendance at bodybuilding competitions.[3] Of these gyms, three were of the health and fitness variety; the other three were of a more hardcore type. Hardcore gyms are distinguished from the former by their sole focus on weight-training, for either bodybuilding or powerlifting purposes. Also referred to as 'spit-and-sawdust' gyms, they consist of basic facilities and do not endorse the luxuries of nice changing rooms or attractive décor.[4] Of the hardcore gyms in the study, two appeared run-down and worn out and, apart from exercise bikes, were kitted out with simple free-weights equipment such as dumbbells, barbells, a squat rack, etc. The other hardcore gym had a far more extensive range of weight-training equipment such as resistance machines and also provided limited cardiovascular equipment (such as treadmills, bikes and rowers) for its clientele.

The fact that I was a qualified personal trainer with over ten years' experience of working in various gyms and knew the basic gym 'linguistics'[5] and 'body techniques' of weight training assisted me in gaining rapport with female bodybuilders. Indeed, my first encounter with my key collaborator 'Michelle' (a bodybuilder of five years) arose when she offered to 'spot' for me in the weights area whilst I was doing a dumbbell chest-press exercise. During the period of the study I immersed myself in the daily routines of this lifestyle by training, dieting and interacting with female bodybuilders. While I did not regard myself as a bodybuilder, I became sufficiently strong for these women to take me seriously when I was working out with them, whilst not becoming so visibly muscular that I was unable to pass as an 'ordinary user' to other gym members and to those friends and family members of female bodybuilders that I interviewed. My willingness to engage in long hours of serious weight training (an activity considered unfeminine and deviant by gender norms) also helped convince the female bodybuilders to whom I spoke that I was sympathetic and serious in wanting to understand their activities and commitments. Being a woman also made it easier for me to raise and discuss intimate issues with them – ranging from unwanted body hair to sexual relationships. Gaining this degree of immersion involved the following practicalities: getting up at 5am to train for several hours with female bodybuilders; learning new body techniques and exercises (including the use of training equipment such as wraps, belts and chalk); going to competitions; waking up aching every day; eating protein every two hours; taking supplements such as creatine, glutamine, tribulus, zinc and essential fatty acids (EFAs); and spending a vast quantity of time talking about bodybuilding, reading magazines, participating in online bodybuilding forums, watching DVDs and building friendships with female and male bodybuilders.

As a result of my feminist stance, I was open with my interviewees as to what my research was about and was happy to discuss any issues with them. There were also times, though, when it was 'impractical to seek consent from everyone involved' (Murphy and Dingwall 2001: 342), such as when I was training and observing in the public domain of the gym. During some fieldwork I did not automatically introduce myself as a researcher, but would explain my presence if asked. In one instance, when I worked backstage at two major bodybuilding competitions (in order to try and capture the ambience and environment of these key occasions in female bodybuilding), I was asked by a couple of inquisitive male bodybuilders why I was there and told them about my research. Generally, though – perhaps due to being a relatively young, slim, toned female – I was accepted in the field and my position was rarely questioned.

During the research I kept a field diary of my experiences which acted as both a research log – detailing significant events during the course of the research – and a reflective account of my experiences of undertaking the research and 'sharing the life' of a female bodybuilder (Krane and Baird 2005: 96). In addition to this ethnographic immersion in the gym environment (and tracing in rich detail the lifestyle of the female bodybuilder via my key informant), interviews were conducted with 26 female bodybuilders to elicit detailed personal narratives (Mishler 1986). These were supplemented by a total of 76 interviews with friends and family members of these women and with other gym users which contextualized the lives of female bodybuilders, allowing an insight into the intimate relationships and interactions that impacted upon the identity of these women. By this means I was able to obtain thoughts and views on a wide range of issues, such as how they felt about the female bodybuilder in question, why they thought she was doing it, and what effects the lifestyle had on both the female bodybuilder and her relationships.

Who were these women?

Of the female bodybuilders in the study, 17 were either competing contemporarily or had competed in the past, and their ages ranged from 23 to 48 years. All the women were dedicated to maximizing their muscular size and definition. While several worked out in hardcore bodybuilders' gyms dedicated exclusively to building muscle, most trained in public gyms that were closer to home and adequate for their needs. Their occupations were concentrated in the working and middle classes (ranging from fitness instructor, to office worker, to university lecturer). Half of the women had degrees, and all but two of them were white British (the others were black British/Afro-Caribbean). The majority of the women were in heterosexual relationships and five had children. The question of female bodybuilders' sexual orientation has been raised frequently during this study. However, it is difficult to find accurate statistics on the general population's sexual orientation, let alone that of female bodybuilders, who may wish to hide their preferences due to the stigma attached. Whilst the majority of the women in my study were in heterosexual relationships, there was a higher than average proportion of lesbians/homosexuals in my sample: 23 per cent, compared to the national average of 5–7 per cent.[6] I do not claim that these findings are representative of British bodybuilders, but more that they give an indication. What perhaps is more interesting is female-bodybuilding journalist Hans Klein's interpretation of the situation, expressed in the following abstract (cited on his blogs and in personal conversations):

> What actually made me start thinking about this issue was seeing the way that female bodybuilders – whether or not they identify as gay – interact with each other. When you see two female bodybuilders together, it's obvious there is an instant intimacy between them, even if they have only just met. I think it comes from a sense of a shared struggle. The idea that female bodybuilders bond with each other in a unique way leads on to another issue. I've heard some female bodybuilders express the view that they are not attracted to women in general but only to other female bodybuilders. In other words, they are not 'lesbians' in the conventional sense but something that is actually far more specific than that term suggests. They are attracted to female bodybuilders not because they fetishize muscle like a lot of male fans of women's bodybuilding, but because they see so much of themselves in other female bodybuilders. This may also be why, when you have two female bodybuilders in a relationship, the urge to merge is so strong.

In this way, it is extremely difficult to categorize and 'label' the sexual orientation of female bodybuilders. What is of most significance to the non-bodybuilding social variables that could be used to differentiate these women, however, is their lack of salience in relation to the responses and comments of both these female bodybuilders and those others with whom they interacted. Thus, the pursuit of muscle was articulated consistently by all the female bodybuilders in the study as the central feature of their self-identities, and this was reflected in the emphasis placed on musculature by their friends, family and others. What mattered, first and foremost, was that these women were devoted to the pursuit of muscle. This is the context in which I identify the female bodybuilders in this study exclusively in terms of the time they spent pursuing this goal.

Confessing the 'ethnographic self'

> As I write this my arm is throbbing. I finished a workout about 2 hours ago and have just refuelled. I've got work to do but all I want to do is go back to bed. I feel physically shattered. My forearm hurts just picking up a cup of tea. My hand hurts, my shoulders, biceps and lats – all of which were pumped with blood and endorphins not so long ago. But now I feel drained, tired, heavy and a little nauseous from the caffeine stimulants… For the first time today I looked in the mirror whilst training back and biceps and saw muscularity. My lats were engorged with blood and flared out, my delts looked defined and the veins on my biceps demanded attention.
>
> (Field notes, 31 July 2007)

On paper, ethnography can appear deceptively simple, and yet in reality it is a 'messy business' (Pearson 1994: vii) that requires the researcher to be both adaptable and persevering in their quest for 'verstehen' (see Ferrell and Hamm 1998). Regardless of how many sanitized accounts of 'research methods' you read, however much you think you have prepared yourself fully for all events, the path of real-life research rarely runs smooth, as I discovered (Hobbs and May 1993). The intention of the following script is to provide a more 'fleshed out' account – warts, bruises, the occasional callus and all – of some of the dilemmas and events that occurred during the research process, and to identify and unravel some of the complex relationships and interconnections between myself and the research. It should perhaps be noted that researchers who have adopted and utilized a theoretical confessional written stance in their research have been criticized for being unprofessional (Willis 2000). Furthermore, 'confessionals' (Van Maanen 1988) are often perceived as narcissistic, self-indulgent, exhibitionist and unhelpful accounts (Lofland and Lofland 1995 [1984]: 14) that dwell in the fictitious subjectivity of the arts and must be separated from 'scientific, objective, value free research'. However, I believe that no research can remain pure, untouched or unpolluted, as it is always constructed by 'subjective' human beings. Moreover, if Conquergood is correct in claiming that 'ethnography is an embodied practice… an intensely sensuous way of knowing' (1991: 180), how can a researcher try to comprehend the world from another's perspective and yet in the same instance remain detached? As Coffey (1999: 8) convincingly points out:

> Ethnographic research is peopled – by researcher and researched. Fieldwork is itself a 'social setting' inhabited by embodied, emotional, physical selves. Fieldwork helps to shape, challenge, reproduce, maintain, reconstruct and represent ourselves and the selves of others.

In this way, regardless of intention, the researcher becomes embedded in the very social world that they are studying; 'it is not a matter of methodological commitment, it is an existential fact' (Hammersley and Atkinson 1983: 15). My ethnographic work is thereby inevitably a product of my own experiences, both past and present, and my own 'sociological gaze'. The findings are inescapably fashioned by who I am, what I have witnessed and those I have encountered. Research findings are furthermore complicated by the actual writing process itself – which is inescapably a mediating experience, consisting of a retrospective account which is inevitably an approximation of experience. Consequently, the writings, quotes and findings belong to a highly edited process that incorporates personal scrutiny, selectivity and interpretation. Reflexivity and reflexive accounts are therefore an essential part of the research process. This reflexivity will not of course prevent bias and politics, but it will allow both myself and the reader 'to consider the implications of these issues on how the research was conducted and the substantive findings that emerge' (Devine and Heath 1999: 7; see also Aptekar 2002). In the sections that follow, I unveil my own relationship with the research enterprise and explore 'how fieldwork shapes and constructs identities, intimate relations, an emotional self and physical self' (Coffey 1999: 5).

Negotiating the field: body work and blending in

Real-life research is a learning curve and challenge with no definitive protocol to follow. It is a continuous and fraught lesson in how to connect with disparate people, create rapport and enable participants to unveil and reveal the subtle complexities which make up social life. Thus building trust and gaining kudos are essential components of ethnographic research, particularly when researching 'deviant' subcultures. Impression management becomes paramount if one is to blend as much as possible in the field, as 'what our body looks like, how it is perceived and used can impact upon access, field roles and field relationships' (Coffey 1999: 68). Conducting research on female bodybuilders inevitably required a great deal of 'body work' – both as a performative presentation-of-self and as physical labour. As I lacked the large muscles that signify being a female bodybuilder, performing an acceptable bodily appearance was particularly imperative. At bodybuilding competitions and during daily interactions with female bodybuilders, I dressed down and predominantly wore jeans and t-shirts in order to blend in as much as possible with the group that I initially 'hung around with', who wore casual and comfortable clothes (such as tracksuit bottoms and combats) and little or no make-up.[7] Coffey (1999: 73) points out that 'ethnographers also span body boundaries during the course of fieldwork'. Supporting Coffey's observation, I found that the very physicality of gym work required me to use my body in different ways than those I was used to. New body techniques and exercises had to be learnt, which were sometimes frustrating, embarrassing or uncomfortable to grasp. Training with others can also be a very intimate and sometimes awkward activity, as bodies are in close proximity and 'spotting' and 'correcting' require touching and physical contact. One particularly 'controversial' exercise, for example, was 'donkey calf raises', which required me to sit on my training partner's back whilst she bent over and did calf raises – much to the amusement of some gym spectators! My bodily postures changed too, as I observed and unconsciously copied my gym partners, realizing that I had done this only as a result of the responses of others. For example, my male gym friends began to tease me that in the gym I walked 'like I had beach balls under my arms'. My body grew in both strength and size during the course of the research.[8] At my peak I put on almost two stone of muscle and water, with an increase of three inches on my thighs and two inches on my arms. Despite these physical changes, compared to a female bodybuilder or even an elite female athlete – for example, a sprinter – I would still be considered just 'toned' to many ordinary people, and especially to bodybuilders.

Whilst the majority of female bodybuilders accepted my presence, acknowledged my empathy and willingly confided in me, gaining this 'access' did not go totally uncontested. In one episode, before a prominent female bodybuilder would let me interview her, she put me through a kind of 'initiation test' to check my seriousness and passion for training, by fixing me up to train with a 20-stone male bodybuilder. Another female bodybuilder directly asked my key informant: 'Can she be trusted? What does she know? Have you told her about steroids?' Personal relationships based on trust are the foundation of any research which desires to procure valid data capturing the sincerity of the actor's perspective and social context (Johnson 1975). However, there is always a cost that arises from creating a relationship based on 'trust', as a researcher cannot selectively decide which data they wish to be 'trusted with' and which events and situations they are willing to be present in, especially when they cannot be foreseen (Punch 1994). Indeed, fieldwork raises ongoing personal and interpersonal ethical concerns. Researchers must not only negotiate their own moral tightrope and decide to what lengths they are prepared to go in order to obtain data, but need also to protect their own academic integrity as well as that of their participants.

Issues of risk, danger and illegality that can arise during ethnographic research have been discussed and documented in some depth, particularly by criminologists who favour ethnographic methods (see Polsky 1971 [1967]; Inciardi 1993; Ferrell 1998; Hobbs 1988; Jacobs 1998; Patrick 1973; Parker 1974; Brajuha and Hallowell 1986). Inevitably, there were times when I too had to negotiate risk and illegality. In my case, one of the most controversial moral, ethical and legal issues was that of steroids. I was sometimes present when drugs were taken or injected, and regularly engaged in discussions around their use.[9] In one instance, a female bodybuilder came to visit me and straight away put hundreds of pounds worth of growth hormone in my fridge. In these situations I negotiated my own moral code.[10] Whilst not participating or condoning the drug taking myself, I did not condemn the actions per se. I felt that if I had removed myself from the situation or voiced disproval, it would have impacted negatively on my research, damaging the rapport that had taken so long to build up. I also felt that to 'label' the drug taker as 'bad', or deviant, or to stigmatize and exclude the issue of drug taking without trying to understand it, would be to ignore the multiple interpretations, motivations and identities of users (Mattley 1998: 156). Interestingly, as I became more immersed within the bodybuilding milieu and developed both my 'scientific' and my social understanding of drug use, my preconceptions and judgements about steroids changed, becoming more complex and less judgemental. Of course, this is where critics of ethnography would be quick to point out that I may have 'gone native' and become desensitized to 'deviant' issues as they became normalized to me within the culture.

Relationships in the field

Relationships based on trust, covering a wide spectrum of intimacy and engagement, are an integral and important part of the research process. This is reinforced in the case of female bodybuilders as they belong to a very small and intimate subculture. Due to this tight network and the controversial issue of drug taking, it was therefore essential that their identity was protected using pseudonyms and that confidentiality was assured. However, even within these 'privacy constraints', I still debated how much I should divulge about these women's lives. As Homan (1991: 154) points out, 'it is common for researchers to be troubled with feelings of guilt that they have betrayed their subjects'. During my research I encountered an exciting soap opera of events; from tales within the lesbian community to sex changes, relationship affairs, party drugs, cosmetic surgery and 'damaged' lives. When writing up, I discovered there was a fine line between capturing an accurate and colourful representation of the daily lifestyle of the female bodybuilder and revealing upsetting and potentially harmful material. As Ribbens and Edwards articulate, in this uncomfortable position I felt 'placed on the edges, between public social knowledge and private lived experience' (1998: 2). Ultimately, though, the protection and welfare of my participants had to be put at the forefront of my research, as without their help, trust, time and dedication, the research could never have taken place. So whilst this book is not a 'bare-all' account, I still believe that it allows a raw and intimate insight into some of these women's lives. From the outset of my research (exploring the relationship between empowerment and female bodybuilding), I had decided that the foundations of my methods were to be built on the premise of feminist research (for more information see Wilkinson 1986; Wise 1987; Bernhard 1984). Whilst it is perhaps more accurate to refer to feminist methodologies in the plural, the core of this ideology, according to Klein (1983), resides in the idea that research is concerned about women's issues, taking into account the needs of women and their experiences with the aim of improving their lives in some way. As unequal power relationships often reside within investigations, feminist researchers actively support a 'partnership' approach that locates the 'researched' on the same critical plane as the 'researcher' (Hobbs and May 1993). Thus, within my study I hoped to diminish the potentially exploitative nature of ethnography (Stacey 1988) by creating a dialectical and reciprocal relationship based upon co-participation (Lather 1988). Some researchers using a feminist paradigm have in more recent times noted, however, that the concept of an oppressed, powerless respondent is at least partially a myth. Although power dimensions inevitably exist throughout the research process, according to Olesen (2000: 255), 'power is only partial, illusory, tenuous and confused with the researcher responsibility'. Furthermore, it is contextual: whilst I am placed in a more powerful position when writing up the findings, during the actual fieldwork I regularly felt that the power dimensions were tipped towards my informants. For example, my meetings/interviews and training sessions were timetabled and to a certain degree governed (as one would expect) by the collaborators in the study.

With regard to the recorded interviews, many female bodybuilders claimed to have found it a positive experience, providing them with an opportunity to speak out ('a voice') and a chance to tell their 'side of the story'. Several commented that they found the process interesting and thought-provoking, giving them a space to reflect upon issues and their own self-identity. Some of the narratives of verbal abuse by strangers and the antagonism that most received for choosing their way of life were hard for these women to talk about. I appreciated their trust, their openness and the bravery they demonstrated in discussing these issues with me. Due to the distressing nature of some of the accounts, I found the ethics of deciding which stories and quotes to select difficult, as even with these women's permission, I was concerned about reiterating their personal pain by having it in print. In the end, after 'conscience-seeking' activity, I decided upon which quotes to use and in most cases double-checked with the participants that I still had their permission. However, the 'transformative consequences of the research process' (Coffey 1999: 246) undoubtedly also had some detrimental effects on the lives of these women. For example, my key informant became far more aware of the negative interactions (stares, comments and so on) that she received from outsiders following the probing of these issues with her during interviews and fieldwork encounters. In another instance, nevertheless, during a particularly challenging time in her life, she cited participating in the research as a motivating factor for bodybuilding that enabled her to carry on 'doing what she was meant to do'. Consequently, I found that the research process has the potential to change the lives of those under study both positively and negatively, regardless of the intention or indeed the desired outcome.

Key informants and best friends

Intimate friendships forged through the research process are not only complex in nature, but also have a considerable impact on the findings of the investigation undertaken. As Coffey (1999: 47) puts it:

> The friendships we experience are part of the contradictions and ambigui-
> ties that denote the essence of fieldwork. Friendships can help to clarify the
> inherent tensions of the fieldwork experience and sharpen our abilities for
> critical reflection... Moreover they firmly establish fieldwork as relational,
> emotional, and as a process of personal negotiation.

Although my background was very different to that of Michelle (my key informant and collaborator), we had many things in common that helped us to establish an immediate bond. For example, we were both of a similar age (late 20s), had a slightly non-conformist approach to society, had been to university, had both been personal trainers at the same chain of health and fitness clubs and had both experienced an initial desire to weight train at a young age. Living in close proximity to each other also meant that we would spend a considerable amount of time in each other's company. Friendships formed during ethnographic research are a contentious issue, with critics pointing out the difficulties of playing the role of both researcher and friend (Crick 1992).

Being immersed so deeply in the research, and as an apprentice ethnographer, there were times when I mishandled events and failed to manage situations appropriately. In one situation I made the mistake of telling Michelle and her partner (Jo) what a gym member had said to me: in this event, a male gym user, who I hadn't spoken to before, came up to me whilst I was training and insisted that I should 'drop the weight' (reduce) so as not to become too masculine and unattractive, like a female bodybuilder. Jo reacted by immediately confronting him, arguing that he shouldn't be allowed to 'get away with it'. By forgetting my role as a researcher, I had 'disturbed' the social milieu unnecessarily and precipitated an uncomfortable and upsetting scenario.

Coffey (1999: 42) notes that close relationships are particularly difficult to maintain when the researcher has left the field, as 'fieldwork relationships are clearly situated within social, cultural and organizational contexts... [and are] tied up with the actual pursuit of fieldwork'. Furthermore, interpreting events and analysis in the write-up can also cause divisions and tension. Using the example of the key informant in her own research, 'Rachel', Coffey explains that in the write-up of events, both interpreted situations in different ways:

> I was writing about Rachel's activities, interactions and career. But I was
> writing for an academic audience and not for her. She evidently felt hurt and
> betrayed by me.

In light of the difficulties Coffey mentions above, when I began writing, I was highly concerned that I may be damaging my friendship with 'Michelle' and

MARK & HELEN OSTERLIN LIBRARY
NORTHWESTERN MICHIGAN COLLEGE
TRAVERSE CITY, MICHIGAN 49686-3061

exposing her private life to public scrutiny. Our friendship consequently had a substantial influence on how I presented my findings. Although I originally planned to focus more on my apprenticeship, body pedagogics and the micro-details involved in my key informant's life, I decided (six months into the research) to broaden out the analysis and depersonalize it somewhat by incorporating more empirical data from different research sites and interviews with other female bodybuilders. As part of this quasi-confessional, it is perhaps worth mentioning that I did enter into a few brief relationships with male bodybuilders during the course of the research. As I became more immersed in the culture, men who were 'normal' in appearance became less attractive to me (and no doubt I to them, as I became more muscular). Whilst this dating experience brought me closer into the 'hive' of bodybuilding, these unsuccessful and stressful relationships must have ultimately impinged negatively on my interpretation of the subculture. In this con-text, key informants, friendships and relationships created in the field have a huge impact on how we navigate the social world – on the study, who we meet, who we initially interact with and how we begin to interpret the world that they inhabit. Inevitably, this in turn affects both the selection and the depiction of events in the write-up, which are themselves shaped by the changes which the researcher undergoes during the research process.

My ethnographic self

Researchers need to be careful, when writing-up, that they are not 'judging lives' simply based on their own viewpoint and biography. As Willis (2000: 120) warns us, '[n]o ethnographer should say "this is how it is", or "I know better than you do about your life"', as what may be a detrimental practice for them may be a posi-tive one for others. Indeed, within my own research I discovered that what was an empowering practice and fulfilling identity for my key collaborator was not the same for me. For Michelle, bodybuilding provided her with meaning, purpose and identity (by way of structure, goals and fulfilling her heroic 'destiny'), whereas I found the culture restricting and self-disparaging. For her, keeping a training diary and monitoring her food habits provided a way of keeping in control and allowed her a sense of measurable achievement and progress as she reached her goals. In contrast, I internally rebelled against any kind of regime and structure or doing exercises that I didn't enjoy or found uncomfortable. Several of my diary entries consisted of complaints regarding how much I hated the leg press and tricep dips, and how I occasionally found the workouts too structured and uncreative. Those were the bad days – the frustrating days, when I didn't achieve my goals or enjoy the process. However, for the majority of the time I felt privileged to be training with such a dedicated and charismatic person, and embraced the adrenaline highs and feelings of accomplishment when the workouts went to plan.

I deeply admired the strong, confident manner of my key collaborator and friend, 'Michelle'. Gender didn't seem important to her – she was simply Michelle. I almost envied her ability to be able to focus on herself, her own goals and desires, rather than the daily juggling act of trying to put other relationships first.

Despite my respect for her and our strong friendship, despite my passion for training, my desire to build muscle and the friendships of the amazing and complex women I met during the course of my research, I could never fully embrace the bodybuilding lifestyle. Reflecting on this, I realize that however much I may try to be neutral, when I began the research I was not a *tabula rasa* mentally or physically. My life experiences, biography, upbringing and socialization had already shaped me. Physically, I had my 'preferred' body techniques and methods of training, and was used to working out by myself and in my own way. Equally, I was contained by my prior feminist perspectives (Lockford 2004). My feminism rebelled against the 'no pain, no gain' mantra of the masculine cosmology of the bodybuilding world and reacted against their obsession with the body's appearance. As my role of gym user changed to that of researcher, I could no longer relax in the gym in the same way as I had previously – I was now continually observing, reflecting and scrutinizing.

If Cooley (1922 [1902]) and Mead (1962 [1934]) are correct that our identities are shaped significantly by our interactions with others (see Chapter 5), then perhaps (risking melodrama) my identity has passed through a 'crisis' during this research project. For example, my self-identity, particularly in terms of body image, regularly felt 'under attack' during the research investigation due to the relentless stream of unsolicited, contradictory comments made about my appearance. This is demonstrated in the following examples:

> Do you take steroids? (male, sports masseuse, Crete)
> Are you a boxer? (male, gym user, Canterbury; male, gym user, High Wycombe)
> Are you a bodybuilder? (male, gym manager, High Wycombe)
> Do you take anti-estrogens? (male, gym user, Kent)

In the same time period that I received these comments, I was asked whether I actually trained at all (especially when people learnt of my research topic) and told on several occasions that I have 'no muscle'. For example:

> How come you were training for two years with female bodybuilders, but didn't put on any muscle? (female, university conference, Bristol)
> You're 'toned', but you're not muscular at all (male, gym user, Kent).
> You haven't got legs, you've got 'pins' (female, gym user, Portsmouth).

These conflicting interactions undoubtedly impacted on my sense of self and added to the confusion of my own position during the research.

Whilst I felt an attraction to bodybuilding, I still had reservations (regarding the self-obsessiveness of the sport and the total focus on physical appearance), and due to my lack of muscularity (not helped by being a tall ectomorph, with high oestrogen levels), I never felt completely accepted as an insider by the bodybuilding subculture. Many of my diary entries refer to the frustration of not being able to build muscle, the impossibility of achieving the desired look of muscles and curves without cosmetic surgery and drugs and the difficulty of coping with ill-nesses and shoulder injuries which prevented training. Through my bodybuilding apprenticeship I learnt to read and value my body in a different way. My inherited vascularity became a source of pride, rather than something that was negatively associated with old age and ugliness in women (a couple of male bodybuilders jokingly nicknamed me 'the vein'). My legs, however – thin by normal standards and prized in wider society – became a hindrance and source of exasperation for me within the bodybuilding culture. Whilst I became desperate to build my legs and 'butt' up, most of my friends outside the culture were trying to slim theirs down. The fact that I neither fitted in with 'normals' nor identified as a body-builder in some ways positioned me in an advantageous location from which to research the subculture, though it wasn't always the most comfortable space to occupy. This further demonstrates the awkward position that the ethnographer must assume and deal with during the research. I have no doubt that my becom-ing hypersensitive to these issues of 'identity', 'body image' and 'belonging' was influenced by my own personality and self-awareness during the research, and it is possible that another 'sociologist' evaluating and exploring the world of body-building would have been less influenced by the impact of their surroundings. For the majority of researchers, however, who wish to empathetically try and 'get into the skin' of their participants, the experience of the research will have a profound effect upon their self-perceptions and the world around them. Thus, in the same way that the natural settings of the field are disturbed by the research process, the researcher's life is also changed.

Conclusion

This chapter has exposed the disparity between the abstract theoretical textbook manual on 'doing' ethnography and what actually takes place in the field. 'Real-life' research is a much more messy, complicated and chaotic business than is often acknowledged. Ethnographic methods provide an unsurpassed insight into the lives and experiences of female bodybuilders. However, accessing this rich and textured social landscape does ultimately come at a cost. As an apprentice ethnographer entering uncharted territory, I had to negotiate my own moral tightrope – by decid-ing to what extent I was prepared to go in order to obtain data, whilst at the same time protecting my participants and being able to justify my actions to my own conscience. As a consequence of these negotiations, my individual choices have impacted vastly upon the research direction, processes and findings. By providing a partial 'confessionary', I have hoped to offer a more open and reflective account that acknowledges the part I have played during the entire investigation and how this will undoubtedly influence and shape my conclusions.

The chapter has also highlighted the importance of friendships and how they are intimately connected to, and forged during, the research process. Furthermore, I have argued that it would be naive to utilize ethnographic methods and try to retain an 'objective' space from which to analyse and observe 'the phenomena', as ourselves, our bodies and our emotions are entangled within the project itself.

Ethnography is a deeply emotional affair; 'we can and do feel joy, pain, hurt, excitement, anger, love, confusion, satisfaction, loss, happiness and sadness' (Coffey 1999: 158). We are not autonomous, objective robots, but human beings with feelings, emotions and bodily sensations. Indeed, how would it be possible to analyse the lives and experiences of female bodybuilders and to ignore my own lived experiences and emotions throughout the process? During the research I have frequently felt guilty, burdened, exhausted, frustrated and confused, but these feelings have been matched by the positive feelings of curiosity, anticipation, excitement, energy, enrapture, bliss, vibrancy and laughter. Ultimately the only way to comprehend this bizarre world, as I have argued throughout this chapter, was to become drenched and saturated in a subculture that has to be experienced as a sentient affair so as to be understood.

3 The history of female bodybuilding

*

This muscular feebleness inspires in women an instinctive disgust of strenuous exercise; it draws them towards amusements and sedentary occupations. One could add that the separation of their hips makes walking more painful for women... This habitual feeling of weakness inspires less confidence... and as a woman finds herself less able to exist on her own, the more she needs to attract the attentions of others, to strengthen herself using those around her whom she judges most capable of protecting her.

(Barthze, quoted in Cabanis 1956, I: 278).

The quote above, from an important eighteenth-century French physician, captures the prominent medical discourse of the Enlightenment period in Western society – highlighting women's supposed weakness, fragility, vanity and male-dependence. Furthermore, it provides a glimpse into one of the patriarchal ideologies surrounding women's bodies that have been used throughout time to justify gender inequalities and legitimize women's subservient status. Historically, women, in Western society, have been positioned as opposite and inferior to their male counterparts on the grounds of their corporeality (see Shildrick and Price 1999; Kristeva 1980; Jordanova 1989; Spelman 1982; Braidotti 1994; de Beauvoir 1949; Weitz 2003; Martin 2001). Bloch (1987: 1) states that this thread of misogyny reaches back to the Old Testament, as well as to Ancient Greece, and extends through the medieval period: the evidence can be found in 'ecclesiastical writing, letters, sermons, theological tracts, discussions and compilations of canon law; scientific works, as part and parcel of biological, gynaecological, and medical knowledge; and philosophy'. Moreover, it has been argued that these oppressive ideas placed around women's bodies actually become culturally inscribed onto the body itself via normalized oppressive practices in the guise of femininity, such as corsets (Eco 1986; Summers 2001; Bordo 1993); ceruse (lead-based makeup) in the Elizabethan era and vermillion rouge (a mixture of mercury and sulphur) in the eighteenth century (Henig 1996; Newman 2000); Belladonna eyedrops (Henig 1996; Donohoe 2006); and more recently, cosmetic surgery such as breast implants (Jeffreys 2005; Saul 2003; Greer 2000).

Set against this backdrop, it is perhaps unsurprising that the body has been an important, if not the main, site of contention for feminists in their struggles against a male-dominated society. Second-wave feminists in particular have argued that women often discover their lack of power and control when they seek to exert autonomy over their sexuality, health and bodies. However, as Foucault (1980: 95) acknowledges, 'where there is power there is resistance'. Following on from this, Grosz (1994: 40) points out:

> As well as *being* the *site* of knowledge-power, the body is thus also a site of resistance, for it exerts a recalcitrance, and always entails the possibility of a counter strategic re-inscription, for it is capable of being self-marked, self-represented in alternative ways.

The body, then, has – at least for some – the potential to rebel and challenge social control, cultural reproduction and social order. In this way, bodies that oppose and transgress the current hegemonic Western bodily ideal of the young, slim and 'unmarked' have the potential to create 'new bodies [and] new pleasures' (Foucault 1981: 157; see also Lloyd 1996; Bartky 1988). This, in turn, provides the potential to release women from an antagonistic relationship with their bodies (Lloyd 1996; Bordo 1988).

It is within this context that female bodybuilders have been heralded by some feminists as resisting hegemonic norms, designing their bodies to their own ideals and creating their own space. Their bodies are perceived by these feminists as being sites of power both symbolically and physically, and as sites of resistance (Tate 1999; Hargreaves 1986). If it is indeed the case that female bodybuilding is possessed of liberatory potential, however, it is a subject that has been underinvestigated. This chapter begins the process of addressing this oversight by chronicling the rise of female bodybuilding.

The birth of female bodybuilding

> This is the first era in all of human history in which women have developed hyper-muscularity for primarily aesthetic purposes. This concept is so totally revolutionary and culturally dangerous that even the physique federations themselves have grave reservations about the idea. Sure, the sport faces its challenges, but you can't have a revolution if everyone agrees with you in the beginning.
>
> (Dobbins, cited in Kaye 2005: 155)

'Amazons', strong women, circus women, female wrestlers, boxers and weight-lifters, whilst rare, have been documented throughout history (see Huxtable 2004; Graves 1992; Todd 2000; Bouissaic 1976; Hargreaves 1994; Roark 1991). However, hypermuscular women who purposely build their bodies and then proudly expose these male signifiers are a relatively new phenomenon. In contrast to men's bodybuilding competitions, which increased in popularity in the 1950s, 60s and early 70s, women's bodybuilding per se was still to be recognized. The only way in which women could participate at these bodybuilding events was in a supplementary beauty contest or bikini show (Lowe 1998). Wennerstrom (1984: 76) suggests, though, that these sideline beauty pageants laid the foundations for women's bodybuilding competitions in the future. Nevertheless, it was not until the late 1970s, against the backdrop of the second-wave feminist movement, Title IX, the rise in fitness consumerism and the relative success of female power-lifting, that female bodybuilding competitions were finally born.

The history of female bodybuilding has been a relatively neglected area of research and thus, like the sport itself, is fraught with inconsistencies. Yet from its conception to the present day, women's bodybuilding has been plagued by the same core issue: how muscular can a woman become and still retain her 'femininity'? Hence, the corporeality of the female bodybuilder is a contested terrain. This physical landscape is staked out by and between the governing bodies of female bodybuilding and the women themselves, causing controversy and ideological conflict. In the remainder of this section I describe, in chronological order, some of the momentous events which shook and in some ways shifted the paradigmatic view of female bodybuilders, exposing the tensions between 'femininity' and muscularity and revealing the dyadic/interlocking relationship between personal agency and structure (Bolin 2011).

Despite 'female bodybuilding arising at a time of great political and social gains for women' (Scott-Dixon 2006: 4), the first widely acknowledged bodybuilding contests still resembled beauty pageants. Female competitors wore high heels with their bikinis and were forbidden from clenching their fists and using other masculine poses such as the 'crab', 'double biceps' or 'lateral spread'. In 1977, Henry McGhee, under the aegis of the United States Women's Physique Association (USWPA), founded the first, notorious female bodybuilding competition,[1] with the intention of using the same judging criteria used in male bodybuilding competitions: assessing muscle size, symmetry and presentation poses (Wennerstrom 1984). McGhee claimed that the purpose of the USWPA was to overcome 'the limited, beauty queen stereotype of what the American women should look like'. However, critics argue that despite the assertion that it was a 'bodybuilding' competition, the first prize was given to a relatively slender woman with small, stringy muscles. A similar tale of events occurred in 1979, when another association was created for female bodybuilders. George Synder established the 'Best in the World' contests under the International Federation for Bodybuilding (IFBB), with the aim of creating a fitness role model for the average American female. However, not only were the women handpicked by Synder himself; they were also chosen and awarded for 'attractiveness and sex appeal over fitness and muscles' (Huxtable 2004: 2).

Doris Barrilleaux, who had previously competed at one of Henry McGhee's events, established the Superior Physique Association (SPA) in 1978: this was 'the first women's bodybuilding organization run for women and by women' (Lowe 1998: 59). However, SPA, like the USWPA before it, disintegrated and was terminated in 1980 due to its inability to compete against the Weider Brothers, who had established the IFBB organization.[2] It was not until 1979, when Lisa Lyon's more athletic physique (and charismatic personality) won the first IFBB

Women's World BodyBuilding Championship, that women's built bodies began to challenge hegemonic notions of femininity and cause a stir in society (Huxtable 2004; Wennerstrom 2000). Lyon's concept of the developed female body was comparable to the dominant strand of feminism at the time. Female bodybuilding, she declared, was about 'redefining the whole idea of femininity. You don't have to be soft; you don't have to be weak. You can be strong, you can be muscular… you can make that visual statement and at the same time be feminine' (cited in Huxtable 2004: 4).

The 1980s: the golden era of female bodybuilding

In wider society, the early 1980s signified a transition from the fashionably thin 'Twiggy' body to one carrying slightly more muscle mass. The female ideal of beauty during this period was dubbed as 'taut, toned and coming on strong' (Corliss 1982: 72). This valued body type continued into the 1990s, led by Hollywood role models such as Linda Hamilton (in 'Terminator II'), Demi Moore ('GI Jane'/'Disclosure'), Angela Bassett ('What's Love Got to Do with It') and Holly Hunter ('The Piano') (Dobbins 1994; Heywood 1998). Within this context, women's weight training began to flourish. For female bodybuilders, this decade has often been regarded as the golden years and the height of female bodybuilding. In 1980, the most prestigious event for female bodybuilders – 'Ms Olympia', sanctioned by the IFBB – took place (Dobbins 1994). As bodybuilding was so new, the guidelines for contestants were ambiguous and no one really knew what was expected (Lowe 1998). The line-up comprised a mixture of abilities and female body types, ranging from the lightly 'toned' physique to ground-breaking muscular physiques: 'Cammie [Lusko] and Auby [Paulick] showed for one of the first times in history real female muscle – not curvy humps of hard flesh, but rippled, vein-splayed muscle' (Gaines and Butler 1983: 66). Rachel McLish's thin, 'toned' physique won the competition, and she consequently became known as the most famous women's bodybuilding competitor in the early 1980s. As bodybuilding progressed, the level of training increased, and in turn the sport slowly began to favour more muscular physiques. However, the public – and, indeed, the bodybuilding community itself – were not yet ready for an overtly muscular appearance which would transgress traditional beliefs about what men and women should look like. This is demonstrated by the iconic movie released in 1985 called 'Pumping Iron II: The Women'.[3] This film documentary followed the lives of several female competitors leading up to and including the 1983 Caesars Palace World Cup Championship Competition. The film pits the incredibly muscular Bev Francis (a world-champion powerlifter turned bodybuilder) against the slim, hyperfeminine reigning champion, Rachel McLish (Moore 1997).

Holmlund (1989) claims that the film was ultimately a marketing strategy by its director George Butler to promote female bodybuilding, albeit in a limited, heterosexual and eroticized manner. 'Pumping Iron II: The Women' does, however, highlight the controversial judging of female bodybuilding and questions about 'femininity', 'muscularity' and 'what makes a woman'. In the film,

Ben Weider (chairman of the IFBB) states, for example, that female bodybuilders must be judged differently to their male counterparts, as 'women are women, men are men, there's a difference and thank God for that difference'. He directs the judges before the contest: '[we are looking for] a woman who has a certain amount of aesthetic femininity, but yet has that muscle tone to show that she is an athlete'. In response, a male judge comments: 'that's like being told there is a certain point beyond which women can't go in this sport... It's as though the US Ski Federation told women they can only ski so fast'.

The competition resulted in the articulate, graceful Carla Dunlap winning the trophy. Whilst her body was more muscular than McLish's, in no way was it comparable to that of Bev Francis, who was placed eighth. Francis was told 'to get feminine or get out of bodybuilding' (Pearl 1989: 51, cited in Mansfield and McGinn 1994: 61). In 1984, Cory Everson (dubbed the 'Female Arnold Schwarzenegger'), weighing 150 pounds, set the new muscular standard. She went on to win the Ms. Olympia competition for six consecutive years before retiring undefeated as a professional. During her reign, the results of the show were even proclaimed on the National Broadcasting Company (NBC) channel. Other competitors were pictured in magazines and participated in television advertisements. Whilst women's bodybuilding had become increasingly publicized, it was still not regarded as a 'true sport', but rather as a fascinating spectacle (Huxtable 2004). Ms. International competitions, second in importance only to Ms. Olympia, were founded in 1986.[4]

Contentious issues in the 1990s: inconsistencies and contradictions in placing

The start of the 1990s was still troubled by contentious and conflicting judging. The Ms. Olympia 1991 competition, which was the first to be televised live, saw the hardcore physiques of Bev Francis and Lenda Murray battling it out to win first place.[5] As a consequence of the increased muscle mass and fears that the women were becoming too 'masculine', and initiated by Ben Weider, in the 1992 Ms. International contest the IFBB enforced a series of 'femininity' rules.[6] These included the rule that 'competitors should not be too big' and presented guidelines stating that women should look 'feminine' and not emaciated. Directions to the judges stated that they 'must bear in mind that he or she is judging a women's bodybuilding competition and is looking for the ideal feminine physique... the most important aspect is shape, a feminine shape, and controlling the development of muscle – it must not be carried to excess, where it resembles the massive muscularity of the male physique' (Huxtable 2004; Lowe 1998). The winner of the competition was the marketable, blue-eyed and blonde-haired Anja Schreiner, who weighed just 130 pounds at 5ft 7. The judge's decision was met with outcry from the audience, whose favourite competitor – Paula Bircumshaw, who weighed 162 pounds at 5ft 7, with similar symmetry and definition to Schreiner – was placed in eighth position. Bircumshaw, furious with her placing, gave the judges the finger and was consequently banned from competing the next year.

Following the unpopularity of the judges' 1992 decision, the rules were yet again rewritten to allow competitors to be judged as physique contestants and not just on aesthetics. Lenda Murray was adjudged to have the ideal combination of both femininity and muscularity and went on to win Ms. Olympia five times in a row. Her main challenger during this time was deemed to be Laura Creavalle, who came second in Ms. Olympia on two occasions and won the Ms. International crown three times consecutively. During the early and mid-1990s other professional bodybuilding shows were established, including the Canada Pro Cup and the Grand Prix events in both Prague and Slovakia. In 1996 Kim Chizevsky won the Ms. Olympia title from Lenda Murray, introducing a harder and more 'shredded' look than had previously existed. She retained the crown for another three years before losing her title in 2000.

More controversy and changes in 2000

In the year 2000, the IFBB decided to amalgamate the men's and women's Olympia contests into the 'Olympia Weekend', which from then on would be held in Las Vegas. The judging guidelines were also updated, stating that female bodybuild-ers would be scored on their appearance, including face, make-up and skin tone alongside 'symmetry, presentation, separations, and muscularity BUT NOT TO THE EXTREME'.[7] Furthermore, female competitors would also be assessed on 'whether or not they carry themselves in a graceful manner while walking to and from their position on stage'. The year 2000 was the only time that weight divisions were incorporated into Ms. Olympia, allowing Andrulla Blanchette (British) to win the lightweight category and Valentina Chepiga to win the heavyweight medal. Juliette Bergmann won Ms. Olympia in the following year, before Lenda Murray returned to win in 2002 and 2003. In 2004, Iris Kyle's extremely muscular physique allowed her to become the new reigning champion. However, in 2005 a new and controversial ruling was passed by the IFBB, named the '20% Solution'. The IFBB announced that due to health reasons and aesthetics, female bodybuilders should decrease their muscularity by 20 per cent.[8] Due to this new ruling, Yaxeni Oriquen won the 2005 Ms. Olympia title, though Iris Kyle returned to the top in 2006 and has maintained her reign to the present day (2012). It is worth mentioning that the elusive equilibrium between femininity and muscularity for female bodybuilders was once again addressed in 2007 at the IFBB Pro League Committee. Betty Pariso, a pro woman bodybuilder, requested 'that the "desired look" for female bodybuild-ers be formalized in writing as part of the IFBB Pro Rules'. In the minutes of the 27 September 2007 meeting it was stated:

> after some discussion, the committee held that majority opinion that the judges were already shaping the look for female bodybuilding with the win-ner they choose and therefore, there was no need for additional criteria than what is currently expressed in the Pro Rules.
>
> (cited in Bolin 2011: 31).

Thus it appears that through these judges' decisions, women's bodies are sculpted, shaped and transmitted, with changing and contested ideas of what type of body signifies acceptable femininity.

The British scene

> I went to see the 'godmother' of bodybuilding today, although unfortunately Diane Bennett wasn't at her gym. Diane is known as the 'British mum' of Arnold Schwarzenegger, who alongside her husband (Wag Bennett) allegedly adopted him and supported him in his bodybuilding career when he came to Britain at the age of 19. Diane is part of the executive committee on the UKBFF and is a Women's Fitness Representative... The gym is fascinating, like a religious shrine to bodybuilding. Signed posters are decorated around the walls. Pictures of bodybuilders are reminiscent of stained glass windows. You feel as though you have been catapulted back through time, especially when you enter Arnie's room. The weights that he had used, such as the globe dumbbells and contraptions resembling instruments of torture chambers, are presented against a backdrop of memorabilia. The sheer mass of newspaper articles and pictures of Arnie are almost overwhelming – I felt like I had set foot onto sacred ground.
>
> (Field diary entry, 20 July 2007).

Despite our tenuous relationship with the most influential male bodybuilders of all time – Arnold Schwarzenegger and Eugene Sandow (dubbed the founding father of modern bodybuilding) – the UK bodybuilding scene remains relatively hidden, and the female bodybuilding subculture remains even more obscure and shrouded in mystery. Carolyn Cheshire claims to be the first UK female professional bodybuilder; however, the origins of female bodybuilding in the UK haven't yet been documented. Grogan (2004) estimates that there are only 30 amateur Women's Physique Bodybuilders who compete during a year in Britain. Exact statistics are difficult to gather, however, as there are several associations in Britain under which female competitors can compete, including the British Natural Bodybuilding Foundation (BNBF), the Natural Physique Association (NPA),[9] the World Amateur Bodybuilding Association (WABBA), the National Amateur Bodybuilding Association (NABBA) and the United Kingdom Bodybuilding and Fitness Federation (UKBFF, formally known as the EFBB). For bodybuilders who want to get the 'pro' card (professional status) and compete in major competitions such as Mr/Ms. Olympia or the Arnold Classic and to get mainstream magazine coverage and sponsorship, however, the key organisation is the UKBFF – the British version of the IFBB.

Amongst the top 100 female professional bodybuilders in the world, only five are British, with none of them being placed in the top 50 (IFBB RAS rankings 2011). In the IFBB RAS rankings of 2011, Wendy McCready, Sarah Bridges, Emma Sue, Carmen Knights and Gayle Moher (although Gayle currently resides in the USA) are listed; other British female bodybuilders such as Dawn Sutherland,

Joanna Thomas, Andrulla Blanchette and Karen Marillier were ranked in the top 100 within the preceding five years. *Flex*, a bodybuilding magazine run by Weider, declares that 'Britain doesn't produce many professional female body-builders but what it lacks in quantity it makes up for in quality… the guys may make the noise yet it's the girls who deliver the medals' (Plummer 2007: 196). Indeed, the last two Brits to win the most prestigious professional shows were both female – Andrulla Blanchette (Ms. Olympia, 2000) and Joanna Thomas (Jan Tana Pro Classic, 2001). Despite this success, in 2005 the UKBFF body withdrew the 'pro' card for female winners at the British finals (they must now compete at the 'Worlds' to get their pro status), but retained it for the men's overall champion. This means that past overall winners at the British championships in Nottingham, such as Aga Ryk (2007), Michelle Jones (2008), Xyleese Burford (2009), Lisa Cross (2010) and Rene Campbell (2011), must now qualify in European or World competitions to become a professional. According to Sarah Bridges (UKBFF judge and professional female bodybuilder), the women's sport has been in decline since its 'heyday' in the 1980s. For example, at the Nottingham finals in 2010 there were only eight female bodybuilder competitors, in comparison with almost 200 males. Whilst some participants claim that the small subculture means there is 'tightness', unity and support, others claim that the community is 'bitchy', fractured, judgemental and secretive. Although it is difficult to judge how cohesive the British female bodybuilding subculture is, I would perhaps suggest that there are clusters of female bodybuilding friendships within the subculture which help and support each other at specific times – although these friendship groups may change and are not static.

The poor media coverage of female bodybuilders has not helped the sport to develop. Similar to Bolin's (2011) findings in the USA (featuring content analysis of 299 covers of *Flex* magazine), which showed the marginalization of women bodybuilders (less coverage, smaller photos, few front-cover photos, etc.), there has been little media coverage in the UK. Even within the British bodybuilding subculture, there seems to be very little support for female physique contestants. This is clearly illustrated by a question-and-answer session in a recent issue of an influential bodybuilding magazine – *BEEF: British Muscle in Action* (2007) – in which Jeannie Ellam (a competitive bodybuilder) writes:

> I would like to express my feelings regarding the disappointing lack of expo-sure for women's bodybuilding in the BEEF: I would like to know why the only reference to the UKBFF BB championships in the BEEF magazine is to the winner of the men's category… Doesn't women's bodybuilding count?

In response, professional bodybuilder John Hodgson replies:

> The sad fact is that it's a male dominated sport…if a bodybuilding show just had male competitors would it survive? The answer is a resounding YES, but the same could not be said if the roles were reversed. Like it or not the overall trend towards the female bodybuilder has been negative and

even more in the current times... Some women enter the stage looking too much on the masculine side – it does detract massively from the feminine image. I do feel that more coverage should be given but at the same time I feel women need to focus on getting the balance right of combining femininity and muscle.

(*BEEF* 2007: 39)

In summary, few British women have recognition either on the stage or in magazine articles. Furthermore, very few are able to gain sponsorships to help support their career and advocate the sport to others.

The decline of female bodybuilding? Fitness, Figure and Bikini competitions

Ever since its genesis, commentators have claimed that female bodybuilding 'is dying of a hereditary and untreatable confusion of purposes' (Gaines and Butler 1983: 69). Questions surrounding the aims of women's bodybuilding have dominated the sport from its conception to the present day: 'Are they about the showing-off onstage of healthy, marketable women to no particular end than that? Or are they about the unhindered development and competition of female muscle?' (Gaines and Butler 1983: 69).

In addition to dealing with the containment strategies previously discussed, female bodybuilders must now also compete for limited resources (in terms of prize money, pro cards, sponsorships, modelling, endorsement, venue space, media coverage, etc.) with more 'feminine' and less transgressive athletic forms of embodiment. Fitness, Figure ('Body-fitness') and, very recently, 'Bikini' competitors have now been added to 'the industry mix of power, labor, and capital' (Bolin 2011: 45).

Scott-Dixon (2006) claims that since the very beginning of female bodybuilding there has been a conflict between those wishing to develop a toned, athletic appearance and competitors who wish to push their bodies to the extreme and develop huge, hard and defined muscles. According to Dobbins (1994), many women felt they had neither the genetics nor the desire to achieve the look of the comparatively muscular Carla Dunlap, who won the Caesars Palace competition in 1983. Therefore, to resolve this difficulty and meet this demand, the Ms. National Fitness contest was founded in 1984 by the Fitness Trade Association. Wally Boyko, who launched 'Fitness', purports:

I had become pretty disillusioned with the whole hard-core bodybuilding scene, especially women's bodybuilding. The steroid abuse was becoming rampant and obviously not a healthy approach to life. I knew there was a demand in the fitness industry for role-models – a healthier, more feminine image for women in particular. I created Fitness to fill that void.

(Kennedy 2005: 116)

Fitness competitions are judged on aesthetics in a similar manner to bodybuilding, but competitors are expected to have a lot less muscle and higher body fat; they are also judged on a dance routine incorporating aerobics and gymnastics (see Bolin 2011). As stated by *Oxygen*, a monthly American magazine dedicated to Fitness and Figure, in comparison to female bodybuilding competitions: 'Fitness contests became more main-stream and competitions showcased more sex appeal' (Kennedy 2005: 116). In 1995 the IFBB picked up on this marketable arena and created Ms. Fitness Olympia. Since then, Fitness has experienced phenomenal growth, creating celebrities and new role models like Monica Brant-Peckham, Susie Currie and Kelly Ryan. As a consequence of these new competitions, it was argued that the sport of female bodybuilding was being undermined. This thought was encapsulated by the *New York Times* in the following quote:

> When the history of women's bodybuilding is written, 1998 will emerge as the year that the weights tipped in favour of the sport's old nemesis, femininity... Fitness competition, a slenderized version of women's body-building, has eclipsed some of the bulked-up muscle shows in participation and popularity.
>
> (Roach 1998)

However, the rise of Fitness has itself come under increasing challenge from Figure contests. Famous Fitness competitors such as Monica Brant-Peckham and Jenny Lynn have successfully switched from Fitness to Figure. Figure is arguably a Bikini-type contest, where women display their 'toned' physiques in 'feminine' poses whilst wearing high heels. To the unknowing eye, these women would still appear quite muscular, but in comparison to Fitness and to female bodybuilders,[10] Figure women have little muscle mass and maintain much higher body fat (see Figure 3.1 and Figure 3.2 for a comparison between a female body-builder and a Figure competitor). As a consequence, their bodies are much more marketable, and competitors are far more likely to gain modelling and sponsor-ship contracts. In 2003, Figure – created by Louis Zwick, the founder of Ms. Bikini America, Ms. Bikini Universe and Ms. Bikini Canada – became a pro sport (Kennedy 2005). Zwick claims that Figure meets the demands of female athletes who want to compete without having the pressures of choreograph-ing a challenging dance routine. He claims that the judges 'look for the woman who has that quintessential naturally beautiful look from head to toe' (Kennedy 2005: 10). Critics, however, claim that Figure shows are 'almost a throw-back to women's bodybuilding contests of the seventies' (Huxtable 2004: 5) and shouldn't be included as a real event.[11] As female-bodybuilding journalist Hans Klein[12] has noted, however, even Figure girls have recently been accused of getting 'too big'. Judges' committee chairman Jim Manion sent out a memo to all Figure pros warning them that their delts (shoulders) were becoming too big and they had too much definition in their thighs, and would subsequently be marked down on these 'defects' in future competitions. Perhaps as a consequence of these concerns, women's Bikini competitions were introduced as a new sport discipline

Figure 3.1 Lynn Grey, female bodybuilder. Courtesy of Rebecca Andrews

by the IFBB in November 2010, aimed at women who do not wish to build their muscle to Figure competitors' standards. Female competitors are expected to display a toned physique with symmetrical upper and lower body development, with no excessive muscularity or conditioning. No specific level of body fat or muscularity is prescribed; rather, it depends on what suits the individual competitor. Due to the infancy of the competitions, interpretation of judging criteria and placing is allegedly inconsistent and confusing. Unsurprisingly, this category has met the

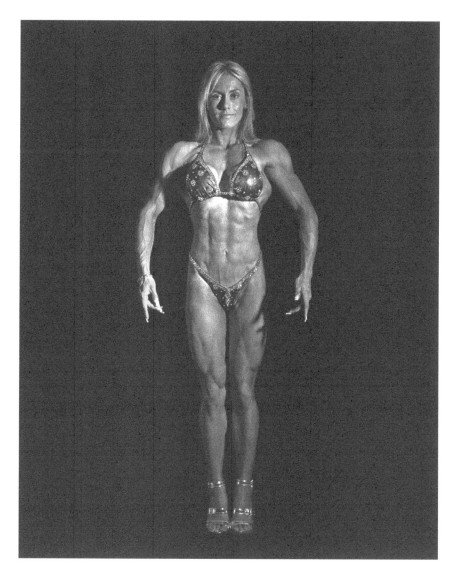

Figure 3.2 Louise Rogers, Bodyfitness/Figure. Courtesy of Rebecca Andrews

greatest reaction from the female bodybuilding community. Lisa Cross, winner of the UKBFF 2010, argues:

> I've read forum posts by girls getting ready for bikini class contests, and all they talk about is teeth veneers, false nails and hair extensions. That's a beauty pageant, not a bodybuilding competition. It's another example of the authorities undermining the hard work done by women who treat bodybuilding as a

way of life. Everyone knows that we are a dying breed, and this is just another nail in the coffin.

(Shahrad 2010)

However, despite the repeated cry that female bodybuilding is firmly on the route to extinction, due in part to the increase in female Bodyfitness competitors (the British equivalent of Figure), I believe the picture is somewhat more complex. For example, the physiques of some female Bodyfitness competitors resemble in size and definition those of some of the early female bodybuilders in the 1980s. Hence, in the late twentieth and early twenty-first centuries, women are still building their bodies to historically unprecedented levels. This trend is also reflected in the number of females engaged in weight training in wider society. Whilst muscular female celebrities such as Madonna, Holly Walcott and more recently Jodie Marsh are still considered deviant by mainstream society, they do spark public interest and place female bodybuilding back in the spotlight.

Conclusion

This chapter has provided an overview of the neglected history of female bodybuilding. As I stated at the beginning of this chapter, feminists have been particularly concerned with 'the body' as a site on which gender ideologies are inscribed. Within this context, female bodybuilding, as arguably the most gender-controversial body modification of all, has received increasing critical inquiry by feminists. Whilst some believe that female bodybuilding has the potential to reclaim the female body from the snares of patriarchy, other feminists are outspokenly cynical regarding this extreme practice. It is to this fiery debate that the next chapter turns – by examining the opposing feminist reactions to this comparatively new phenomenon.

4 Muscle is a feminist issue

> Muscles on women clearly have meaning, but exactly what they mean and how they are valued is not agreed upon even amongst feminists.
>
> (St Martin and Gavey 1996: 47)

The controversial nature of female bodybuilding has caused significant rupture on feminist ground. Whilst proponents claim that female bodybuilding is a way of empowering and liberating women, others see it as another form of corporeal entrapment in the guise of choice and agency (Bordo 1988). This chapter provides a literature review of the small corpus of research to have been conducted on this practice, by briefly examining the two key opposing feminist reactions towards female bodybuilding. It begins with those who herald female bodybuilders as resisting hegemonic norms by creating 'new styles of the flesh' (Bartky 1988). I then turn to the counter-argument put forward by feminists who declare that female bodybuilding is simply another form of oppressive control over women.

Feminist reactions: the female bodybuilder as a feminist icon

> '[The] muscular woman is not just a look; it's a social rebellion'.
>
> (Fierstein 2000: 32)

Space: invading the male domain and transgressing the 'slender' feminine body

Cashmore purports that historically, sports have 'validated masculinity' and 'made possible a strong and assertive proclamation of men's strength, valour and, above all, superiority over women' (Cashmore 1998: 84). On the reverse side, sports also then offer women 'the potential for reducing physical power imbalances on which patriarchy is founded and verified' (Castelnuovo and Gutherie 1998: 13). Bodybuilding has conventionally been perceived as the ultimate masculine activity, as a celebration of male embodiment and muscle power. However, through struggle, perseverance and determination, female bodybuilders have accessed this 'ovary-free' male domain (Klein 1985; Mansfield and McGinn 1993; St Martin and Gavey 1996). Advocates claim that by doing this, female bodybuilders have penetrated this homosocial area and challenged and undermined divisions and traditional understandings of men's/women's space (Hanson and Pratt 1995; Blunt and Rose 1994; Massey 1994).

Muscles have always been associated with men, as signifiers of masculinity, strength and power. Thus, women who embody these allegedly male attributes are antithetical to traditional notions of women as weak, fragile and soft. Tate (1999: 36) also posits that women with hard, muscular bodies transgress the contemporary feminine ideal of the 'slender' body. Indeed, Bartky's (1990: 73) comments made over 20 years ago could still be said to resonate today: 'Women are forbidden to become large or massive; they must take up as little space as possible... a body lacking flesh or substance, a body in whose very contours the image of immaturity has been inscribed'.

This sparse, insubstantial female hegemonic ideal of embodiment symbolizes both invisibility and weakness. In direct contrast, the female bodybuilder constructs a body that takes up space and demands attention. Consequently, in a society where females are presumed to be physically weak (Choi 2000), and where physical weakness is readily associated with mental weakness (Orbach 1988), strong women both physically and symbolically embody power. This counter-hegemonic body has caused feminists such as Fierstein to declare that female bodybuilding 'is the liberation of the flesh – it's very threatening but also very exciting' (Helmore 2000: 32). These spatial issues are explored in more detail in Chapter 7.

Body projects for themselves

Fierstein believes that through bodybuilding, women are finally achieving the right to manipulate their bodies in whatever way they choose and are creating new discourses of femininity (Bartky 1988). Likewise, Tate (1999: 33) claims that when these muscular women design their bodies according to their own ideals, gaze, self-image and desire, 'their bodies become sites of empowerment'. Indeed, she states that female weight-trainers

> [c]onstruct themselves almost as art forms, from the inside out. Their inscriptions on their bodies then come to represent them. Their identities are not ruled by the symbolic violence of the gendered habitus and the tyranny of slenderness... she seizes power by operating outside the system which would judge her on the femininity of her appearance.
>
> (Tate 1999: 47)

In this way, the 'body projects' (Shilling 1993) created by female bodybuilders are argued to disrupt gender-hegemonic norms and generate new bodies that challenge the oppression of conventional beauty. Hewitt (1997) believes that women who customise their bodies in extreme ways are not only rebelling against society, but are also taking back control over their bodies and identity. In addition, she argues that the actual experiences/process of modifying the body can potentially be cathartic. Similar to other extreme female body modifications (such as hardcore piercings, tattoos, scarring, sadomasochism – see Pitts 2003), Hewitt (1997) suggests that pain-inducing body customs can be used as a 'self-help' process of psychological healing. Likewise, Heywood (1998) postulates that bodybuilding enables women to reclaim control over their bodies and to heal the wounds left by sexual abuse and harassment. Moreover, MacKinnon adamantly argues that strong, muscular women actually challenge the very foundations on which patriarchy is verified and maintained:

> It's threatening to one's takeability, ones rapeability, one's femininity, to be strong and physically self-possessed. To be able to resist rape, not to communicate rapeability with one's body, to hold one's body for uses and meanings other than that can transform what *being a woman means.*
>
> (MacKinnon 1987: 122)

Power over nature

Women, due in part to the symbolic possibilities afforded to others by their possession of reproductive systems, have always been perceived as more embodied and less cultured than their male counterparts. Women's different and subordinate role in society has therefore been viewed as an ordained and inevitable consequence of the natural order. Specifically, women have been viewed as tied to the natural conditions of their embodiment: menstruation, pregnancy and childbirth. Men's embodiment, in comparison, has been seen as far less restrictive, enabling their minds much more freedom to engage with and pursue activities within the cultural sphere (Shilling 1993: 43). Thus, whilst men have been associated with reason and rationality as 'minds', women have long been associated with bodily, biological processes and seen as 'walking wombs'. Women's bodies have therefore been perceived to control their minds, whilst men's minds have been viewed as controlling their bodies. Furthermore, feminists have argued that the female form has been treated with fearful abject fascination, as the place where life and death are reconciled (Kristeva 1980). Championing this perspective, Shildrick and Price (1999: 3) put forward the following argument:

> The very fact that women are able in general to menstruate, to develop another body unseen within their own, to give birth, and to lactate is enough to suggest a potentially dangerous volatility that makes the female body as out of control, beyond, and set against the force of reason.

This vivid depiction contrasts sharply with the image of the self-contained male body and the heroic masculine ideals of a 'strong, stoic, resolutely independent, self-disciplined individual who holds himself erect with self-control, proud of his capacity to distance himself from his body' (Bologh 1990: 17). Against this backdrop, Tate (1999) argues that dedicated female weight-trainers enter into the ultimate male realm of having power over nature. Self-management, discipline, control and power have been typically associated with notions of masculinity, whilst 'leaky', 'unruly' and uncontrollable bodies have been equated with the subordinate feminine body. However, female bodybuilders challenge this traditional belief by exerting extreme control over themselves – creating muscled, 'fat-free' bodies. More importantly, perhaps, as female body-builders strive for 'hard', low body-fat, 'vascular' and 'shredded'[1] bodies, they challenge the binary oppositions of the identities dictated by the 'gendered habitus' (Tate 1999: 41).

Deconstructing the feminine and breaking down dichotomies

Proponents argue that female bodybuilders not only break down the feminine/ masculine dichotomy, but also contest other traditional Western binaries such as nature/culture, body/mind and sex/gender. This deconstruction of gender results in both a questioning of the 'natural' and an undermining of the 'natural gen-der order' (Kuhn 1988: 17). The female bodybuilder, then, 'threatens not only the current socially constructed definitions of femininity and masculinity, but the system of sexual difference itself' (Schulze 1990: 59). Aoki (1996), from a slightly different perspective, also believes that female bodybuilders disrupt gender categories by appearing to create a hybrid human being – a woman's head on a man's body. Aoki (1996) argues that due to the radical gender-destabilizing potential of this practice, female bodybuilders negotiate their bodies by becoming hyperfeminine through emphasizing supposed feminine attributes such as posing, hair, make-up, breasts and dance routines. Indeed, Mansfield and McGinn (1993: 64) claim that 'the female body is so dangerous that the proclamation of gender must be made very loudly indeed'. However, Aoki (1996) points out that far from making female bodybuilders' bodies more acceptable, these feminizing activities actually raise more questions over the natural body and the social construction of femininity, in a similar fash-ion to the 'man/woman in drag' and/or 'female impersonator'. Butler (1990) asserts that as 'drag' discloses the artificialness and unauthenticity of 'gender', it has the power to undermine traditional notions of a natural gender/natural sex binary. Championing both Aoki's and Butler's argument, Coles (1994: 452) explains the confusion caused by the female bodybuilder:

> [She] enact[s] a double impersonation, her 'female' body fills out a mas-culine body drag, laced with super-feminine embellishments. The spectator cannot resolve what she 'ought' to be – a woman – and what she appears to be: the impossible juxtaposition of feminine/masculine, female/male, femme/butch.

The 'uncodability' of the female bodybuilder, then, challenges not only the essentialism of gender, but the very foundations of reality itself. As Aoki

(1996: 65) notes, her contradictory appearance 'is the disturbing intrusion of the real'. The potentially subversive appearance of the hyperfeminine bodybuilder is further elaborated upon in this comment by art historian Maria-Elena Buszek (cited in Frueh 2001: 104):

> I, myself, read it as holding a very sneaky potential for the feminist 'bait-and-switch' that I love in pin-ups. I mean, if these women wore no make-up, cut their hair very short, dressed extremely butch and were all fairly young, they'd be living up to the stereotype of what a female bodybuilder (much like the lesbian) is supposed to be – a male wannabe.

Furthermore, Frueh (2001: 104) declares that bodybuilding defies an ageist society: 'the older bodybuilder/pinup/fatal woman is a killer; she destroys erotically outworn strictures of female beauty'. Thus even the aesthetic erotic presentation of the female bodybuilder could be seen as holding possibilities for liberation and empowerment. Unlike any other professional sport, many bodybuilding competitors reach their peak in their 30s and 40s, with many athletes still competing at Ms. Olympia in their 50s. Frueh consequently argues that bodybuilding has the potential to give women confidence in their bodies, appearances and sexuality regardless of their age.

Third-wave gender activism

Heywood (1997: 57) believes that female bodybuilding can be seen as a form of third-wave gender activism. Not only, she claims, does it empower and liberate the individual, but it can also 'work to facilitate change [in society] particularly on the levels of perception and consciousness'. Thus third-wave feminism, according to Heywood's perspective, can not just impact on an individual's self-development, but can also be used to improve women's role in life. This occurs, she claims, 'on an individual level, one woman at a time, women change how they see themselves and their positions in relation to the larger world, and how they are seen by others' (Heywood 1997: 57). For example, as a woman increases her strength in the gym and bench presses more than she previously believed possible, the suggestion here is that this in turn trickles into all areas of her life and empowers and enriches her to strive for more. She starts to believe that she can achieve greater things and begins to shrug off the internal socialized cultural beliefs that 'women can't do that'. Heywood consequently argues that female bodybuilding has the potential to transform a person, to make them more confident, more in control, more assertive and more positive in their work and home lives. Against the criticisms of female bodybuilding (which will be explored in the next section of the chapter), Heywood declares:

> I have to believe that consciously or unconsciously, intentionally or not, any babe who sports a muscle symbolically strikes a blow against traditional ideas about male supremacy and such practices of male domination as domestic

violence.... that any woman with muscles makes a statement in support of women's equality, self-realization, and women's rights.

(Heywood 1998: 192)

In a related argument, Nelson (1994: 31) claims that 'feminism is about freedom; women's individual and collective liberty to make their own decisions. For women, sports embody freedom... women find it, use it, and insist on retaining it'. Bodybuilding allows women time for themselves, for their own project and their own needs. As Nelson (1994: 58) asserts, '[t]hey become the person, the project, who needs care. They take care of themselves. For a group of people who have historically been defined by their ability to nurture others, the commitment to nurture themselves is radical'.

If Heywood's and Nelson's arguments are to be believed, then spending time on sports – such as bench pressing in the gym – could be seen as 'committing feminist acts'. I now turn to the opposing feminist perspective, which declares that far from empowering women, female bodybuilding is a destructive and detrimental practice.

Feminist reactions: female bodybuilding as another form of control over women

The searching, the waiting, the hoping... Using bodybuilding as a way of filling the void in people's lives, giving purpose and meaning. The absurdity of it all. Ghosts play in masquerades of femininity and masculinity. Hollowness. Void. ... deluded souls trying to make a stand, make a mark against backdrops that reveal every moment their absurdity, their puny selves, their delusions, their heartrending, pointless futility.

(Heywood 1998: 124)

The myth of the empowered female bodybuilder: the similarities between anorexia and bodybuilding

Bordo (1988) questions the 'so-called empowerment' of female bodybuilders. She claims, from a Foucauldian perspective, that while the phenomenologist centres on the malleability of the body (as evident in the notion of 'body projects'), power over the body in terms of regulation and discipline is often overlooked. She believes that activities such as bodybuilding and jogging lay on the same 'axis of continuity' as anorexia. According to Bordo, there are at least three interconnected yet distinguishable axes: first, the 'dualist axis' (dualism of separated mind and body); second, the 'control axis' (over the 'unruly' body); and third, the 'gender/power axis' (fear of women 'as too much'). Bordo refers to the 'dualist axis' as the Western philosophical binary that privileges the rational, intellectual and spiritual mind against the 'unruly passions and appetites [of the body] that might disrupt the pursuit of truth and knowledge'

(Shildrick and Price 1999: 2). Thus the body here becomes 'alien', representing 'confinement and limitation', 'the enemy' and all that 'threatens our attempts at control' (Bordo 1988: 92).

In the second axis, the 'control axis', Bordo asserts that modern society is even more obsessed with mastering the 'unruly' body. She claims that anorexia is primarily a result of a sufferer becoming 'hooked on the intoxicating feeling of accomplishment and control' (Bordo 1988: 96). Likewise, sporting activities (such as jogging and bodybuilding) are purely about control and appear to be self-destructive and self-loathing practices that 'have no other purpose than to allow people to find out how far they can push their bodies before collapsing' (Bordo 1988: 97). She goes on to claim that whilst 'on the surface', the woman who builds her body appears to be the direct opposite of the diminishing and frail anorexic, in actuality they are very similar: in both cases the women feel alienated from their bodies and there is an emphasis on control and invulnerability, with little attention directed to matters of health. Furthermore, both the anorexic body and the muscled body are united against 'a common platoon of enemies: the soft, the loose; unsolid, excess flesh' (Bordo 1990: 90). In accordance with this perspective, bodybuilding is then yet another way to control and create docile bodies (Foucault 1981).

In the 'gender/power axis', Bordo (1988: 108) points out that the 'female body appears... as the unknowing medium of the historical ebbs and flows of the fear of the woman-as-too-much', in the sense that women's anxieties spill out over their uncontrollable hungers: wanting too much, needing too much, being too emotional, too loud, too passionate and so on. Dieting and exercise are consequently implemented as a contemporary form of control, in order to discipline, chastise and contain the disobedient body. Bordo therefore argues that the anorexic, the compulsive jogger and the female bodybuilder are all trapped in a relentless and compulsive battle with their bodies: forever encaged in a life of self-destructive obsession, self-monitoring and surveillance, damaging both their health and their imagination.

In a later work, Bordo claims that the modern heroine, as presented in the media and advocated by 'power' and 'muscle' (agency[2] and third-wave) feminists, must have 'as much guts, willpower, and balls as men, that they can put their bodies through as much wear and tear, endure as much pain, and remain undaunted' (Bordo 1997: 28). In capitalist consumer society, she further posits, the 'Go for it! Know no boundaries! Take control!' mentality has taken hold. This has resulted in the celebration of plastic surgery, jogging, bodybuilding and other practices as personal and individual decisions, which people take purely for their own gratification. However, Foucault (1981) and Bordo challenge this 'self-belief' and point out that in reality, many of these products are actually 'normalization' agents – conning people into believing that such undertakings are *their own choice*. Bordo critiques 'agency' feminists (such as Davis 1995) who view this as a way for women to take back control over their lives. She claims that 'freedom', 'choice', 'autonomy', 'control' and 'self-agency' are delusions that cover up the pain, self-doubt, compulsions and disorders which result from trying to live up to societal ideals. Thus Bordo argues that the image of the female bodybuilder as confident, proud and accepting of her body is an illusion. Instead she is driven by self-imposed cultural enslavement, strict self-discipline and body dysmorphia, resulting in dangerous and oppressive acts.

Elite male bodybuilder Sam Fussell's 1991 autobiography is an insightful view into the trials, tribulations and irony involved in the world of bodybuilding. Although seen exclusively through the eyes of a male, some of his descriptions resonate beautifully with Bordo's work, pointing out the pain and despair of an encaged life forever doomed to a routine of self-surveillance and discipline. Fussell claims that bodybuilding is about a 'masculine cosmology', where the need to rule, control and conquer dominates every aspect of their everyday lives, including sleep, food, sexuality and training. When he steps on stage to collect his trophy at the San Gabriel Valley bodybuilding contest he is struck by the irony and the discrepancy between how he appears and how he feels. He claims that the façade of the 'joyful and spontaneous' image of composed strength and power is faultless, and yet:

> Thanks to the rigors of my training, my hands were more ragged, callused and cut than any longshoreman's. Thanks to the drugs and my diet, I couldn't run for 20 yards without pulling up and gasping for air. My ass cheeks ached from innumerable steroid injections, my stomach whined for substance, my whole body throbbed from gym activities and enforced weight loss. Thanks to my competitive tan, my skin was breaking out everywhere. Vinnie and Nimrod explained that all this was perfectly normal… 'Big Man, this is about *looking* good, not feeling good'.
>
> (Fussell 1991: 193)

For critics of bodybuilding, this extreme practice is simply another form of control and masochism. Academics from various disciplines have concurred with this perspective and pointed out the low self-esteem and insecurity of the elite amateur and professional bodybuilder (Fisher 1997; Klein 1993; Pope *et al.* 2000; Roussel and Griffet 2000; White and Gillett 1994).

Hyperfemininity and the compulsory heterosexuality of the female bodybuilder

Feminists who argue against the possibility that women can be liberated through bodybuilding highlight the destructive criteria of hyperfemininity and compulsory heterosexuality that is prominent within the bodybuilding subculture. Schulze (1990: 15), whilst acknowledging that the physically strong and muscular woman's body is potentially dangerous, asserts that it is pulled back into the hegemonic system using 'the markers of the patriarchal feminine'. These 'markers', as mentioned earlier in the chapter, often consist of dyeing hair blonde (suggesting innocence and vulnerability), elaborate hairstyles, hair and nail extensions, breast implants (emphasizing a fetishized part of the female body)[3] and wearing high heels, corsets and often bondage outfits for photo shoots. Subsequently, Frueh (2001: 108) argues that they become 'pin-ups in order to court stereotypical sexual fantasy'. Lisa Bavington, a professional female bodybuilder herself, explains this by arguing that patriarchal society over-sexualizes 'women's bodies in a concerted effort to diminish them from achieving any real power', thus it is 'much easier to accept a muscular woman if she is portrayed as overtly sexual' (Bavington 2000). Pornographic representations thereby minimize female strength and act as a containment strategy. For example, photography shown in muscle magazines, pictures and on the internet is the main outlet for the representation of bodybuilders (and often provides a source of income; Heywood 1997); yet the female bodybuilder, in contrast to her male counterpart, is often portrayed in pornographic or 'erotic' ways for the 'male gaze' (Coles 1994; Heywood 1997; Mansfield and McGinn 1993; St Martin and Gavey 1996; Holmlund 1989). The lack of sponsorship money for female bodybuilders means some make their living through 'schmoes' who pay for private 'muscle worship' sessions, which may include posing, wrestling or more erotic acts (Ian 2001). Thus, in direct contrast to Tate's body-project argument, the woman who builds her body becomes 'a being-for-others rather than a being-for-self' (Heywood 1997: 105). Muscle worship is discussed further in Chapter 6.

In their research, Rich (1980) and Hargreaves (1994) both expose the compulsory nature of heterosexuality in sport as a form of social control, particularly in reference to women and sexuality. As female bodybuilding pushes the boundaries of gender more than any other sport, the woman who builds her body must be 'anchored to heterosexuality; if she is not, she may slip through the cracks in the hegemonic system into an oppositional sexuality that would be irrecoverable' (Schulze 1990: 11). Schulze claims that due to a complex combination of homophobia and patriarchy in society, the female bodybuilder is labelled as a lesbian and a 'male-wannabe'. Consequently, Hargreaves (1994) believes that muscular women counteract this negative stigma by embodying images of hegemonic femininity based upon conventional heterosexual assumptions. Thus Heywood (1997: 182) argues that female bodybuilders' self-determination is undercut by their desire to be (hetero)sexually appealing; indeed, she writes ironically, 'femininity, it seems, is synonymous with sexuality'. Against this background, Heywood (1998: 113) believes that the sexual representation of female bodybuilders 'effectively subverts any disruptive potential of this new version of the feminine form'.

Competitions as controlling the female bodybuilder

Many sociologists have focused on Physique Women's Contests as a detrimental force for the liberation and empowerment of women (Aoki 1996; Mansfield and McGinn 1993; St Martin and Gavey 1996). As was demonstrated in Chapter 3, in contrast to men's competitions, female contestants have been judged on the basis of symmetry and 'feminine presentation' (including appearance, posture, posing, mannerisms, display, make-up and skin tone) more than on muscularity.

This 'femininity' factor has continuously changed over the years, depending on what is deemed to be the ideal feminine muscular physique of the time. As Lisa Bavington (2000) points out, 'femininity' is not a 'natural', inherent condition but a social construction that cannot be defined objectively; 'rather, it is open to a wide degree of interpretation and subjective criticism'. According to Lowe (1998), confusion regarding the ambiguous 'feminine' quality causes conflict and disparity between female contestants, who are never sure exactly what the judges are looking for and what will be considered 'feminine'. One conclusion to be drawn from this is that the competitive female bodybuilder is argued to be controlled by hegemonic markers of femininity, which undermine the potential to create a liberated female form.

Klein (1993) claims that bodybuilding is, ultimately, a subculture almost entirely run by men for men, as a predominately capitalist enterprise. Maria Lowe expands upon this irony:

> Bodybuilding with its almost monopolistic power hierarchy, creates an opportunity for a new physically strong look for women, yet at the same time is run by a handful of men [officials, judges, promoters and sponsors] who have the power to determine the 'appropriate' images of women's bodies.
>
> (Lowe 1998: 73)

These 'appropriate' images, according to Lowe, change periodically in order to include a wider commercial audience. She concludes, in her American study of elite female bodybuilders, that

> although, at first glance, female bodybuilders appear to embody an empowering image of women – one that exudes physical strength and emphasizes impressive musculature – when placed in the patriarchal and capitalist context of … bodybuilding organizations; their strength and power are tempered significantly.
>
> (Lowe 1998: 159)

If Lowe's study is to be believed then, despite changes over time, female bodybuilding is still dominated by men who ultimately dictate how far the sport – and women's bodies – should be allowed to evolve.

Conclusion

As it presently stands, there appear to be two viable and strong critically opposing arguments concerning women's potential liberation through bodybuilding. On the one hand, it is claimed that women who pump iron resist physical restrictions of imposed femininity. On the other, critics argue that female bodybuilders are engaged in an ultimately oppressive quest for perfect bodies of another kind. So far, no suitable empirical work exists that would allow us to properly adjudicate between these views. I argue that without further investigation into the daily lives and experiences of the female bodybuilder, it is impossible to assess whether female bodybuilding can empower and emancipate women by disrupting 'habitual practices of femininity' (Bordo 1992: 167). However, before I present the findings of my study and invite the reader into the fascinating world of British female bodybuilders, there is another critical point to make here. Despite the fact that these perspectives are diametrically opposed, both claim to have a monopoly on the truth. Moreover, both present their arguments in a simplistic fashion – either claiming that female bodybuilding is empowering or that it is disempowering – and suggest that there can be no room for manoeuvre between the two perspectives. Without more attention to the potential complexities and contradictions that may characterize the life world of the female bodybuilder, this seems a premature conclusion. Rather than simply joining one side or the other of this argument about female bodybuilding, then, I want to allow for the possibilities of a more nuanced understanding of this activity by recognizing that power is never a simple possession, but is constituted through multiple and shifting practices and discourses (Foucault 1980; Rich 2002). Such an approach can help us embark upon a more 'open' method of enquiry, allowing us insight into the nexus of subjectivities open to the female bodybuilder in relation to fluctuating relations of power – which renders them 'at one moment powerful and at another powerless' (Walkerdine 1981: 14).

Despite a small but increasing corpus of academic work centred on this research area, the majority of studies have frequently neglected the actual practices and daily experiences of the female bodybuilder, focusing instead on the textual meanings and symbolic representations of these women's bodies. In contrast to this superficiality, Schulze (1990) acknowledges that in order to appreciate and thoroughly examine the life of the female bodybuilder, we must engage with and submerge ourselves within the subculture itself, instead of trying to analyse and explain it from the outside. This is the downfall of Maria Lowe's interesting study of professional female bodybuilders in America, which does not appear to entail immersion into the subculture itself. The work of Leslie Heywood and Anne Bolin, as female bodybuilders themselves, has made vital contributions in this area, using the authors' own experiences as reflexive participant observation. However, as yet, there exists no comprehensive ethnographic study of female bodybuilders in the UK. In particular, there is a dearth of investigation into those phenomenological issues involving either the lived experience of how the female bodybuilder's physique is constructed, or how their 'assault' on conventional norms of feminine appearance is received both inside and outside of the gym.

Against this background, there is a strong argument for suggesting that it is only through detailed ethnographic work and researching the subculture from the 'inside out' that we can begin to answer and assess the question of whether female bodybuilding can be empowering for women. The purpose of the following chapters is, subsequently, to try and rectify this absence of adequate empirical work by providing an insight into the lives of these extraordinary women, uncovering the answers to mysteries such as: what precisely do these women do? How do they construct their identities? What social relations do they enter into? How do they experience and feel the reciprocal jostling that exists between their bodies and machines/weights? What does it mean and feel like to compete? It is only after examining issues such as these, I suggest, that we can construct more adequate answers to questions regarding the liberatory or oppressive character of female bodybuilding. In the next chapter I begin my exploration and presentation of my findings by focusing on the identity and daily lives of female bodybuilders outside the gym environment.

Sarah's story: part I

The beginning: becoming a female bodybuilder

There's no one reason as to how it all started. I was brought up on bodybuilding in some respects. My parents weren't into bodybuilding so much as training, but the gym where they trained was what you would call a 'spit and sawdust' gym – there were some 'hardcore' bodybuilders at the gym, and I guess what was going on in my mind subconsciously, that I was picking up on this bodybuilding thing and I really liked the look of the girls in the 80s such as Tonya Knight. As a family we were very fitness orientated – Dad had his protein powders around and we would eat well. Dad would have me up before school training, or running and after school – and so that lifestyle to me was always a normal way of being. I was just destined to take things to the extremes.

I started training from the age of 12 and by the age of 16 I knew I wanted to compete. By that point Dad had started running one of the natural bodybuilding shows, so for me it was always like a normal thing, whereas to most people it's kind of like an odd or strange thing to do. I competed at 18 and 21, back then I didn't really know what I was doing, and then I didn't compete again until 2006 (age 27?) – although my (weight) training was always like my anchor...

However, I don't think my parents ever wanted me to look like I do now, it wasn't their vision. As far as they were concerned they were encouraging me into a health and fitness lifestyle... but me being me, I have this kind of in built thing of 'how far can I push my body?' 'How much can it take?' 'Where are its limits?' and it's all or nothing – just a fascination with what it can do. If you do it, then you give it everything. If it wasn't bodybuilding then it would just be something else.

I remember being 14/15 and I was home on my own and it was absolutely belting it down outside, absolutely chucking it down... This is where I think I have this mental toughness thing – 'do I have what it takes to mentally make myself physically do something difficult?'... I remember putting on my jogging bottoms, my t-shirt, my Walkman; I was listening to Bon Jovi. I jogged to the end of the road where there was a playing field with a small running track. Jumped over the fence to see if I could make myself do ten laps of the running track in this absolutely pelting down rain, freezing cold – and I did it. I felt so good after that I'd done it and that I hadn't stopped or given in. The first time I felt that I really connected with someone, was when I heard Bev Francis [female bodybuilder] on the film 'Pumping Iron II' say that when she was a kid she would set challenges for herself such as how long she could hold her head under water. And I remember thinking that's me. I get that.

I used to be into every sport. Running, football, roller skating. I used to just go out on my bike – normal everyday activities. I wanted to do rugby, rather than football, but I wasn't allowed. I found football a bit cliquey and I wasn't very good at it... I always preferred the solitary stuff like running or doing weights in the garage... I didn't like team sports, although I was competitive.

I first competed when I was 18, in the old NAB natural show. My family loved it, they thought it was great – I was bang into sport anyway. I don't remember much about the day, only that I loved it on stage and didn't want to leave. I remember thinking prior to it, that if I enjoyed it then I would do it again – if not I'd just continue training for my own pleasure. But that was it, I was bitten. I didn't want to get off that stage. And that's all I remember.

See when I was a baby (although of course I don't remember much of it), from the age of four having had my hernia, I was told that I had to do sit-ups every day and I used to do up to 20 a day. I was a very sickly child; I would wake up in the middle of the night and be sick for no reason. And my poor mum had to change all my bedding – and I hated it and I didn't want to be this weak kid. And my Dad doesn't tolerate weakness. My brother was quite a soft-natured child and my Dad couldn't deal with it. He always said that me and my brother should have been born the other way round and he wanted Jack to be this rufty, tufty kid. Whereas I felt that I was that kid but he wanted me to be, you know, kind of his little girl, but also that. He didn't really know how to deal with me. To be fair to my parents they didn't mollycoddle me – that's probably why I am the way I am with my health, because I potentially could have had a colostomy bag, and there's no way I would have been training now. Fortunately, surgery second time round worked... so there was a massive side of my life which was really privileged by what my parents gave to me and my brother... the way they made us. They were very much 'go out there', 'get on with it', 'if it hurts then push through it, it will make you stronger'. 'If you fall over you get up and you carry on'.

I didn't want to be this weak, sickly kid. I wanted to be strong and fit and able to, like, take care of myself and not have to be reliant on anybody, but there was a side of my Dad that was... he was terrifying, aggressive – we lived in fear of him... for example, we were driving back from somewhere, me and Jack were kids sitting in the back, Mum was in the passenger seat and the next thing we knew the windscreen had shattered. Dad had punched it. Just an outburst. And you never knew when it was coming. My brother took the brunt of it really badly. He bullied my brother. He really beat him, and I felt bad and felt guilty that Jack got the brunt of it. I think Dad was wary of me because of my health, he wasn't quite sure... If me and my brother were acting up then he would bang our heads together and I'd get an awful nose bleed and blood would be pouring out of my mouth... that's not an unnatural thing for parents to do... but I think my Dad was a little bit frightened of how fragile I was... Once I was older he was more verbally aggressive towards me – I think a lot of [my desire] to be strong came from my Dad's behaviour. It was about protection, but I think it's also that nature/ nurture thing though. As he was re-enacting his Dad's behaviour. So, I think it's partly in my genes. My Dad won't remember – a combination of brain damage from an accident and alcohol has made him forget. My parents never talked about things and were never open about things. They always kept everything in. And I guess that's why they have ended up where they are now (Mum dead and Dad an alcoholic).

Despite everything, Dad always knew me in a way that Mum didn't. He always knew that I wouldn't fit into the mould, that I was going to be different. I don't think he anticipated how I would be. It's hard. It hurts a bit. Because at the end of the day, they set this ball rolling, they surrounded me in this environment and set me up in this environment and they probably didn't do themselves any favours in the respect that they didn't educate me on steroids. But they rammed down my throat natural bodybuilding, and they rammed down my throat about everything negative about steroids. So of course, when I started to learn for myself, when I realised that I wasn't going to get what I wanted naturally, I discovered that everything they were saying to me wasn't true. And I guess it's just one of those things, isn't it? You tell a child not to do anything... 'you created me, you inspired me in this environment, you told me to be different, you told me to push myself to the max, to always do my best' – they must have been times when it must have crossed his mind that I would come to a T junction of 'do I or don't I?' – but he never spoke to me about it. And now he wouldn't be able to talk to me about it anyway. He is so judgemental with me and my brother, yet look at him. And yet he seems so disappointed. I'm not what he hoped for when I was born and he was 22.

5   The identity, lifestyle and embodiment of the female bodybuilder

> It is the drive, it is the passion, it is the desire, it is the goal of perfecting your body as much as you can with the genetic limitations and blessings that you were born with. It is the life of dedication, stress, pain, pain, and more pain, and then the joy of reaching even your smallest goal... [Female bodybuilders compete] against themselves and against society. Bodybuilding is a sport and an art and the driving force that propels so many of us to sacrifice ourselves and punish our bodies and minds for goals that, to most others, seem unreasonable or even ridiculous. THAT is a bodybuilder. THAT is the female bodybuilder.
>
> (Sharon, bodybuilder of 12 years, in response to the question: 'who is the female bodybuilder?')

The costs and sacrifices involved in being a female bodybuilder are high. Her identity is under assault from many quarters. However, she also has various strategies to try to keep her sense of self unspoilt and sustainable. In this chapter I explore the identity, experiences and daily lifestyle of the female bodybuilder. I begin by outlining sociologically how identities are forged and shaped by the social interactions we have with others and exploring the consequences of not conforming to social norms. Next, I look specifically at female bodybuilders and how both the pursuit and the appearance of muscle make them deviant in society's eyes. After looking at the stereotypes, stigmatization and marginalization of the female bodybuilder, I examine the motivations and strategies that these women employ to create and preserve their identity against all this adversity.

The interaction order

People's identities are shaped significantly by the interactions they have with others. Theorists, such as Cooley (1922 [1902]) and Mead (1962 [1934]) argue that a sense of selfhood can only develop through our participation in social relationships. Cooley used the concept of the 'looking glass self', for example, to illustrate how the identities of individuals are formed via the 'gaze of the other'. These perspectives suggest that humans can only understand themselves in relation to other people, by 'comparing themselves with others, or seeing themselves through the eyes of others, that is, by taking a statistical and objective view of themselves' (Merleau-Ponty 1962: 434). As Brace-Govan (2002: 404) argues:

> The symbolic meanings conveyed by bodies are very important because people cannot be in the world without bodies. The demeanour, the presentation, the look, the size, and the physicality of bodies is… read like a text at an automatic and deep level of perception.

This 'feedback loop' on bodily appearance and self-presentation is a continuous process involving a reciprocal dialogue that spans the entirety of a person's life. According to the likes of Mead (1962), furthermore, this dialogue between others and ourselves involves more than a simple exchange of information, as we need positive approval from others in order for our lives and actions to have meaning and purpose. For example, as Crossley (2006a: 97) points out, 'it is difficult to find yourself beautiful if others do not'. These processes may affect all social actors, but feminists have been quick to point out that women in particular have historically experienced such dialogue as an objectifying, estranging and alienat-ing experience (Simone de Beauvoir 1949; Bartky 1988; Young 2005: 44). Men have been 'freer' in the interaction sphere to be more communicative, whilst women have been judged more on their physical appearance, as visual objects (Crossley 2006a: 85). Erving Goffman's work becomes particularly relevant here. Influenced by Mead's theory of self-identity formation through social interaction, Goffman (1989) looks at how we present our bodies in public and the impact that this presentation has on our capacity to sustain a specific self-identity. Goffman (1971: 185) argues that the self is created through the 'tenuous encounters' and precarious nature of the 'social interaction order': 'the individual does not go about merely going about his business. He goes about constrained to sustain a viable image of himself'. Interactions are complex and risky affairs that entail the 'actor' always being vigilant and self-monitoring in order to allow the encounter to go as smoothly as possible. For Goffman (1979, 1987), 'impression manage-ment', including the crucial first impression, is paramount in preserving both social and personal identities. Within the interaction order, social expectations, norms, values and roles are constantly being maintained, and nowhere is this more evident than in the case of culturally acceptable notions of gender.

Kessler and McKenna (1978) argue that individuals automatically make a 'gender attribution' every time they see a human being, consigning others to the sex of male or female based upon Western assumptions of masculine and feminine. As children, our gender is one of the first things that we learn and is central to developing our sense of self (Oakley 1972). According to Coveney *et al.* (1984: 31), furthermore, 'masculinity and femininity have been and are constructed in relation to one another to create and perpetuate male supremacy'. This is reinforced by the pressure on women to be inherently sexual in *appear-ance*, compared with expectations for men to be sexual in *behaviour* in terms of dominance and power. Fitting gender norms therefore becomes vital for a person's bodily presentation to be likely to facilitate social interaction and to be accepted generally by society. These norms of 'gender interaction' are not imposed by any brute force or physical control, but are conveyed in a more subtle manner. For instance, Goffman argues that 'men often treat women as faulted actors with respect to "normal" capacity for various forms of physical exertion' (1974: 196–7). Bartky (1988: 68) extends this analogy by arguing that 'a man may literally steer a woman everywhere she goes'. The man's movement 'is not necessarily heavy or pushy or physical in an ugly way; it is light and gentle but firm in the way of the most confident equestrians with the best trained horses'. In this way, Goffman (1979: 9) believes that gender inequality within the ritual order of everyday encounters is 'carried via the positioning of the body even into the gentlest, most loving moments without apparently causing strain'.

Against this background, it is not surprising to learn that there are high costs for those who transgress and do not fit the norms, appearances, behaviours and actions deemed appropriate for their sex. These 'costs' can involve violence. More usually, however, they relate back to the need for validation of self through the social approval of others. If an actor's body betrays him or herself during the public ritual, that individual risks 'losing face' and subsequent ostracization and stigmatization. In his landmark book *Stigma: Notes on the Management of Spoiled Identity* (1963), Goffman describes stigma as 'an attribute that is deeply discrediting within a particular social interaction' (ibid.: 3). The person with the attribute becomes 'reduced in our minds from a whole and usual person to a tainted, discounted one'. They are judged and found morally culpable. Exclusion from the interaction order makes it incredibly hard for deviant individuals to develop and maintain a positive identity. Actors are not, however, passive entities, and do have some agency: they can, albeit with difficulty, disregard negative feedback by focusing on only the views of the people they deem to be important and, even within this feedback circuit, carefully select and interpret the information that they decide to take on board (Cooley 1902; Franks and Gecas 1992). Stigmatized people can also try to protect their identities by surrounding themselves with other similarly marginalized people and 'sympathetic others', away from the 'normals'. Subcultures can therefore provide marginalized groups with at least some positive reinforcement, although ultimately, as Crossley (2006a: 95–6) points out, it 'is difficult not to be affected or bothered by the views of significant others'.

Female bodybuilders, like other stigmatized groups, are marginalized and condemned by their 'deviant aesthetic' and because they are subverting 'the stylistic certainty and aesthetic precision' related to the smooth functioning associated with social control (Ferrell and Sanders 1995: 5, 11, 15). However, the fact that the appearances, actions and desires of female bodybuilders may threaten not only institutional norms, but the *gendered foundations of social interaction* itself, separates them from many other deviant groups within society (Downes and Rock 2007). In a culture where the 'appearance and (re)presentations of women's bodies are key determinants of feminine identity and cultural acceptability' (Brace-Govan 2002: 404) and 'muscles are *the* sign of masculinity' (Glassner 1989: 311), female bodybuilders deviate forcefully from gendered interaction norms. The transgressive nature of female bodybuilders lies not just in the shape and size of their muscular bodies, moreover, but in their *choice* to pursue this transgression. This choice poses a considerable challenge in relation to the task of sustaining a viable sense of self-identity. It also raises questions about what identity-affirming resources, or vocabularies of motive (Mills 1940), are made available to these women during their time as female bodybuilders.

The stereotypes, stigma and marginalization of the female bodybuilder

The troublesome and disturbing body of the hypermuscular woman is deemed so outrageously deviant by society that it provokes and evokes harsh attributions and acts of discursive violence (Reid-Bowen 2008), as typified by and encapsulated in the following quote:

> It is disgusting! These are NOT WOMEN anymore. They are beyond the point of no return. Whoever would do that is SICK! YOU HAVE TO BE SICK TO DO THIS TO YOURSELF! THERE IS NO NEED TO LOOK LIKE THAT! IT IS DISGUSTING! MALE BODYBUILDERS WHO OVERDO IT LOOK HORRIBLE TOO BUT SEEING A WOMAN MUTILATE THEIR BODY IN THIS WAY IS SICK! UGLY UGLY UGLY! [emphasis in original].[1]

Furthermore, Fierstein (2000: 15) argues that these 'monsters' are considered to be 'grotesque, manlike, androgynous, virile, freakish, dumb, narcissistic, obsessive, excessive, unhealthy, pornographic, offensive, and scary; she is a steroid user, a bulldyke, a dominatrix and an exhibitionist', amongst other derogatory terms. Perhaps less aggressive, albeit still negative, stereotypes were found in Forbes *et al.*'s (2004: 487) research, which discovered that female bodybuilders are perceived as less likely to be good mothers, less intelligent and less socially popular and attractive than average women. Literature by Lowe (1998), Shea (2001) and Steinem (1994) argues that men find muscular women who challenge traditional notions of male supremacy threatening and repulsive. As Forbes *et al.* (2004) point out, ordinary women also see female bodybuilders as violating gender norms and rebelling against 'nature'. The female bodybuilder's body 'presents a clear and present danger... to what a woman is and ought to be, but also to the constitution of maleness' (Fierstein 2000: 17; also see Chapter 4).

In the context of these highly negative cultural views, it has been suggested that the hypermuscular woman's body must be 'constantly policed, a nightmarish fantasy-body that is forever under the sign of prohibition' (Aoki 1996: 66). In this regard the media acts as a powerful enforcer, portraying these women as 'scary monsters' who are 'at war' with society and with their own bodies, looking and sounding like men and rejecting what is culturally normal, acceptable and even tolerable (Theroux 2000; *The Independent* 2008; Maume 2005).

The pursuit of female muscle as deviant

The witch-hunt begins right at the very beginning of the female bodybuilder's pursuit of muscle, even before there are any visible markings of deviance. The decision and *choice* of these women to embark on a quest for muscular size and definition immediately ostracizes them and renders them abnormal in relation to gender norms. Friends, families and work colleagues, noticing this initial interest in bodybuilding and progression from light weight training to training for muscle mass, often feel compelled to articulate their concerns, acting as a form of social control. In the case of Lucie (a bodybuilder of eight years), she recalls her mother getting quite angry at her, asking, 'Why are you doing this? What are you trying to prove?' Similarly, Sascha (a bodybuilder of three months) remembers her father saying: 'I'm concerned about you; I'm worried about your health. I don't understand why you're doing this to yourself'. These comments illustrate the social unacceptability of a woman wishing to build muscle. She is thought to be psychologically deviant or pathological, or even considered to be deliberately trying to upset other people. The idea that a woman wants to build muscle and yet still retain her identity as a female is incomprehensible when seen in terms of the hegemonic gender norms of society. Indeed, most female bodybuilders, at some point in their lives, have been asked: 'Why do you want to look like a man?'

The perceived deviance of female bodybuilders stems from cultural assumptions about masculinity and femininity which have historically influenced how women's and men's bodies have been perceived. According to these norms, men and women are opposite, and should consequently be, *and* desire to be, aesthetically disparate. Differentiation between the sexes is commonly considered to be exaggerated during puberty, when hormones trigger the visual display of secondary sex characteristics. Whilst there are several physical markers which signify the transition towards male adulthood (for example, enlargement of the testes, development of facial and pubic hair and changes to the voice), it is the growth of size and strength which are the principal symbolic badges associated with 'manliness'. Muscularity is not only a visual marker of masculinity, interpreted ordinarily as a manifestation of naturally higher levels of testosterone, but informs the kinesthetic expectation that men dominate social and cultural spaces (Goffman 1974; Young 2005). The male body, then, is not just a physical entity but a way of orienting the world through embodiment. As Connell (1987: 297) explains:

> The physical sense of maleness is not simply a thing. It involves the size and shape, habits of posture and movement, particular skills and lack of others, the image of one's own body, the way it is presented to others and the ways they respond to it, the way it operates at work and in sexual relations.

In this context, strength and muscles belong to the man's domain, representing power, authority, force and capability.

Against this background, women who participate in male-dominated sports and activities emphasizing their strength and increasing their muscularity are perceived as a threat to this social order and risk having both their femininity and their sexuality scrutinized and questioned (Nelson 1994: 45; Rich 1980; Hargreaves 1994). Females learn from a young age the importance of looking attractive to men (McRobbie 1991), which in Western society has never included feminine strength, size and muscle (Gorely *et al.* 2007). If a woman desires these masculine traits, she is perceived as rejecting both her sex and heterosexual relationships. For instance, one of my interviewees, Pat (a bodybuilder of seven months) recollects her mother saying: 'What's wrong with you? Don't you want a boyfriend?' Similarly, Deborah (a bodybuilder of six months) recalls her brother telling her:

> Female bodybuilders look sick and repulsive. They are transsexuals... Why does anyone want to look like that? Who finds female bodybuilders attractive? Gay men? Lesbians? Who?

Thus when a woman displays (or even desires) the aesthetics of muscularity, it impinges on most people's sense of propriety and normality in relation to gender and sexuality. Not only do female bodybuilders lose out in terms of physical capital (Bourdieu 1978), placing themselves beyond the borders of conventional notions of beauty; they also risk 'censure for so deliberately transgressing the normative ideal for the female body' (St Martin and Gavey 1996: 55). This censure comes not only from the media, but also from the general public, work colleagues, friends, family and lovers.

Paying the price for defying the gendered social interaction order

As found in many other research studies (Lowe 1998; Brace-Govan 2004; Dobbins 1994: 8; Ian 1995; Fisher 1997; Heywood 1998; Schulze 1990; Frueh *et al.* 2000: 8), the women in this study regularly had to deal with unsolicited derogatory remarks. Their bodies, exuding stereotypical notions of masculinity in terms of size and shape, were no longer allowed to be their own but became objects of public property. However, it was not just strangers' stares and muttered comments that these women had to contend with, but also confrontational remarks and challenges regarding their physique, femininity and sexuality. Whilst none of my interviewees spoke of the violence that other research into this area has highlighted (Ian 1995), many female bodybuilders spoke about the discursive animosity they received for crossing the boundaries of acceptable femininity. Caroline (a bodybuilder of 17 years) reflected upon some of her negative experiences:

> People can be so cruel... I've had people shout out their car window at me, 'are you a geezer?', or stop me in the street or when I'm out shopping and ask me 'are you a man or a woman?'. People can be so extremely rude, harassing and hurtful... when I was younger some of the comments would upset me so much that I'd cry and Daniel [her husband] would say that if it upset me so much I should stop...

Alice (a bodybuilder of 18 months) recalls an incident in a pub where a stranger walked straight up to her and wanted to arm-wrestle her. On another occasion, at a local nightclub, a man came up to her and grabbed her bicep, declaring in abject fascination that she had the biggest arms he had ever seen on a woman. In the public sphere, the female bodybuilder is then under constant interrogation from the 'gaze' (and actions) of others. There are, however, other gender interactions that are unintentionally damaging to the identity of the muscular woman (Devor 1989: 47–9). For instance, Sharon (a bodybuilder of 12 years) spoke with anger and exasperation of being refused money in a bank because the cashier did not believe she was a woman (her first name appeared on the debit card). Similarly, Christine (a bodybuilder of five years) told me:

> People look at the size of me – they look at my height, my build... especially my back... and just assume that I'm a man. I get called 'Sir' all the time. It really frustrates me... that's one of the reasons I've decided to grow my hair long.

The assumption that a muscular body must be synonymous with manhood also affected Katie (a bodybuilder of six years) who has on several occasions had to deal with the embarrassment of being asked to get out of the women's toilets.

Whilst some of the families became more accustomed to and accepting of the female bodybuilder's lifestyle, showing either resignation or signs of support, for the majority this quest for muscularity continued to cause conflict and emotional distress. Amy (a bodybuilder of four years) mentioned how her sister became belligerent whenever the topic of bodybuilding was brought up. For example, she said to Amy: 'your back is disgusting, really lumpy – you'll look like a freak'. This was by no means an unusual reaction: most family members felt they had a licence to censure and recriminate. As the following observation illustrates, the lifestyle choice of the female bodybuilder causes friction and strain on immediate relations:

> Family meals and get-togethers have become a nightmare. I avoid them whenever I can... They expect me to eat the fatty foods that they prepare and feel rejected if I bring my own and yet I never lecture them to eat more health-ily because they are overweight... they won't accept my lifestyle choice at all – they seem to think I'd be happier if I got married, settled down and had children.
>
> (Katie, bodybuilder of six years)

Against this background, further misunderstandings and fear are generated, as bodybuilding not only appears to be 'gratuitous, dysfunctional and purposeless' (Frueh 2001: 81), but also transgresses against gender roles and norms concerning how women are expected to spend their time. Traditionally, participation in sport has been seen as a form of escapism for men, a place where they can focus on activities purely for their own pleasure (Messner and Sabo 1990). In contrast, women have been expected to be selfless, caring and nurturing, focusing their attention on close relationships and starting a family of their own (Heywood 1998). Even in families where parents have participated in the bodybuilding subculture themselves and have actively encouraged their daughter's endeavour, there are still limits and borders that should not be crossed. Michelle (a bodybuilder of five years) described how her father used to be supportive of her training until, after much contemplation, she decided to take steroids: 'Since I turned to the "dark side" [steroids], I've hardly been in contact with my dad... he doesn't like what I'm doing now... there's now this gulf between us'.

Some of the female bodybuilders spoke of the challenges and difficulties of not only trying to maintain intimate relationships with others, but also finding and dating heterosexual men who did not feel threatened or repulsed by their bodies. Alice (a bodybuilder of 18 months) illustrates this in a recent conversation in which a man told her: 'You are an attractive woman, but your arms are just too big... They intimidate men'. Indeed, several of my single interviewees similarly spoke of the problems involved in trying to date 'normal' men, who treated them as 'abnormal' and unappealing on the assessment of their physique. Whilst being overlooked as suitable 'dating material', rejected as unattractive and even found disgusting by mainstream society can be potentially detrimental to the identity of the female bodybuilder, female muscle challenges the gender order so much that it can also actually break down serious long-term relationships. Monica's (a bodybuilder of two years) decision to break up with her cohabitant boyfriend exemplifies this: after trying to persuade her not to train and to lose weight for many months, the situation came to a head when he told her: 'I don't want you to train anymore... Having sex with you from [behind] is like having sex with a man'.

These previous examples show just how truly deviant female muscle is considered by society, and demonstrate the high price that is paid, both in the public and the private sphere, by the women who decide to become female bodybuilders.

The quest for muscularity: motivations, embodied pleasures and identity

In light of the stigma and reactions by 'normals' to the transgressions of female bodybuilders, many questions are raised: why would a woman choose to take up bodybuilding in the first place? What motivates these women and spurs them to subvert societal gender norms? How do female bodybuilders seek to maintain a positive sense of identity in such a hostile world? As Webber (2007: 139) posits, it is only by exploring 'the lived reality of transgression', including the desires, motivations and pleasures of these extraordinary women, that we can begin to understand their devotion to an interactional order based upon the pursuit of muscle rather than the cultivation and reflection of gendered ideals.

In the same way that these individual women come from very diverse backgrounds, the motivations that propelled these women into bodybuilding were equally heterogeneous. For some women, the slide into the 'ministry of muscle' came about simply as an extension to their training, a sport they realized that they both enjoyed and excelled at. Others, such as Amy (a bodybuilder of four years), 'got hooked' after using weight training as a prescribed form of rehabilitation from other sports-related injuries. In some cases, my interviewees spoke of the lure of intense weight training as a consequence of a particular event in their lives. Lucie (a bodybuilder of eight years), for instance, spoke of her desire to regain control of her body after giving birth to her son:

> I remember standing in front of the mirror and being horrified by what I saw in front of me... I saw what I had become and wanted to do something about it... I'd always been active in the past but somehow I'd let myself get out of shape. I didn't want this to be 'it', if you see what I mean? I didn't want to be defined for the rest of my life as just a mother. I guess I wanted to take control of my body and my life again and say 'this is me!'

Resonating with Victoria Pitts' (2003) body modifiers, other women spoke of their involvement in bodybuilding as a form of healing. Katie (a bodybuilder of six years) believes that her immersion in the bodybuilding lifestyle literally saved her from a reliance on alcohol:

> Instead of drinking every night – and, let's face it, most of the day too! – I put all my time and energy into the gym. I started to look after myself more and have more respect for my body... it wasn't easy... and I relapsed a few times – but you can't drink and build muscle, it was one or the other...

Rachel (a bodybuilder of two years) and Mary (a bodybuilder of 12 years) also spoke of the cathartic and therapeutic power of extreme weight training, but this time as a route of recovery from anorexia. In a society where women are preoccupied with slimming and losing weight, female bodybuilders defy convention by eating a high-calorie, high-protein diet in order to increase their body mass. Rachel explains how her negative and destructive relationship with food changed as a direct result of becoming more involved in bodybuilding:

> I used to see food as the enemy and would use loads of different avoidance strategies... [such as] drinking loads of coffee and diet coke, eating foods with as few calories as possible, eating fibre tablets and so on... I'd exercise for hours if I'd overeaten and even force myself to be sick at times... I tried to eat only one meal a day... but now I'm no longer afraid of food as I know I need it to build a bigger and healthier body. I no longer avoid fats for example and I make sure I eat protein every couple of hours... I exercise less and rest more. I feel so much better for it, both mentally and physically.

Similarly, Mary spoke of the remedial properties of embracing the bodybuilding world:

> I took up bodybuilding because I didn't want to be weak anymore… I wanted to be in control of my life but in a powerful and positive way… I used to hate my body, but now because of bodybuilding I have learnt to really appreciate it.

Echoing the narratives of other female body modifiers (see Pitts 2003), female bodybuilders emphasize the importance of taking back 'control' over their bodies in a beneficial manner. As Barbara (a bodybuilder of seven years) articulates:

> Control is central to it all, control of my body means control of my life… If things are getting out of control in your life, the one thing you can control is yourself; when you train, how you train, when you eat, etc.

This emphasis on control over the body can be read as a way of 'anchoring the self' (Sweetman 1999c) in the context of an increasingly unstable and uncertain society – a time when individuals are experiencing a sense of loss and disorientation in the whirl and confusion of postmodern life (see Introduction and Chapter 1). As Polhemus and Randall (1998: 38) explain, 'in an age which increasingly shows signs of being out of control, the most fundamental sphere of control is re-employed: mastery over one's own body'.

Despite the diversity of motivations to become female bodybuilders, all these woman realized that they were different, or at least desired to be different, from hegemonic norms of femininity. For some, this incompatibility with dominant gender norms became apparent at a young age:

> I've always felt I was different from other females. Even as a girl… I was a real tomboy… and since I was little I've always gone 'feel my arms'.
> (Corina, bodybuilder of four years)

For other female bodybuilders it was more of an epiphanic moment:

> I was reading through my boyfriend's *Muscle and Fitness* magazine when I saw a picture of a Fitness girl, and I thought I want to look like that… She looked amazing, strong, independent and beautiful, like she could do anything.
> (Danielle, bodybuilder of five years)

> I became interested in bodybuilding when I was 17. I was exceptionally tall for a woman and very thin, weighing under nine stone. People used to tease me… One day I saw a picture of a female bodybuilder… and decided that I wanted my body to look like that. I wanted to be big and strong.
> (Emma, bodybuilder of 19 years)

Such reflections illustrate how these women not only felt distanced from *at least* one element of the gendered norms associated with the interaction order, but also became committed to identities and actions placing them outside of the respectable boundaries of interaction. This is evidenced further in their reactions to the changes wrought in their *own* bodies. Whilst the significance placed on visual display (especially in competitions – see Chapter 9) has obvious affinities with the feminine concern with appearance, it is accompanied here by an emphasis on physical empowerment focused on the *dominance* of space and *enjoyment* of self, rather than with passivity (Young 2005). This is illustrated by the delight expressed by both Christine and Amy:

> I love looking like I do when I'm cut [defined] and at my peak. I feel so strong, like I could do anything and nothing could stand in my way.
>
> (Christine, bodybuilder of five years)

> It's really exciting when… you suddenly notice the definition and striations in the muscle group… I love it. I think it looks really beautiful.
>
> (Amy, bodybuilder of four years)

These findings coincide with comments in other interviews with female bodybuilders:

> Thanks to bodybuilding… I feel powerful, emotionally and physically. I feel strong and in tune with my body. And I feel more alive and sexy than ever before.
>
> (Skye Ryland, cited in Dobbins 1995: 125)

> When I look in the mirror I see someone who's finding herself, who has said once and for all it doesn't really matter what role society said I should play. I can do anything I want to and feel proud about doing it.
>
> (Irma Martinez, cited in Rosen 1983: 72)

The focus on muscular aesthetics for these women thus becomes a somatic representation, symbolic of strength, power, control, mastery and independence. The women derive a sense of achievement through activity shaping their bodies for themselves. Furthermore, as Monaghan (2001: 351) points out, there is an intimate connection between bodybuilders' physical appearance and their sense 'of physical and emotional wellbeing'. Within this context, Williams' (1998: 451) notion that 'transgression is pleasurable' becomes especially applicable to female bodybuilders, whose transmogrification becomes not just a visual display but an embodied union of empowerment and pleasure. The desired textual appearance of muscularity at its most positive becomes intricately woven with the motivations and pleasures of the female bodybuilder, resulting, at its best, in an amalgamation of the mind and sensuous embodiment.

Body projects and feminine identity

Female bodybuilders get intense pleasure out of constructing a body to their own design. They become the architects of their own body projects (Shilling 1993). As Charlie (a bodybuilder of four years) comments: 'Isn't the beauty of the human body the opportunity to mould it into whatever we want it to be? We are doing this so that we can feel good about ourselves'. Female body-builders are well aware that their corporeal self-expressions are not perceived as beautiful or even acceptable by mainstream society. Despite the animosity received from 'normals', many of these women declared that they did not care about other people's views of their appearance. This is illustrated by Danielle (a bodybuilder of five years):

> It doesn't bother me at all… because I'm proud, I do it for myself, you know, I do it because of how I want to look… to me that appeals… I prefer that; a fit body, to me that looks like she's working at it, meaning she takes care of herself, not that she's just done it naturally.

Similarly, Corina (a bodybuilder of four years) acknowledged that whilst perhaps some men found her body unattractive (or even repulsive), 'it's not the male view that counts, is it? It's your own personal view of your body'. In this way, female bodybuilders confront and challenge conventional notions of women as docile, erotic spectacles for the enjoyment of men (Bartky 1988). Instead, they reclaim power from the objectification of women in patriarchal society, by carving out a territory for themselves in which they can revel in their own definitions of beauty and pleasure. Their bodies become signatures and self-authorships of their own desires (Tate 1999: 50).

Fierstein (2000: 17) declares that 'the hypermuscular woman is a woman… who wants and has big muscles and who identifies herself as female and squarely within the parameters of feminine identity'. How then, in the context of subvert-ing all societal understandings of femininity, do female bodybuilders not only see themselves as possessed of their 'feminine identity', but also manage to sustain it? Comparable to Lowe's (1998) and Tate's (1999) studies, each female bodybuilder in my study has her own interpretation of 'femininity' and her own aesthetic boundaries that should not be crossed in order to maintain it. One professional competitor (and UK female judge), for example, expressed this view when com-menting on the issues involved in balancing femininity and muscularity:

> I think I look like a woman – though I know other people don't always per-ceive me in this way. Femininity is very important – your skin tone, the way you look, walk, your posture, the way you act. Make-up, hair, nails (even the way you pose on stage needs to be feminine). Femininity can be destroyed if people abuse drugs rather than use them – go overboard and develop masculine characteristics.

However, when I asked the same UK judge if male bodybuilding competitors were judged on a 'masculinity' factor, her reaction was one of confusion. It appears that masculinity is perceived as 'non-performative' and innate, compared to femininity, which is perceived to be more fluid and transferable (Halberstam 1995). In contrast, for Michelle (a bodybuilder of five years), femininity takes on a different meaning:

> I think many female bodybuilders misinterpret femininity and they do this – over the top femininity thing, you know, which I don't necessarily think means femininity. I think men and women can be feminine in other ways, without it having to be the whole hair, make-up and big boobs, if you see what I mean…

Other female bodybuilders also actively interpret their definition of 'femininity', as illustrated by Corina: 'Femininity is whatever I decide it to be. I would love to be huge'. Debbie (a bodybuilder of seven and a half years), when reflecting on this issue, recognized the constricting oppression of contemporary gender norms:

> Girls can be feminine with or without muscles. Do people ever criticize men for being unmasculine because they don't work out and have no… muscle definition or size… a girl can come across masculine because of attitude and you don't need muscles for that… on the other hand people confuse the confidence that being strong and in good shape gives you for masculinity because women are 'supposed to be weak and incapable'… I am a girl, I like being a girl, and yes I would love to get a lot bigger and more muscular… and I am very feminine.

Female bodybuilders are therefore reflexive, self-conscious agents who live out their own definitions and understandings of femininity. Like Tate's (1999: 35) serious weight-trainers, these women, firm in their identity, do 'shape their body to their own liking', perceiving their quest for muscle as 'a personal challenge' that does not seek 'the approval of men, women, or society'.

However, as noted at the start of the chapter, our identity is in constant negotiation through interactions with others. Female bodybuilders therefore employ several other strategies in order to maintain a positive identity. Similar to other deviant and stigmatized people who are excluded from mainstream society, these muscular women pursued social relationships among like-minded and like-bodied individuals (Hall and Jefferson 2006). Social comparison theorists claim that in order for deviant individuals to retain a positive sense of self, cognitive and physical boundaries are erected between themselves and vilified others (Rosenburg and Kaplan 1982; Widdicombe and Wooffitt 1990). Female bodybuilders consequently cultivate an attitude of superiority to 'normals', valuing themselves as unique, special and different to other women (Fisher 1997). In comparison, outsiders are frequently perceived as lazy, unmotivated and unattractive. Negative and cruel comments made by these unimportant 'ignorants' (Christine, a bodybuilder of five years) are thereby dismissed and ignored. Instead, these extraordinary women surround themselves with partners and friends who are accepting, encouraging and complimentary of their appearance and endeavour. For instance, as Lucie (a bodybuilder of eight years) stated defiantly:

> My husband thinks I'm sensuous and hot… among other flattering descriptions. Just because some people might not comprehend a certain aesthetic look, doesn't mean that other people don't appreciate and love it.

These crucial interactions with 'kindred souls' create an alternative frame of reference, enabling female bodybuilders to deflect the wider stigmatization that they face in their daily lives (Cohen 1955). Furthermore, the identity of the female bodybuilder is reaffirmed by engaging in activities that support their lifestyle and goals. For example, reading and buying bodybuilding magazines, books, DVDs, posters and pictures normalizes the image of the female bodybuilder (Tate 1999), whilst interacting on bodybuilding forums and attending competitions allows them to be part of a collective identity. Indeed, the internet has provided an increasingly important source of information and interaction for female bodybuilders. Cyberspace has created a place where geographically scattered female bodybuilders can not only feel valued, but also come together to create a kind of 'sisterhood' (a group of similar women whose shared struggle gives them a unique emotional connection), supporting each other by offering friendship and practical advice. Although not all of my interviewees believed that the bodybuilding subculture provided a supportive network for females (see Fisher 1997, Klein 1993 and Lowe 1998 for pessimistic claims about 'hypermasculinity' and 'devaluation of women' within the culture), some of the women found great comfort in mixing with their 'own'. For example, Alice (a bodybuilder of 18 months) claimed: 'bodybuilders are… unique… I have found more compassion, thoughtfulness, encouragement and sense of community in my short time being a bodybuilder than anywhere else'. This sense of camaraderie is reinforced by the fact that these women occupy the same 'social field' and recognize, and pursue, the same form of physical capital (Bourdieu 1978).

Body dissatisfaction: the price paid for investing too much in the body's appearance

Even though the defiant, positive narratives of desire, motivations and pleasures in embodiment articulated by these women are real, to leave their story there would offer only a partial analysis of what it is to be a female bodybuilder. Like other human beings, muscular women are complicated, complex individuals who can hold apparently opposing beliefs simultaneously. This section, then, explores the more negative aspects of embodiment experienced in the daily lives of these women. Despite the various strategies employed to sustain their identity, the female bodybuilder still has to contend with arguably the most powerful critic of all – herself. Tate (1999: 42) argues that female bodybuilders become slaves to the 'tyranny of the[ir] latent image', which 'rules women's lives – how they perceive themselves, their diets, training routines, leisure time, relationships… fear of what they would become if they didn't train'. The 'male gaze' is rejected, but is arguably replaced by yet another voyeur. The women become driven, obsessed and self-disciplined by their ideal of perfection – spurred on by their own concept of beauty and the perfect female form. Thus, far from creating a body that they can be content with, many of my participants concurred that 'bodybuilding makes you even more critical of your body' (Lucie, a bodybuilder of eight years). As Danielle (a bodybuilder of five years) contends: 'I think bodybuilders are all hypercritical of themselves. It's an art form where precision is everything and there is always something that can be improved'.

Bodybuilders have commonly been diagnosed and pathologized by psychiatrists as suffering from 'reverse anorexia' ('bigorexia'), or what has been more popularly classified as 'muscle dysmorphia'. Symptoms include the preoccupation with 'excessive' muscularity (to the extent that it impairs and impacts upon daily lifestyle) and are accompanied by feelings of poor body image (Connan 1998) and low self-esteem (Olivardia *et al*. 2000). Despite continual reassurance from the tape measure, fat calipers, weight scales and other people, the 'bigorexic' still perceives themselves as too small and 'not muscular enough'.[2] The condition is believed to be under-diagnosed due to the societal acceptability for men to be or to desire to be big (Pope *et al*. 2000). Until relatively recently, only men were attributed to be suffering from this disorder. However studies such as that of Phillips *et al*. (1997) are quick to point out that women can also develop characteristics of muscle dysmorphia. Fisher (1997) claims that, similar to the anorexic, female bodybuilders see themselves through a distorted lens and fail to see themselves equitably. Michelle (a bodybuilder of five years) illustrates this point in the following quote:

> I still don't see it (the muscularity). Though… I caught a glimpse of myself in the mirror and it was one of those moments where I could see myself more objectively and I thought fucking hell I'm actually quite big. But most of the time I just don't know – I always think that I'm small and not good enough and that this body part needs bringing up.

The pleasures in the body, then, can become secondary to the discontent and dissatisfaction these women felt from their perceived physical flaws and inadequacies. Similar to many female bodybuilders in this study, Emma (a bodybuilder of 19 years) explains: 'You can't ever be "happy" with your body – you are always trying to improve it'. The continual struggle to achieve their "latent" image (Tate 1999) can generate discord between their mind and body, potentially allowing the body to become an object of hate, resentment, loathing and fear. This is demonstrated in the words of Amy (a bodybuilder of four years) and Sharon (a bodybuilder of 12 years):

Every time you look in the mirror you just feel like you're a million miles away from the ideal that you're striving for… I just think what more do I have to do?!

(Amy)

I keep striving for the light at the end of the tunnel and hope that eventually I'll get where I want to be. But the thing about bodybuilding is that I'm never satisfied… nothing ever seems good enough… I hate the summer, I don't like wearing shorts and tops, or being on the beach, I prefer covering up – maybe one day I'll feel differently.

(Sharon)

Female bodybuilders do not therefore escape the relentless need for self-improvement associated bodily dissatisfaction experienced by other women in society (Bordo 1988). As Smith (1990: 19) notes in research into the effects of fashion magazines on female body image, 'the body, for the feminine subject, is the object of the subject-at-work'; the body is always inadequate, 'there is always work to be done'.

Food

Feminists such as Steiner-Adair (1990), Bordo (1997, 2004) and Frost (2001) claim that in Western society women are expected to be preoccupied with their weight and dieting, and indeed to be 'at war' and in an antagonistic relationship with their bodies (see Chapter 4). However, female bodybuilders have a particularly complex relationship with food. Although they need surplus 'quality' calories and a regular high protein intake throughout the day in order to create the optimum conditions for muscle growth, for the muscles to actually show (to mark them out from being simply 'big' women, or even worse considered 'overweight' women), they need to have low body fat (this is discussed further in Chapter 9). The women in my study dealt with this dilemma in two different ways. The first group felt that the desire for muscle and strength far outweighed any additional increase in body fat that might be inadvertently acquired as part of their quest. Within this category, the women were divided between those who embraced the opportunity to eat on a regular basis, declaring that they spent so much time 'dieting for competitions that they wanted to enjoy their food as much as possible' (Michelle, bodybuilder of five years), and those who were committed to this muscle-building philosophy but developed an alienating and negative relationship with their bodies as a result. This is illustrated by Amy (a bodybuilder of five years):

I know that in order to grow [muscle] I have to put on this extra layer of fat. But I hate it when I can't see the definition in my abs. I just feel flabby and uncomfortable in myself… I end up wearing baggy training tops and clothes so that it doesn't show.

The second group of women in my study, however, spend a lot of time and energy trying to 'balance' their food intake and exercise output, in order to retain a body of low fat percentage, with defined muscularity. This is supported by Mary (a bodybuilder of 12 years):

> I need to eat more [in order to put on size and muscle], which goes against the grain of everything... But I have a big appetite... I have had to cut down on CV [cardiovascular exercise] a lot, it's a bit of a mental thing... It was my birthday last week and I ate out so many times, I needed to do boxercise and I really worked hard ... Otherwise I would become so fat.

The negative and detrimental attitude to food cited by many of my participants has been confirmed by other studies. In Tate's (1999) work, for instance, the desired image becomes so powerful that the women feel compelled to perform excessive amounts of cardiovascular work in order to 'burn' off any 'bad', fat-laden food to which they have 'given in' and eaten. Confirming Bordo's (1993, 2004) claims that there is a direct link between bodybuilding and anorexia (see Chapter 4), one judge told me that 'eating disorders are rife within the industry'. Both bodybuilding and anorexia effect an investment of everything into outward appearance and are connected by the anti-fat theme which permeates our society, and which particularly affects women (Lloyd 1996). Furthermore, whilst male bodybuilders also struggle to eat the 'right' foods, it is female bodybuilders who have the most difficult relationship with dieting. Not only is it harder for them to lose fat due to natural hormones and genetics, but there is still more pressure for women to retain a 'slimmer' appearance throughout the year for the purposes of photo shoots, promotional endorsements and opportunities within the subculture (Lowe 1998; Heywood 1998).

Female bodybuilders, like their male counterparts, accumulate vast knowledge about nutrition. Their diet becomes regulated with extreme precision and it is not unusual for strict diet plans to be adhered to on a daily basis, determining the exact number of grams of protein, carbohydrates and fat that is allowed. As Tate (1999: 43) explains, the 'relationship with food becomes one in which food does not necessarily need to be enjoyable', but is used scientifically and calculatedly as a fuel for the formation of muscle. These diets become extremely monotonous and structured, requiring immense self-imposed discipline in order for them to stick to 'plan'. The body, then – especially in relation to food – becomes 'a territory that must be cherished, yet overcome, as a best friend and worst enemy' (Yates 1991: 168).

The regime

In order to achieve their 'ideal' body and to lay the foundations for optimum muscle growth, female bodybuilders construct a very rigid, structured lifestyle. As Jennifer (a bodybuilder of two years) put it, time is ordered on a basis in which bodybuilders 'wake up, eat, "medicate", work out, eat, work out, eat, "medicate", sleep'. The lives of female bodybuilders therefore revolve around their muscular endeavour. As Michelle (a bodybuilder of five years) articulates:

> Bodybuilding is all-consuming. I think about bodybuilding from the moment I wake up to the moment I go to sleep. Sleep, eat, drink, think of bodybuilding... all the time you are either thinking about training, or supplements, or you've got the next feed to sort out etc.

The pursuit of muscle takes over every aspect of their world, including relationships and work commitments:

> My partner knew what I was like when she took me on, she knew first and foremost that I was a bodybuilder and that would take first place above everything else including her.
>
> (Emma, bodybuilder of 12 years)

Lucie (a bodybuilder of eight years) captures some of the ongoing sacrifices and strains on relationships that are a consequence of the regimented lifestyle in the following quote:

> It's the early nights, eating at certain times, not going out to BBQs in the summer... it takes a lot of time management and a lot of stress... it's okay for me but I can feel the stress on my friends and family because they don't understand it and they really don't like it.

The highly structured and regulated day-to-day world of the female bodybuilder makes life much simpler and more straightforward, in a comparable manner to the highly organized life of the army or monastery. By immersing themselves in routines and rituals, female bodybuilders help to retain their self-identity, giving themselves focus, meaning and purpose, as 'habits lie at the very base of our sense of self' (Shilling 2008b: 13). However, habits can also function to 'restrict our relationship with the world' and become a negative, self-imposed doctrine (ibid.). Barbara (a bodybuilder of seven years) encapsulates the pressures of this constraining lifestyle and the consequential problems in striving for perfection:

> If I've had a bad day and I haven't trained or trained hard enough, or my diet's gone to pot, then I feel a failure. Bodybuilding makes you monitor every aspect of your life from how and when you train, to diet and sleep. It makes me irritable if my routine gets disturbed and it has to come above everything else in my life...

In this context, far from being a liberating experience, the daily lifestyle of the bodybuilder could be seen as a good way of controlling women who break away from societal norms. The obsession and inward focus on the body prevents them from causing any real challenge to society (Bordo 1988).

The regime, like Foucault's Panopticon, becomes a mechanism of self-regulation and self-surveillance which results in self-monitored docile bodies (Mansfield and McGinn 1993: 53).

These findings of body dissatisfaction amongst female bodybuilders appear, at least ostensibly, to provide evidence supporting academic and other critics of female bodybuilding. The women's relentless compulsion to 'work on the body', spurred on by an internalized judging self who is never satisfied by the mirror image, arguably eliminates any subversive potential the activity may have possessed. In Fussell's (1991) biography, bodybuilding is depicted as a form of armour against the world. Immersion in a life dedicated to muscle is understood as a form of escapism from personal insecurities and protection from getting hurt in relationships of love and intimacy. He declares: 'as long as I hated myself, I still believed that it mattered (bodybuilding). My deepest fear was that it didn't matter' (ibid.: 248–9). To Fussell, Bordo and other critics, all bodybuilders are living under the illusion of control and empowerment, but subconsciously just want to be accepted for who 'they really are', and are in fact 'craving recognition and self-assurance' (Fisher 1997: 15). In this way bodybuilders are yet another victim of exploitative consumer capitalism, whose mantra decrees that we are never good enough as we are.

In the context of these criticisms of female bodybuilding, it is interesting to note Lloyd's (1996) suggestion that in order to liberate and empower women, physical activities need to transcend the 'tyranny of slenderness' and be 'totally free from patriarchal pressures'. Hence, motivations to participate in and sustain fitness practices must be, and remain, 'pure'. This criteria could easily be used to reinforce the above criticisms of female bodybuilding. However, in agreement with Grimshaw (1999), I believe that Lloyd's (1996) proposal is somewhat naive. Bodies are always constructed within a cultural context and can never be disentangled from the discourse in which the body operates. In this way, I argue that there can never be a body that can simply 'transcend' society and 'free' women from 'patriarchy'. Furthermore, I support Grimshaw's related argument that 'the body can never be a wholly unproblematic something, which one can be "happy" with, in a simple, stable or permanent way' (Grimshaw 1999: 115). She argues that when Bordo and Lloyd talk about 'being happy with oneself', they slip into an almost essentialist feminist perspective that believes an authentic, real 'relationship with one's body' is possible, 'free of cultural norms and pressures' (ibid.). A more 'fluid' understanding, then, becomes useful in interpreting the body dissatisfaction expressed by the female bodybuilders. 'Doing looks' (Frost 1999) might be better viewed as an ongoing conversation, which can be the cause sometimes of despair and at other times of pleasure (as demonstrated by the apparently contradictory comments made by the women in relation to their body image within this chapter).

On the basis of the complexities and contradictions revealed in my ethnography thus far, I find myself becoming increasingly sceptical of second-wave feminist claims that there is 'a female body' which can be 'reclaimed' from 'patriarchal' society. Rather, I would prefer to take forward my study by adopting Grimshaw's

(1999: 99) perspective that there can never be a resistant 'female body outside of discourse, or a resistant body that can stand as a simple exception to forces of normalisation or domination'. For this reason I am doubtful that female body-building can provide any form of 'pure' empowerment, but I think it is equally simplistic to reduce this activity to an act of patriarchal domination. Consequently I am drawn to the following position cited by Grimshaw:

> There can be no guarantees that any practice is free of normalising pressures; no assumption of ideological 'purity' in any motivation; no clear dividing line between what is internally or externally imposed. And no body practice, in all its manifestations, can be understood wholly in terms of subjection or capitulation to normalizing pressures.
>
> (Grimshaw 1999: 100)

Conclusion

This chapter has explored the daily lifestyle and interactions of the female bodybuilder, a 'gender outlaw' who is heavily penalized for transgressing normative gender roles and consequently battles against stigmatization in both her private and public life. However, her identity is under constant attack not just from 'normals' but also from her own internalized, self-policing gaze. It is this inner critic (creating negative body image, obsession and insecurities) which has caused opponents such as Bordo (1990) to argue that women's bodybuilding, far from empowering them, merely produces differently feminized bodies imprinted with the gendered meanings of culture. However, there are two related problems with this argument. Firstly, it would be wrong to treat bodybuilding merely as a site of 'femininity's recuperation' (St Martin and Gavey 1996: 54). If this recuperation actually occurred, how do we explain the continued hostility that female bodybuilders experience in the interaction order? Instead, the choices, appearances and behaviours of these women place them firmly outside the bounds of respectable interaction. Secondly, critics have failed to engage with the 'biographical agency' (Davis 1995) of these women by ignoring the complex motivations and vitalistic satisfactions they gain from this activity. In the next chapter, I continue this exploration by turning to the most deviant aspects of female bodybuilding – muscle worship and steroid use.

6 The 'dark side' of female bodybuilding

In the last chapter I explored not only the lifestyle and motivations of female bodybuilders, but also how they managed to maintain a positive sense of self in such a gendered and hostile world. This chapter follows on from that theme to explore, through a more empirical and 'fleshed-out account', the most deviant, yet underexplored, aspects of female bodybuilding. The first part of the chapter reveals the vocabularies of motive for, and provides accounts of, female bodybuilding muscle worship activities through the voices of the participants themselves. These narratives expose the complexity of the situation, which fits neither femininity's 'resistance' nor 'recuperation'. In the second part of the chapter, the phenomenology of drug taking (particularly steroids) is explored, focusing on how female bodybuilders maintain their sense of identity as female in light of the masculinizing effects of the drugs.

Part 1: muscle worship

> Congratulations, slave, you are here because you need me. The seed of my female superiority had been planted the minute you entered into my private chambers. You have often fantasized about someone like me dominating you, overpowering you, enslaving you and forcing you to do my bidding. You yearn to reveal your true self, explore your fantasies, shed your inhibitions and expose your most intimate yet intoxicating details of your darkest desires.
>
> (http://www.mistresstreasure.net/servitude.htm, accessed 8 July 2012)

The deviant world of muscle worship sprang into the limelight ten years ago through TV documentaries such as 'Muscle Worship – Hidden Lives', 'Super-Size She' and Louis Theroux's 'Weird Weekends'. At the same time, the subculture has flourished on the internet through blogs and websites dedicated to muscle goddesses, picture and DVD sales and webcams, and is argued to provide female bodybuilders with the necessary income to survive – yet very little scholarly activity has been conducted in this area, other than Nicholas Chare's (2012) and Niall Richardson's (2008) fascinating textual analyses of 'female muscle worship'. Richardson's (2008: 289) pioneering article highlights that rather than female bodybuilding being simply feminist resistance or erotic spectacle, its nature depends on the context and how it is coded within the representation. My research builds on this analysis by focusing on the experiences and interpretations of the participants themselves. Chare (2012) argues that female muscle worship is formed through mutual dependence/co-existence between the muscular women who need financial support to aid their lifestyle and the men who need the female bodybuilders to satisfy their sexual preferences. In the work that follows, I explore this relationship further. Are female bodybuilders simply sexual commodities for the satisfaction of male fantasies, or, can muscle worship celebrations be positive self-affirmations for these women, which at the same time subvert traditional notions of gender? Before we can explore these questions, it is necessary to briefly explain the unusual phenomenon of muscle worship.

Eroticism, fetishism and muscle worship

A useful definition of 'muscle worship' comes from the entry for wrestling in *The Encyclopaedia of Unusual Sex Practices*, which lists sthenolagnia ('sexual arousal from displaying strength or muscle') and cratolagnia ('arousal from strength') as paraphilias associated with the practice of wrestling for erotic purpose. It is perhaps unsurprising that a female muscle fetish would be located at the bottom of Rubin's (1984: 281) hierarchy of sexual value/desire and that muscle worship has often been portrayed as a seedy and dangerous underworld of domination and submission (see Arnoldi 2002). Female muscle worship is described by Richardson (2008: 290) as no different to any other sexual fetish, in the sense that it is about 'the adoration of the fetish object itself rather than copulation'. However, what is even more subversive here is that the muscular woman's body becomes eroticized – a 'deviant body' which rebels against hegemonic norms. Fetishes are often pathologized and labelled obscene and disgusting by mainstream society. Whilst popular psychological theories, in particular Freudian perspectives, focus on the fear of castration and parental relationships as being the cause of these 'abnormal' physical desires (see Richardson 2008), sociological explanations look at the social context in which these fetishes become labelled deviant and at subcultural understandings of the phenomena. Weber (1948 [1915a]: 345) perceives eroticism as a sensual and creative force which, through the 'boundless giving of oneself', culminates in a heightened physical state of 'unique meaning'. For Weber, eroticism is a direct response to the hardness and mundanity of modern rational society, allowing transcendence through sensation and desire. The self becomes lost in/obliterated by the all-consuming carnal sensations of the moment, providing an escape from reality. These feelings of heightened euphoria are captured by one female muscle worshipper who claims that 'muscular women can literally make me lose my ability for rational thought... [I become] intoxicated' ('6ft1Swell', interview).

A plethora of 'female muscle worship' information is readily available on the internet, from blogs and chat rooms which hail and celebrate the muscular female form (such as femalemusleslave.com and Saradas.org) to sites selling DVDs and photographs (wpwmax.com), to female bodybuilders providing webcam services at a price. Websites such as Wb70, Ironbelles and The Valkyries will also promote wrestling and muscle worship sessions with individual women. Sessions may include the following services: muscle worship (may include flexing or licking and touching the muscle), shirt ripping, strip tease, light domination, posing, submission, video production, lifts/carries, personal training, massage, lingerie posing/modelling and wrestling (wrestling might include fantasy wrestling, oil wrestling, competitive wrestling, headlocks, head scissors, body scissors, grapevine leg holds and so on – see Kaye 2005 for further information). Some sessions also provide a dual act where two female bodybuilders will act out the fantasy of the muscle fan.

For many men who are female muscle worshippers (as yet, no women muscle worshippers who pay for sessions have been identified), there appears to be a masochistic drive, with the desire to be dominated or controlled. As Mary expresses (quoted in Kaye 2005: 117) 'they are just in awe… some want to be picked up and carried around or squeezed really hard or held like a baby. They want to feel your power, feel your strength. They want to be overpowered or dominated'. However, this understanding cannot be accepted uncritically. As '6ft1Swell' explains in the following quote, muscle worship means different things to different people:

> Regarding muscle worship and S&M, I think that for some female muscle fans it is pretty much the same thing and for others it's completely different. I've had contact with some guys for whom the whole attraction of muscle women is their ability to dominate. These guys' idea of heaven is having the crap beaten out of them, or being choked into unconsciousness between a pair of muscular thighs etc. There are some who want to be dominated on a wrestling mat, forced to submit and then worship, others more into the Robert Crumb lift and carry thing. For me, it's never been about this. In my fantasies about female bodybuilders (and actual experience with muscular non-FBBs), muscle worship is like the foreplay. Not that I would object to (nor have I objected to) a bit of flexing during sex (or before, or after for that matter!). But I have no interest in being battered, dominated or 'forced' to do anything that would be classified as S&M, and I'd rather see a woman demonstrate her strength in the gym than on me… it all depends on what each person's version of muscle worship is.

Muscle worship is a lucrative business for female bodybuilders and can be an option to sustain the women's lifestyle and enable their financial independence and economic empowerment. Sessions in the UK usually cost £300–£325 per hour (although discounts may be offered to repeat customers). Whilst there may be some element of a sliding-scale cost depending on how famous the female bodybuilder is and the kind of session required, costs can range from £200–£500 an hour. Likewise, the price of webcam sessions depends on the desired session and female bodybuilder. One muscle worshipper explains this in more detail:

> Most performers will begin in free chat, then you request a private show. Just flexing is around $2 a minute, but some women don't do anything for free,

so they start in what they call premium chat, which can go up to $5, and is basically a way of getting you to pay just to see the performer. Many of the women also have fantasy (i.e. fully nude) chat, which can be up to a few dollars on top of that, while others require you to request what they call one-on-one before they go fully nude, but it's usually a similar price, and may also involve more overtly sexual displays.

Thus webcam sessions can cost £50–£70 for a ten-minute fantasy session with a famous female bodybuilder. Some websites, which are often run by the female bodybuilder themselves, will charge £35 a month for worshippers to view new pictures and clips, allowing some women to make up to £45,000 per annum from the website alone. It is important to point out, however, that not all female-muscle fans engage in sessions and in sexual transactions. Some may simply wish to sponsor female bodybuilders in their sporting endeavours. Others may wish to sponsor muscular women in exchange for their time or friendship, or indeed for training with them. As Corina (a bodybuilder of four years) states, 'some just want to discuss training with you and see a bit of flexing'.

Views from the women

Despite the burgeoning trade in muscle worship, very little is known about how female bodybuilders experience these events. Do they participate in these sessions purely for money or are there other motivations and pleasures to be found? The community of female bodybuilders is divided on this topic between those who believe it is debasing and damaging to the sport, those who believe that it is a legitimate way to make a living due to the limited opportunities available to them in the sport (see Chapter 9) and those who engage in sessions for individual pleasure and sexual satisfaction. Charlie (a bodybuilder of four years) points out that due to the high financial costs of female bodybuilders' lifestyles, it is difficult to survive without supplementing their income with muscle worship: 'the pros can't really have a regular job… the male bodybuilders also do it but that's even more taboo'.[1] Although female participants claim that a high proportion of female bodybuilders do it, it is impossible to find numbers due to the secrecy commonly involved in any form of sex work. Kaye (2005) estimates, very broadly, that between 20 and 80 per cent of competitors are involved in muscle worship sessions in America – demonstrating how little is known about this activity. However, it is not difficult to find female bodybuilders in the UK who do sessions, as they either have their own website or are listed on others.

Some female bodybuilders are horrified by the commercialization of female muscle and the financial transactions of muscle worship. Barbara (a bodybuilder of seven years) states: 'I just think it's disgusting, it's bad for the sport; it's no different to prostitution really'. A leading figure in the world of female bodybuilding, and a UK judge, has also spoken out against these sessions, arguing that they degrade the women and bring the sport into disrepute. These opinions correspond with the feminist argument (see Chapter 4) that despite female bodybuilders creating a body which defies hegemonic norms of femininity, the women are recuperated once again into patriarchal society by becoming erotic spectacles for the pleasure of men. However, Lisa Cross (winner of the UKBFF 2010) retaliates:

> Some people argue that it's bringing bodybuilding into disrepute. As far as I'm concerned, it's putting bodybuilding on a pedestal, making it available to people who would never consider attending an actual show. It's a huge industry in the US, and it allows me to spend 99 per cent of my time totally focussed on my career. The federation would probably have less of a problem with it if they were making money from it themselves.
>
> (Shahrad 2010)

Another female bodybuilder stated that she 'did it for cash pure and simple'. Rather than the women being coerced in any way, there is a suggestion of choice and free will and feelings of being in control:

> We get £210 for muscle worship, compared to the regular girls who only get £100 (£40 taken for commission) and have to sleep with them… Depends on the client and what we decide… it leaves the ball in our court. There's no pressure to do what we don't want to do… There's really no assumptions there, which surprised me at first because of the way things are portrayed – the hardcore muscle worshippers are simply that – hardcore worship fans… some want the 'girlfriend experience', others just want you to flex, sometimes there's no sexual stuff at all. It's really up to the woman herself and what she wants to do.
>
> (Danielle, bodybuilder of five years)

Thus the female bodybuilders have agency and are not passive dupes, but are complicit in the performances. In addition to the financial incentives, for some female bodybuilders, there was pleasure to be found in both the recognition of their hard work and the dedication that it had taken to create their physique, and the worshipper's admiration:

> If someone wants to make money out of something for what they've done, and what they've achieved – then why not? You spend so long being slated for what you do and having to put up with negative press… And then someone comes along and offers you £200 to say how fantastic you are for an hour – then who's going to turn that down? Regardless of what they do?… I just think that if you can make money out of it and provide a stable financial way of living and stuff…then I don't think that's a bad thing… for people to tell me I'm great.
>
> (Mary, bodybuilder of 12 years)

As Erin (a bodybuilder of seven years) articulates,

> [E]very human being appreciates and desires recognition for something and thoroughly enjoys having the opportunity to feel sexy and wanted. If a female bodybuilder gets that from her muscles, how is it wrong or different from other women being desired for their chest size or pretty face?

Thus, in the face of the negative reactions that female bodybuilders often contend with, muscle worship may affirm their identity as sensual and feminine.

For some women, muscle worship is not about financial reward at all, but about a mutual and sexual appreciation of their physique and individual empowerment. For example, Nathalie Gassell articulates her sexual desire to be worshipped and submitted to for her own pleasure:

> But back to my muscles, to that capacity to dominate and enslave a body for my pleasure and yours, to that seizure, the consumption of another's flesh, willing, sacrificed on the altar of my thirst.

> I gently caress his slender body and then, when he asks for it, I become brutal. His delicacy is striking and beautiful beneath my hands. His body lays belly down, and I lay on top without any fighting; a motionless test of strength – where our bulks come face to face with their differences in thickness, in muscle tone, in power – suffices to make my body, concretely in its own flesh, the guiding element of our encounter. Our minds are impregnated with these differences. He is consenting. If my body were not the stronger, I could not be pleased. I could not get any carnal pleasure.
>
> (cited in Frueh *et al.* 2000: 118–19)

Thus on the one hand, the 'deviant' female body is being fetishized and eroticized by men, whilst on the other, the female bodybuilder is actively seeking individual pleasure.

Other female bodybuilders have also expressed their desire to revel with admirers in their own muscular glory. This is captured by a male muscle worshipper when discussing a previous relationship:

> Having her muscles 'worshipped' was how she warmed up for sex. It sometimes involved her doing her kung fu moves in varying states of undress while I watched and told her how sexy she looked and how turned on I was getting, and then move onto me touching her. Or we would skip the first bit and get straight to the kissing, stroking and oiling. But as I say, this was all a prelude to the sexual act, not the be all and end all itself.
>
> ('6ft1Swell')

An American female bodybuilder[2] who participates in muscle worship sessions with partners/potential partners purely for enjoyment believes that 'for the female bodybuilder, it can most certainly be an empowering and equally sexual experience'. She expands upon this in the following quote:

> Even aside [from] the sexual high, other thrills are just knowing how turned on your body is making somebody else, having your body and your muscles appreciated for what they are, being the one who is in control and has the power over the other person.

> Thus for my sessions, most of them have been incredibly sexual, both as an intense form of foreplay before more happened, and also where the worship has been the sex, or taken the place of actual sex... it's often times a more intense sexual experience than the actual sex itself.

In this way the eroticism of the muscle worship becomes more important than sexual intercourse itself, thus challenging the supremacy of the phallus and creating new pleasures of the flesh (see Chapter 8). Empowerment is found both through the power to sexually excite and in the physical knowledge that she is in control:

> I had always been physically larger and stronger than the guys I had dated. Therefore it was empowering in the literal sense in just knowing that if I wanted to, I could literally pick this guy up and throw him around, or I could have my way with him and he wouldn't be able to resist. It is also empowering on the mental sense in that knowing how aroused these guys got over female muscle, I could make them do what I wanted simply by withholding from them what they really craved.
>
> (Erin, bodybuilder of seven years)

Although the female body remains an erotic, sexual symbol subject to the male gaze,[3] as Richardson (2008: 297) points out, 'muscle worship [also] challenges conventional heteroerotics and demonstrates the potential for alternative sexual pleasure outside the reductive idea of not only penetrative sexuality but also traditional gender-based power dynamics'.

The muscle worshippers

Despite these female bodybuilders' openness in sharing their views, there is still much secrecy about what goes on behind closed doors. Many female bodybuilders seemed hesitant or unwilling to discuss these issues. As one muscular woman stated: 'I don't know how many women are honest about it – I don't believe that people are willing to talk about it'. At this point it appeared that my research had come to an abrupt end. I had found a wall of silence or even of outright threat. It appears that even more than steroids, muscle worship sessions are shrouded in mystery and 'taboo'. The following diary extract not only demonstrates the controversy and delicacy of this issue, but also highlights the problematic nature of investigating forbidden territory:

I received an email a couple of days ago from a famous female bodybuilder demanding that I stop my investigation. It was brash and harsh, and most of all shook me to the core. Questions kept whirling round my head: had I been totally naive to think that female bodybuilders would wish to talk about muscle worship from their perspective? Had I handled the situation insensitively? Who was I writing for? Myself? My readers? On behalf of the female bodybuilders? What right did I have to go poking my nose into people's business in the name of academia? And yet, should I be censured by threats?

I re-evaluated my research and turned for more information to those who appreciate female muscle – the worshippers themselves. As demonstrated in Chapter 5, for a female to build muscle is to transgress the gender norms of society, risking exclusion, censure and a lack of appeal to heterosexual males. However, there are a minority of males who do appreciate and are sexually attracted to muscular women. Little is known about these males, and whilst I call for more research to be conducted into this area, this work provides an introductory insight into the subculture of muscle worship.

As hegemonic masculinity and hypermasculinity consist of traits such as dominance, power, strength, independence and muscularity, perhaps it is unsurprising that males who have been attracted to deviant muscular female bodies have been depicted in a negative light. Stereotypical muscle worshippers have been portrayed in documentaries such as Louis Theroux's 'Weird Weekends' as weedy, nerdy, pathetic, 'living with their mothers at 40 and saving every penny for sessions', repressed homosexuals, lacking in social skills and having something mentally defective about them. So far, no comprehensive study has taken place which interrogates this common knowledge. These 'mad monks' (as one male worshipper jested in his description of the reverence and secrecy of this subculture) are hidden from view and mocked by hegemonic society. Indeed, 'coming out' or confessing to being sexually attracted to muscular women is taboo.

Furthermore, as the muscular body has been coded 'male' (and therefore the muscular female is coded male), there is an assumption that in order to be attracted to muscular women, one must be homosexual. This is demonstrated in Slave's scenario: 'When I told him [his brother] the truth he laughed. But not at me, at himself. He'd found my stash of magazines when we were young, and he'd assumed I was gay!' Very few muscle worshippers are open about their fetish, however, due to stigma and concern about how people might react. For example, Douglas said that he can't tell his friends or family in case they 'rip it out of him'. In Slave's case, however, he found his brother very supportive: 'He had no problem with it at all. He too has a fetish, for fat girls with huge tits. We decided we were both totally normal in our abnormalities!' From a young age, many of the female-muscle fans believed that there was something inherently 'wrong' with them, that they needed to be cured of this unique and lonely obsession. The internet, however, has made life much easier, bringing 'like-minded' people together. Blogs and chat rooms have provided a kind of sanctuary for these men; a space where they can share their appreciation of female bodybuilders and exchange photos, thoughts and experiences. This subculture can create comradeship and shelter in a society which doesn't understand and condemns their desires. As one male worshipper articulates:

> Having kept my love for female muscle secret since the start, the internet gave me the push I needed to finally speak about it. Knowing that there are not just a few, but thousands of people out there who have a similar passion is kind of empowering.

Who are these people?

It is extremely difficult to establish how many muscle worshippers there are. One of the largest worldwide forums has almost 20,000 members, although there must be far more who do not subscribe or actively participate. A UK blog such as Femalemuscleslave can receive up to 200 visits from the UK per day. In Kaye's (2005) book, 'Mary' claims that there is no single type of muscle worshipper – that they are of all ages (20–80 years old), ethnicities, classes and appearances. Despite great methodological issues,[4] my research in the UK found that the majority of muscle worshippers were middle-class, university-educated, and aged in their late 20s–late 40s. The majority were heterosexual and were active gym members. That several weight trained is perhaps surprising and contradicts with other scholarly works, such as Chare (2012: 207) and Richardson (2008: 296). These academic commentators claim that 'schmoes' may deliberately 'cultivate flabbiness or lankiness, perfecting a feeble physique incapable of lifting heavy weights… [in order to] better contrast their bodies with the images of the powerful figures of female bodybuilding'. However, according to interviewee '6ft1Swell':

> I'm not surprised you have found that many of us in the sample do train, as I think this is connected. Wisdom among the brethren (the more mature ones anyway) is that training yourself is the best way to arouse your partner's interest in training, or at least getting into the gym for some kind of physical activity.

These demographics clearly offer a counter-presentation of the stereotype of muscle worshippers as weak and economically dependent.

A common thread between the muscle worshippers is that their attraction to muscular women developed in their teens:

> My interest in FBBs began with seeing muscle magazines in my teens, I had an immediate fascination with women like Lenda Murray and Kim Chizevsky. By my late teens and early 20s my access to the internet was daily and so I was able to access a lot more online, and my interest increased as a result.
>
> (Kiyone)

> I was young when I first saw a slot on news where a bodybuilder appeared, a male, then I started like watching athletes… When I was a teenager I started

buying bodybuilding magazines, but as time went on female bodybuilders became less common in the magazines, but the magazine WPW was available in some places.

(Aiden)

I'm not sure how it all got started exactly but like many I grew up with American comic books with some strong sexy female superhero characters… Way back maybe late 70s, early 80s, there was a bookshop in London's Charing Cross Road, near where the Cass Arts shop is now, which had what I now realise to have been early editions of the Women's Physique Publication and possibly Women's Physique World Mag… Well, feeling self-conscious about doing so, I used to quickly try to browse them, but I was too embarrassed I think to actually take one to the counter to buy, the guy at the counter was usually always talking to another staff member and I kept thinking that they would say something like 'you don't like this stuff do you?'

(Patrick)

Whilst muscle worshippers often stated that they did find 'normal' women attractive in terms of personality, all distinctly expressed their preference for a muscular physique and not the 'glamour norm of thin with large breasts' (Aiden), thus subverting the hegemonic norms of desire. For the fans, muscle symbolizes power, strength, independence and vitality, and creates a visceral effect which is difficult to capture in words. The women take on superheroesque qualities. As Kiyone explains:

To me muscle represents power, strength and confidence, aside from how much I like the look. There's a primal aspect to it I find very appealing. It is hard sometimes to verbalize what I like about muscle though.

Traditionally, eroticism has been critiqued by feminists as often being about masculine dominance and power over the female. In the words of Bologh (1990: 204), it becomes 'a patriarchal arrangement in which the stronger party accepts and expects the devotion of the weaker'. However, muscle worshippers often wish to be overpowered by the female bodybuilder. They are in awe of these muscular goddesses and wish to celebrate their muscles, their strength and power – thus transgressing traditional gender roles. As the woman becomes hard, tough, unbending and powerful, the man becomes weak, passive and subservient. The popular fantasy of the muscular dominatrix puts her in control; the worshippers are reduced to slaves and must submit under her powerful influence. Whilst this is a pervasive argument, it is worth noting Chare's argument that despite 'gender bending/gender trouble' (see Butler 1999), there still exists an 'exultation' of hardness or muscularity and strength. The male muscle worshipper desires the women to be hard, with low body fat, vascular and in competition state. The softness and fluidity associated with feminine traits are pronounced as weak, whereas traditional masculine traits of hardness and strength are heralded as superior.

Female bodybuilders as sexual commodities

Media portrayals of sessions, such as 'Muscle Worship – Hidden Lives' and 'Highway Amazon', show women travelling to different hotels/motels to perform for individual muscle fans, with suitcases full of props to fulfil males' fantasies. In this light, muscle worship may be viewed as simply a sexual fetish service performed in exchange for money. The women's muscular bodies are their commodity. However, the pleasure some women take from this and the forms of control mentioned above question this simple interpretation. Do the women become the passive, fetishized commodities so representative of patriarchal capitalist society, or can intimate relationships be forged on complementary needs?

For some female bodybuilders, the situation appears relatively clear-cut:

> My view [is that] guys who actually hire female bodybuilders for a worship session are viewing them as a sexual commodity. They have a female muscle fetish, they get highly aroused by female muscle, thus they hire female muscle in order to experience a sexual thrill.
>
> (Barbara, bodybuilder of seven years)

Another female bodybuilder who participates in sessions only for mutual enjoyment, and does not take payment, voices her frustration at being viewed simply as a sex object for men's pleasure:

> I suppose my biggest annoyance with most guys who want sessions is that they are only thinking with their 'guy part' and thus think I am an object who is here solely to allow them to live out their fantasy. Wrong! I'm a real person who is due courtesy and consideration as any other person.
>
> (Erin, bodybuilder of seven years)

However, the writings below by one male muscle worshipper demonstrate the complexity and difficulty involved in coming to a conclusion on this debate:

> I had seen photos of all of them, and I was attracted by their size, as well as the good amount of muscle definition all of them had. I would say the physique was the only real factor that came into my decision. That and I had seen on one forum I frequent, that people who had done sessions with them had nothing but good things to say. I was given some of choice in what I wanted in the sessions, whether I wanted mainly muscle worship, wrestling, nudity (all my sessions offered nudity) etc. One of the Americans offered anything except sexual intercourse, the other offered everything but I decided to stop short of asking for intercourse. The British one offered everything except intercourse until our last two sessions where she started to offer that too. But the main aspect of all these sessions for me was muscle worship and to some extent a being-dominated aspect… I enjoyed the sessions with both Americans a lot, they were both very nice and friendly. One was very intimate, with the other you could sense a little reserve. The British one and I have a very good

rapport and level of intimacy in our sessions and she always seems like she enjoys it as much as I do.

(Kiyone)

Whilst there is a suggestion here of choice and 'purchase' of the women purely on the basis of their looks and recommendations by other worshippers, the women appear to be in control of their actions and decide in advance how far they want to go. Indeed, some women appear to engage in mutual enjoyment of these sessions – not only for the purposes of financial stability, but also to reconfirm a sense of positive self, sexual potency and indeed even friendship. Furthermore, we cannot ignore the pleasures of the flesh and the feeling of empowerment that some female bodybuilders spoke of experiencing during their sessions. It is with these complex thoughts and contradictions in mind that I turn with some hope to 'sex-radical' feminist perspectives to help shed light on this matter. Some 'sex-radical' feminists (see Colosi 2010: 13) believe that within patriarchal society, women participating in sex work (including pornography and prostitution) are both agents and victims, and thus form 'sites of ingenious resistance and cultural subversion' (Chapkis 1997: 29). Consequently, 'sex work' can be viewed as a complex site (Frank 2003) in the struggle for empowerment. As Lockford (2004: 100) points out, researchers must discern 'the nuances of consent within actual situated experiences' and in order to do this, 'the voices of those involved need to be listened to'. In addition, she requests an abandonment of hierarchies of sexual value which privilege heterosexual monogamous coupling, and calls for a 'sex-positive' view that respects everyone's unique sexual preferences. Championing Rubin's (1984) argument, Lockford suggests that a new feminist approach to moral judgment of sex acts is needed: 'A democratic morality should judge sexual acts by the way partners treat one another, the level of mutual consideration, the presence or absence of coercion, and the quantity and quality of the pleasures they provide' (Rubin 1984: 283).

In conclusion to this section, the situation appears complex and contradictory; indeed, it does depend on the individual circumstances and biographies of the female bodybuilders and muscle worshippers. Whilst methodologically this sample is not representative, and like all research, contains many flaws, it does undermine stereotypical notions about this subculture and calls for more research to be conducted into this area. In the context of the stigmatization and marginalization that a female bodybuilder can experience in society due to her choices, actions and appearance, muscle worship can potentially reaffirm her self-identity and her sexuality, as well as potentially providing much-needed income.

Part 2: steroids

It is clear that AAS use is not equally as dangerous for everyone... [It is] by far the most dangerous for women and girls as the female body is simply not equipped for exogenous male hormones.

(www.steroidabuse.com/steroids-and-women.html, accessed 14 August 2012)

Why female bodybuilders are shunned for anabolic steroid use is because they INTENTIONALLY inject or swallow anabolic steroids to induce muscle growth and INTENTIONALLY face the risks of side effects. Many women are willing to risk the side effects to have bigger, harder muscles. This is considered unacceptable by mainstream society because she shouldn't have muscle in the first place!

(www/albertabodybuilding.com//abffeature8.htm, accessed 12 July 2007)

In Chapter 5, the penalties for and costs of transgressing corporeal norms of femininity were explored. Women who chose to build their bodies were perceived as gender freaks who violated the natural order. However, as was demonstrated, female bodybuilders managed this social stigma by creating their own desired views of femininity and through interactions with 'kindred souls' (Cohen 1955). In the work that follows, I delve into arguably the most controversial aspect of this body modification – steroid use. Locks (2003: 254) convincingly argues that as bodybuilding not only shapes the textual appearance of the user, but engrosses and permeates the whole body through the use of drugs, this makes it not 'just far more transgressive and rebellious, but far more problematic and resistant to narratives of recuperation'. Moreover, for women to pursue such a contentious type of body modification is viewed as doubly deviant. Female bodybuilders become seen as 'monstrous' in their appearance and are pathologized as unfeminine drug takers (Heywood 1998). In this section I explore the lived experiences of drug taking (particularly steroids), focusing primarily on how muscular women maintain their sense of feminine identity in light of steroids' masculinizing effects.

The physical effects of steroids have been documented in some detail by scientific and medical literature (see Hartgens and Kuipers 2004; Korkia 1994; Kashkin 1992). In addition, anabolic and androgenic drugs' psychological impacts on users (with regard to aggression, emotions, body image and so on) have received much scholarly attention (e.g. Gruber and Pope, 1999; Malarkey *et al.*, 1991; Grimes, 2003). However, as Grogan *et al.* (2006: 846) point out, 'most previous work on anabolic steroid use has focused on men, as most bodybuilders are men; and most steroid users are male'. Furthermore, there has been a dearth of information into the lived experiences of female bodybuilders in relation to steroid use. Whilst Grogan's work has tried to rectify this gap in knowledge, the pleasures and intimate details involved have remained unexplored. Although the following work can hardly do justice to this endeavour, it does hope to provide some understanding of the use of steroids by female bodybuilders.

Women who take steroids as doubly deviant

Anabolic-androgenic steroids (hereafter abbreviated to 'steroids') are usually synthetic derivatives of the male hormone testosterone. 'Steroids are taken by bodybuilders or athletes to increase strength, stamina and muscle size. In this respect steroids work primarily in the muscle cells by increasing protein synthesis, creatine phosphate synthesis and glycogen and fluid storage' (Frueh *et al.* 2000: 19). Serious documented long-term side effects of steroids include diarrhoea, dizziness, chronic rectal bleeding, thyroid problems, depression, high blood pressure, heart complications, kidney and liver malfunction, hepatitis, gallstones and cancer. However, despite these potentially dangerous risks to health, it is often steroids' masculinizing effects on women that receive the most media attention. A typical comment is captured in the following newspaper article, entitled 'Bulked up Barbie girl waging war on her body': '... she sounds like a bloke and she's got a five o'clock shadow... She's put through her paces by her friend Debbie, who looks like Sly Stallone and sounds like Tom Jones' (Maume 2005). Female bodybuilders are far more often demonized for taking steroids than their male counterparts are. Indeed, during my research I found that whilst male bodybuilders frequently told me about their pharmaceutical endeavours, perhaps as a masculine badge of honour, women were sometimes less forthcoming due to the associated gender stigma. The reasons for this were articulated by a casual gym user in my study, who remarked: 'men taking testosterone are just enhancing what is already in their bodies, whereas women are putting something into their bodies which isn't "natural" and is therefore mucking around with their sex' (male, gym 1:3). There are two points to be made here. First, far from being unnatural, women *do* of course have testosterone in their bodies. Denial of this can be seen as a tactic employed to erase the commonalities between the sexes and assert a fallacious biological dualism upon which social and cultural inequalities can be justified. Second, however, this assertion makes reference to a hormone that is key not only to *cultural representations* of male and female, but to actual *physical transformations*. Consuming testosterone to 'excess', via steroidal drugs, is associated with several bodily changes in female bodybuilders, including receding hairline, growth of facial hair, growth of clitoris size, lowering of voice tone and, often, increased sex drive. The issue of drugs and female bodybuilders is therefore particularly controversial, as it impinges on so many people's sense of what is natural and central to biological sex. The irony of this, however, is that men also suffer gender side effects from taking steroids which have the potential to emasculate them. Men risk prostate cancer, painful urination and infertility – most frequently there is a reduction in testicle size, low sperm count and sometimes impotence. Gynecomastia – the embarrassing development of male breasts, referred to by bodybuilders as 'bitch tits' – can also be a problematic issue (see Fussell 1991).

Although steroids are used widely by bodybuilders and athletes, both professional and recreational, the illegal nature of steroids (see Chapter 2) means there is little formal medical knowledge (by way of clinical and scientific studies) about these substance interactions. Bodybuilders therefore become pharmaceutical experts, creating their own subculture of ethnopharmacology (Monaghan 2002), negotiating risks and inadvertently becoming their own 'human guinea pigs'. Supporting Grogan *et al.*'s (2006) study, female bodybuilders were critical about how little information is available to them in relation to steroid use. The men have access to 'steroid bibles' and forums devoted to sharing information, and it is not unprecedented to overhear discussions around drug use at the gym.

For women, however, due to the taboo nature of this area, less information and support is available. Indeed, there is a 'veil of secrecy', and women often deny or underplay their use of steroids. It appears that even within the subculture, the stigma of females using drugs means that women will seldom admit to taking steroids, and even more rarely to which anabolic substances they are using. Traditionally, women have relied upon trusted male and female bodybuilders to guide them; although recently, female bodybuilders have begun to post and share information about steroid concerns through bodybuilding internet forums, asking questions about matters such as which steroids are the most suitable for women, and how contraceptives might react with testosterone-based drugs.

Motivations, self-fulfilment and pleasures

The women felt they needed to use steroids in order to create the desired and coveted look discussed in the previous chapter:

> I'd train so hard, eat well and follow all the advice I could find on body-building – but I still couldn't put on muscle. Every week I would take my measurements, and look at my reflection daily in the mirror but I couldn't see any changes. I was strong but I didn't look like I trained. I loved the look of muscles, and I wanted them for myself. It took me a while to realise that I couldn't achieve muscularity without hormonal supplements.
>
> (Debbie, bodybuilder of seven years)

> In the bodybuilding world, I think I waited 15 years, probably longer, for someone to really tell me the truth about what it would take for me to be a successful bodybuilder [in terms of drugs]. Very few women – those with amazing genetics – can put on muscle without steroids… It became clear that in order to build muscle I was going to have to turn to the 'dark side' as it were.
>
> (Caroline, bodybuilder of 17 years)

The decision to use steroids was not something that the women took lightly, and many had spent time researching and seeking advice from trusted others who had reputations for being knowledgeable within the subculture. This is captured in the following quotes from Barbara (a bodybuilder of seven years):

> I decided obviously to be cautious about it… I wasn't going to go in silly with it and take everything under the sun. I'd been training long enough and been clean for eight years already, so I was going to go on this route wisely… Yes, it was a big decision, when the reality came, that I was going to be doing drugs, it really hit me – I thought it's now or never.

These 'constructive rationales' and justifications are echoed in other works on subcultural theories around drug taking (Schaps and Sanders 1970; Monaghan 2001, 2002).

After the decision had been made and the process begun, the women recalled noticing even the most minuscule and mundane changes as the steroids began to work. Barbara (a bodybuilder of seven years) recalls the excitement that she felt when she first noticed the changes in her training and physique:

> The first time I took anavar, within three or four days I noticed a significant change in my strength, where a 12.5 kg dumbbell would feel like a 5 kg dumbbell to me, it would be light as anything and I remember thinking that this is ridiculous, that I'm pushing weights that used to be my maximum… I'm pushing men's weights – and even more than men's weights, and it gave me that confidence and even more that feeling of invincibility.

These feelings intensified towards the end of the first course:

> I was strong, had more energy, felt confident, 'didn't give a shit'. I was pumping weights left, right and centre – and kept pushing beyond my max. And when I was at my peak and on the primobolane in with the anavar and I was decline pressing about 90 kg, I was dumbbell pressing 32 kg in each hand… I was bicep curling 20 kg, I squatted 3.5 plates a side and on leg press I was pressing 400 kg… front squat a plate and a half and two plates a side…

Other female bodybuilders also noted vast increases in strength, along with increased muscle size. Barbara illustrates: 'my upper pecs grew quickly through the gear – they have changed from being my worst body part to my best… my quads increased to 28 inches and my biceps grew to 15–16 inches'. In addition, the women reported recovering from their workouts more quickly, aching less and feeling that their training was 'easier'. Increased vascularity and pleasure in 'the pump' (see Chapter 8) were also articulated by co-participants:

> I'd get pumped really easily… my biceps, I'd literally only have to do a couple of reps on my first set and they would be pumped.
>
> (Emma, bodybuilder of 19 years)

> 100 per cent better pump on gear – that's when you feel like your skin is going to split… training without it doesn't feel the same. You really miss it when you are not on a course.
>
> (Michelle, bodybuilder of five years)

As each woman began to embody their latent image, other people began to comment on their physical transformations, thus validating the women's identity as female bodybuilders. As Barbara explains:

> It definitely increases your confidence when people start looking at you and asking how you are getting on and all that – and it's good, and it's that bit of

vanity as people are paying attention... Even at work customers would ask me if I was a bodybuilder and that would put a big smile on my face as I was starting to look [like] who I am.

In relation to this, another female felt that steroids enabled her to present her true self to the world. As her strength and size increased, so too did her confidence and her ability to be taken seriously by other people:

> Before I took gear I was always determined on the inside, but now I have the confidence to show that on the outside. I'm sure that before I was a more placid, softer person, but now I'm more confident... I think it's a combination of lots of things, partly the change in emotions, but also the confidence that comes with size and strength. I think I've also become more hardened to people as you get judged... you feel more empowered and feel able to stand your ground. People appear intimidated by you just by your presence – they seem to take you more seriously.
>
> (Michelle, bodybuilder of five years)

Other female bodybuilders have expressed changes in their emotions and outlook on life brought about by taking male hormones. These included feeling 'harder', 'colder', 'more distant and less emotional', 'more confident' and 'invincible' – all emotional traits associated with men and traditionally prized. However, different female bodybuilders reacted in different ways. In particular, Barbara (a bodybuilder of seven years) denies the inevitability of 'roid rage' which is so prominent in the media and popular discourse:

> Most of the time I was quite placid I felt, I was quite content and happy... and I was just getting on with things... I just liked what gear done to me in terms of the fuel. Because it fuelled my training and gave me adrenaline it fuelled my focus to lift the weights but I certainly didn't get angry or 'roid rage' or snap at people outside the gym.

The sexual effects of steroids, such as increased sex drive and an increase in the number and intensity of orgasms, have also been documented in great detail in academic literature (Mansfield and McGinn 1993; Ferguson 1990). This was found to be no exception in my research:

> ... my sex drive was ridiculous... felt out of control, although I never did anything!
>
> (Katy, bodybuilder of six years)

> Sex drive goes through the roof... if you have a break or change what you are using you become aware of it again... improves the intensity of orgasm.
>
> (Michelle, bodybuilder of five years)

… the first time I took anavar it was ridiculous; it really was. … I was think-ing about sex all the time. Even sitting on a seat in the gym… I was aware. I'd never experienced that before in my life. My clit became puffy and enlarged through the gear. I was a bit conscious of it, it was a bit weird, a bit of a real-ity check to think that it was a result of taking gear… luckily although it has enlarged, it's not too noticeable, just a lot more sensitive…

(Barbara, bodybuilder of seven years)

Although one female did state that having an enlarged clitoris made her slightly hesitant and self-conscious when embarking on new relationships, most female bodybuilders articulated the sexual side effects of gear as a positive phenomenon which increased their pleasure and sense of identity as sexual and erotic women. This sexual agency of muscular women also subverts and undermines gender scripts which have historically portrayed men as sexually active, with women more passive reciprocates.

In this way, steroids are viewed as a form of ignition which enables women to see the results of their labour, allowing them to create a muscular body of which they can be proud and which fulfils their self-image of a female bodybuilder. Through the side effects of the drugs, the women enjoy an increased feeling of wellbeing and energy, decreased recovery time from workouts, heightened sex drive, increased orgasm intensity and self-confidence.

Side effects, negotiations and femininity

Mary Wollstonecraft, writing in the late eighteenth century, described femininity as a prison and akin to slavery. Later on, second-wave feminists picked up this theme and protested against compulsory femininity by abandoning conventional beauty regimes, in order to free women's bodies from being constantly patrolled, inscribed and self-surveyed by the beauty doctrine that Dworkin (1974: 113–14) captures in the following quote:

> In our culture, not one part of a woman's body is left untouched, unaltered. From the age of 11 or 12 until she dies, a woman will spend a large part of her time, money and energy on binding, plucking, painting and deodorising herself.

Feminizing actions are encouraged by bodybuilding competitions, sites described as submitting to 'the femininity project in terms of the almost hyper-feminine ornamentation, posture and demeanour required for competition' (Daniels 1992; Guthrie and Castelnuovo 1992; St Martin and Gavey 1996; see also Chapters 3 and 9). Whilst these expectations encourage a veneer of femininity to be placed over the project of muscularity there is no complete transformation into acceptable hegemonic norms regarding how a 'female' should look and act. Nevertheless, for the majority of female bodybuilders, femininity is a calcu-lated 'balancing act' (Grogan 2004) which takes time, money and effort. In this section of the chapter, I turn to the ways in which the women manage the masculinizing side effects of steroids in order to maintain the appearance and identity of a feminine woman.

Steroids will enable a woman to increase her strength and muscle size, but at the same time she will have to cope with the virilization-related side effects. For the women involved, the increase in testosterone and the decrease in oestrogen (further expounded by oestrogen blockers such as Clomid and Tamoxifen) are comparable to going through male puberty. Women will usually have to contend with acne, increased appetite, increased body and facial hair and the lowering/'breaking' of the voice (Ferguson 1990). Individuals will react differently depending on their chemical sensitivity and genetic disposition/susceptibility. As Michelle (a bodybuilder of five years) explains:

> Not all people respond the same way, it depends on what receptors you have. I knew for example that I would have hair problems. I'm hairy, therefore I am most likely to have male pattern baldness as I have a lot of hair receptors that respond to testosterone… I used to have bad skin, so I knew that acne would also be an issue for me.

However, any amount of steroid which is introduced into the female endocrine system will cause a reaction – and this is usually irreversible. The women who choose to use steroids are aware of these consequences and the risks that the side effects pose for their 'femininity'. This is demonstrated by Barbara (a bodybuilder of seven years).

> We are not naturally able to look like bodybuilders; for example, you can't achieve the rippedness on your quads due to oestrogen and water. So in some ways you are removing your femininity and replacing it with masculinity.

Muscularity, vascularity and hardness are increased as estrogenic fat, usually situated on areas of 'womanly curves' such as thighs, hips and breasts, decreases. As women's breasts are a signifier of femininity, with erotic/aesthetic and fertility-related associations (Yalom 1999), losing breast tissue and fat can be devastating for some women. Several of the women had already had plastic surgery to enhance their breasts before I conducted my research; however, one female bodybuilder, who had initially been adamant that she would not compromise, decided after two years to undergo breast augmentation when she became tired of being mistaken for a man. Another female bodybuilder was seriously contemplating breast enhancement as she felt 'unattractive' with 'saggy boobs', which had decreased by two cup sizes and damaged her confidence in sexual relationships as a result of her dieting and taking oestrogen inhibiters. Danielle (a bodybuilder of five years), however, claimed that whilst she didn't like the look of her breasts when dieting, the steroids had no effect on her chest size or shape. Similarly, Michelle (a bodybuilder of five years) stated: 'I never had boobs anyway… so I don't feel it's made any difference'.

Amenorrhea (absence of periods) frequently became an issue for female bodybuilders whilst on steroids. Regular menstruation, being associated with fertility, is often viewed as a vital part of being a woman (Kitzinger and Willmott 2002). Yet whilst one female bodybuilder did articulate concern that steroid use may prevent her from conceiving at a later date, most expressed their relief that they either did not have periods whilst on a cycle or that PMS symptoms, including period pains, were diminished and periods were lighter and shorter. The women who did light/moderate steroid cycles of less than three per year found that menstruation returned to 'normal' after two or three months; however, those on a heavy course or who continually used steroids found their periods ceased indefinitely. Interestingly, acne did not feature as a significant problem for the female bodybuilders. Whilst several used topical over-the-counter acne medications to control 'breakouts', some of the women claimed they did not suffer from any skin problems at all. The following quote by Corina (a bodybuilder of four years) is a typical comment on the topic: 'my skin's not too bad, but I've got a few boils on my back. My skin gets worse after shows, as all the toxins come out'.

In comparison, the steroids' effect on the women's hair did make an impact, to a greater or lesser extent. Our hair, according to Weitz (2004), is not only a broad language which tells others about ourselves, but is also a symbol of femininity. In modern society, ideals of femininity are personified by long, flowing, thick, shiny and healthy hair. The majority of women experienced some effect on their hair's thickness and texture. Receding hairlines and thinning hair are well-documented consequences of steroid use and many women compensated for this by getting hair extensions – although, as Barbara (a bodybuilder of seven years) claimed, 'lots of the professional female bodybuilders wear wigs'. As the following extract shows, however, women may have different experiences:

> Touch wood, I've not lost any hair on my head… it's really thick and drier now. That's the Oxy's – it changes the texture and makes it wiry. I have to get it thinned, but it's better than it all falling out and getting a receding hairline.
> (Caroline, bodybuilder of 17 years)

Body hair also plays a central role in constructing both masculinity, femininity and sexual identities (Oberstein 2011). In contemporary Western society, for a woman to have excess/dark hair, facial hair, underarm hair, hair beyond the 'bikini line' or hairy legs is considered taboo, unhygienic and disgusting by hegemonic norms. For female bodybuilders who use steroids, and whose body hair increases as a result, this can be an ongoing and frustrating area to manage. One female bodybuilder describes it as a 'mammoth task. I have to shave my arms and stomach – use close grade clipper as otherwise my skin gets really sore… My partner shaves my back' (Emma, bodybuilder of 19 years). Whilst some females shave every day, others use creams or wax to get rid of their hair. Intense Pulsed Light (IPL) is also a popular method, despite being expensive; however, whilst 'it definitely works', it is not a permanent solution for these women who will need regular appointments. Some of the women reported only growing 'fine, blonde, baby hair on their chin', which was 'disturbing but manageable'. Another reported plucking hair from around her nipples and from her stomach, which had become routine since taking a course of steroids several years previously.

Another serious 'gender' defect that women have to deal with is the effects on their vocal cords:

> When people start talking to you on the phone and keep asking you whether you have a cold… and you wake up in the morning and your voice in very deep. Then you become very conscious… I could feel the voice being quite grainy and my vocal cords feel quite thick. Even now I feel that I have to clear my throat at times by coughing… [and] get a bit hoarse.
>
> (Barbara, bodybuilder of seven years)

> People sometimes call me 'sir' on the phone and I have to correct them. Like the other day I was changing my car insurance and the guy on the phone assumed I must be getting it on behalf of my partner.
>
> (Michelle, bodybuilder of five years)

All but one of the muscular women claimed to deliberately soften their voices as a result, particularly on the telephone. However, Michelle claimed that it no longer bothered her: 'My voice has changed; I think I sound like my brother… I don't care anymore, I think I've got used to it… I think that I might sound like a camp man'.

In this section I have discussed some of the negotiations that muscular women undertake to maintain dominant ideals of femininity. These include breast implants, hair extensions/wigs, extreme hair depilation and softening their voices. Such actions are frequently undertaken as a response to the effects of taking steroids/oestrogen blockers in distancing their bodies from gendered norms. This suggests that there are limits to the transformations many female bodybuilders are prepared to display. Instead, actions that compensate for a loss of femininity comprise the 'dull compulsion' of gender norms. These female bodybuilders pursue muscle, but also pay respect to presentational norms by donning some of the accoutrements of femininity. Felshin (1974) refers to this as the 'feminine apologetic'. These compromises, if compromises they are, may not be unreasonable if they enable female bodybuilders to pursue their primary goal, but do illustrate the efficacy of wider presentational norms. Of course, it is also important to consider that these women want to maintain a feminized muscularity, and the combination of muscle and hair extensions, physical bulk and make-up, refined vascularity and prominent breasts are all expressions of a single coherent identity.

Managing the risks

Grogan *et al.* (2006) argue that the masculinizing effects of steroids could act as a deterrent for female bodybuilders. However, the women who chose to take the steroid route (the majority in my sample) learned to manage the drugs' side effects and risks. Some did this by keeping drug dosages low and cycle lengths short (a maximum of eight weeks), with extended periods of recovery between courses. Likewise, highly androgenic compounds (such as testosterones and dianabol) were often avoided; popular steroids (with potentially less virilizing side effects) for women included anavar (oxandrolane), winstrol (stanozolol) and primobolan depot (methenolone enenthate). For each female bodybuilder there appears to be a line which they are unwilling to cross, as illustrated in the case of Barbara (a bodybuilder of seven years):

> When I was on my second course of taking primo and anavar – seven weeks into that my voice dropped… I was almost at the end of my course so I just carried on. My hair went fine – just the texture and the way it looked. It looked a bit lifeless… Although if I'd noticed any hair loss I would have stopped there. That would have been the line for me… [I] washed my hair a bit more to make it look more full-bodied and I tied it back more to stop people noticing.

Another woman stopped using steroids altogether when she noticed her voice becoming 'scratchy'. However, in the case of the women seeking to become professional competitive female bodybuilder, higher 'risks' were taken with drugs such as decca and trenbolane. Unsurprisingly, a greater amount of unwanted and harmful physical effects developed too, as demonstrated in the following quotes:

> I'll also use Oxy's, which are known to be quite toxic – that's what done my kidneys in.
>
> (Caroline, bodybuilder of 17 years)

> I had a really bad experience with tren… you can get it from gear sometimes… it's like a cough, like an anaphylactic reaction… I did a shot of tren and I couldn't stop coughing and it was really painful… it was quite frightening.
>
> (Michelle, bodybuilder of five years)

> When I was dieting for competition, the steroids along with the fatburners (clenbuterol, ephedrine and caffeine) made me feel lightheaded and shaky. It felt like a continual tightness in my head and congestion in my nose. My eyes were bloodshot… I just didn't feel right in myself.
>
> (Barbara, bodybuilder of seven years)

> I used to use decca in the off season, but I tend to stay off it now. It makes me massively hold water and my hands and feet become unbearably painful.
>
> (Emma, bodybuilder of 19 years)

Supporting the findings of Grogan *et al.* (2006) and Monaghan (2002), female bodybuilders often spoke about drug 'use' rather than 'abuse' – that is to say, using drugs for the purpose of building muscle and creating low body fat with muscular definition, at the same time as being knowledgeable about and minimizing side effects. However, there is a fragile divide between these two things. Although I can only skim the surface of this important discussion here, the drugs' side effects were managed in a variety of ways by the female bodybuilders, including the following: injecting rather than taking oral tablets (as this is understood to be less harmful on the liver), 'keeping a clean diet', avoiding recreational drugs (including alcohol) and taking health supplements such as milk thistle to support the liver. Despite the pleasures articulated earlier by the women, some female bodybuilders did express a fear for the future and the wish that they did not have to take steroids in order to achieve their goals:

> I hate the side effects from gear... you can't stop it, you can't go back. And that's what frightens me for the people who are so young that they might decide in a few years that bodybuilding is not for her and she can't go back.
>
> (Michelle, bodybuilder of five years)

> No one really wants to inject themselves... I know the risks and yet somehow I don't think it will happen to me... Little is known about the long-term health risks of heavy use.
>
> (Katie, bodybuilder of six years)

These reflections are similar to those found in Grogan *et al.*'s (2006) study, in which one woman called steroids a 'necessary evil' in order to compete.

Despite the masculinizing effects of steroids and the other physical risks involved, for the female bodybuilders the pleasures and desires outweigh the negative side effects and provide them with the ability to fulfil their goals. Further research is needed into how female bodybuilders manage the risks associated with their lifestyle and the long-term consequences of their choices. Whatever compromises the female bodybuilders made, none were prepared to revisit their primary aim of developing a muscular body. There is for these women a pleasure intrinsic to building muscle that overrides the costs associated with breaking social taboos, a finding consistent with Grogan's (2004) suggestion that the development of female muscularity can be used positively to help resist certain gendered norms.

Conclusion

This chapter has focused on the 'dark side' of bodybuilding, exploring muscle worship and steroid use through the lived experiences of the participants themselves. By doing this, it has offered more complex and multi-dimensional insights than have previously been documented. Indeed, there has been a tendency in academic literature to disembody female bodybuilding by presenting a picture 'devoid of women's experiences, feelings, and practical activities with regard to their bodies' (Davis 1995: 169). Yet without exploration into these processes, physical pleasures and practices, it is difficult to fully comprehend the lives of these women, which appear hard and difficult, despite periodic moments of pride and enjoyment. As Grosz argues, 'understanding the body means examining what things it performs; what transformations and becomings it undergoes; the connections that it forms; and the capacities that it can proliferate' (Grosz 1994: 165). It is for this reason that the next two chapters focus on the place where these women feel most at home and experience the 'workout' as the peak phenomenological heightened pleasure in their daily lives. It is to this exploration of female bodybuilders in the gym that I turn in the next chapter.

Confession of a muscle slave

The first time I saw a female bodybuilder I was in my family home, watching a BBC popular science programme. I was about 13 or 14 I think, and the show, called 'Body Matters', had invited Carolyn Cheshire on to demonstrate the way muscles work in tandem. She came down a set of steps through the audience, tanned, oiled and wearing an orange bikini. Then she started to pose, and my life changed forever.

I have been attracted to female bodybuilders and women with muscle in general ever since. I can't really explain why this is so, not in the sense of 'Where does this attraction come from?' I'm just wired that way. But I can try to explain what I find attractive and erotic about them.

First of all, I love their muscles. This may seem obvious, but it needs to be said nonetheless. Muscles on women turn me on more than anything else. Any amount of muscle will do it for me, but the more muscle there is, the more defined it is, and the more proportional it is, the more turned on I will be. I simply find muscular female physiques to be more aesthetically beautiful than any other body type.

I love the way they look whether relaxed or flexed, in motion or frozen in a photograph. A common criticism of female bodybuilders is that they don't have the 'curves' of a conventionally sexy woman. I've never understood this. Muscle women have curves in places that most women don't have places. To me, they are the most curvaceous, and therefore the sexiest, women of all. I'm pretty sure that the reason for my reaction to female bodybuilders in those first few years was that they were truly unique women. I had never seen anything like them, and they were so different from the norm that this must have been the reason for the intensity of my physical response to them.

I also think that this is a key factor in my response to seeing muscular women in the course of my everyday life – not that this happens often! A muscle woman looks totally different from other women. The shape of her body is different, and her muscularity means she carries herself differently. She radiates strength and confidence, which is not something that many conventionally bodied women do.

Confidence is a quality that most people (male or female) find appealing, and I am no exception. A muscular woman has it in spades. She's such a unique creature that it is almost inevitable that she will attract attention when she is in situations outside the gym or the contest, and unless she is supremely comfortable in her own skin, this attention will be unbearable.

One of my favourite female muscle clips is of Gayle Moher walking through the streets of New York in a revealing red dress. People gawp at her, necks snap round in disbelief, pure shock on their faces – they can't believe what they have just seen. And Gayle just keeps walking on, seemingly oblivious to it all. She looks absolutely magnificent of course, but the sexiest thing about this clip is the way she just keeps walking serenely through the crowd, radiating total self-confidence. It's a fantasy of mine to be with a muscle woman in such a situation, to be walking through the crowd with her and to observe the reactions myself.

Furthermore, since I started training myself, I have come to appreciate the dedication and sheer hard work that it takes to sculpt such a body. The physical and mental effort necessary is so great that only the most determined, single-minded women achieve the kind of look that I find most erotic. Again, the ability of someone to set goals and reach them is something that most people find attractive, whether male or female, straight or gay. Both of these aspects of my attraction – the confidence and the achievement of goals – are things I would expect anyone to admire, and not just in muscular women. There are other factors in my attraction for them that are more personal though.

The first is that muscle women subvert their traditional gender roles or arche-types completely, and this is another aspect of what makes them sexy to me. I am generally attracted to things that exist outside the mainstream. I don't know whether my inclination towards an unconventional, even subversive lifestyle and life choices is a result of my admiration for muscular women, or whether the admiration is an aspect of my inclination, but I do have a tendency to sympathize with outsiders, original talents, new ways of thinking and so on.

Moreover, there is the use of steroids, and their apparent effects on the women who use them. I'm not the kind of person who thinks that 'drugs are bad'. I've never been averse to recreational drug use, even though I no longer partake. And while anabolic steroids are quite different from other, let's say 'party' drugs, my point is that I know from experience that drugs can have very positive effects as well as very negative ones.

Through my interest in muscular women I have come across articles and inter-views in which the effects of steroids on women have been reported. I have to admit, I find a lot of what is said extremely erotic: the increase in sex drive and the enlarged clitoris particularly. I've never, unlike many fans of female muscle, been into the idea of being physically abused by a huge female bodybuilder, but I do fantasize about being picked up in the gym by a pumped-up, uncontrollably horny and virtually insatiable woman who uses me to satisfy her steroid-induced sexual cravings.

And even though I have never had sex with a woman on steroids, my own per-sonal experience of women with muscular, or at least toned, fit bodies is that the sex is more frequent, they have more stamina, are more flexible and are more willing to experiment. In short, the sex was better. In one or two instances, much, much better. And the women I have known were dancers, physical education *teachers, a martial artist and a gymnast. 'If they were so much better in bed', my female-muscle lovin' head says, 'imagine a woman who is really really muscular. She must be truly earth-shattering between the sheets!'*

To sum up, then, my attraction to female bodybuilders and other muscular women is based on their aesthetic appeal and their confidence; my admiration for their unconventional lifestyles and their achievement in creating such unique bodies; and finally a suspicion that they are better lovers than any other women. Actually, I sometimes wonder why I feel the need to justify my attraction to them – either to myself or to others. Shouldn't the question be put the other way round and those who don't like muscular women be asked 'Why not'?

After all, what, exactly, is there not to like about them?!

7 Exploring the 'empowerment' of female bodybuilders through concepts of space

I become acutely sensitive of my surroundings: sounds, smells and sensations that I am normally so accustomed to that I barely notice. Loud music is blaring out, echoing and booming against the warehouse walls. The machinery hum of treadmills and other cardiovascular equipment can be heard in the background. Within the weights area, male grunts, groans of exertion, and shouts of encouragement can be heard, occasionally interrupted by a fleeting eruption of laughter. The thuds of heavy weights as they are dropped or thrown to the floor vibrate through my trainers. Smashing sounds are heard as iron hits iron. Audible twangs and clicks. There's a sense of anticipation, tension and excitement in the atmosphere. Scent glands emit bodily uriniferous and musky smells, which vaporize into the air and mingle with other sweat odours, characteristics of food eaten the night before such as garlic, onions, and curry.

My training partner prepares to squat 160 kg. She moves into the squat rack and mentally prepares to psych herself up. She looks directly in front of her, straight into the eyes of her reflection. She wears no makeup, her hair is free and loose. She does not smile. Her clothes consist of a baggy t-shirt and tracksuit bottoms, allowing her to move freely. She wears a weights belt around her waist to support her lower back, signifying the seriousness of her weight-training endeavour. I stand behind her silently, ready to act as her 'spotter', should she need me. She stands up straight, taking the full brunt of the weight, allowing the barbell to lodge itself into her traps. She starts. Sounds of 'Shhh', 'ghrurr' 'Arhh' and gasps for air issue from her lips as she pushes the weight up through her heels. Grimaces cause lines to become etched out upon her face. She has the look of determination. Another female weight-trainer encourages her: 'that's it drive it', 'drive 'em out', 'come on', 'nice depth', 'light weight'. … She completes the set and leans on the squat rack for support. Her face is flushed, she breathes heavily and appears exhausted… a minute later, she looks me in the eye and gives a little nod and a smile of satisfaction – 'your turn', she says.

(extracts from field notes, 15 March 2008)

Chapter 6 explored how the identity of the female bodybuilder is constantly under attack, making it difficult for her to sustain a positive sense of self. In this chapter, it is argued that although it is not without impediments, female bodybuilders perceive the gym as 'home' – as a hospitable sanctuary that, at least in part, shelters them from the negative interactions of wider society. By navigating substantial obstacles in the male domain of the gym, female bodybuilders carve out a space of physical and mental liberation for themselves, which in turn provides a key source of motivation and identity affirmation. Also in this chapter, using ethnographic data, I explore 'what actually happens in the gym' by focusing methodologically on the under-explored area of 'space'. The first part of the chapter describes how the environment of the gym is organized into highly distinctive gendered spaces, moving beyond a focus on 'place' to an investigation into how identity is constructed and expressed, as well as how social relations are produced, negotiated and contested in this area. In the second part of the chapter I employ a more phenomenological understanding of space in order to explore how female bodybuilders, despite stigmatization, use their spatial transgressions and deviance to their own advantage.

Sexed space: building gendered bodies

The health and fitness gym environment is organized through conditions of time and space.[1] Peak training hours occur at lunch time and between 5 and 7.30pm, when the majority of gym members finish work. Sassatelli (1999: 4) points out that whilst 'gym crowds can rarely be reduced to one socio-demographic at any time', there is a tendency for different groups of people (e.g. students, professionals and the elderly) to attend at different times of the day. Bodybuilders as a rule, depending on their work commitments, prefer to train at the extreme ends of the day, when the gym is at its quietest and is not 'polluted' by the presence of casual users (Douglas 1966). However, although time is a relevant aspect of the gym culture, providing a 'time out from life' as well as being a central component of training programmes and used to monitor progression (for example, ten minutes on the treadmill), it is the analysis of space that provides us with more useful insights into exploring the empowerment of female bodybuilders. Feminist geographers insist on the importance of researching the interconnections between gender relationships and space studies. According to Hanson and Pratt (1995), feminist geographers were the first to point out that women live spatially restricted lives, believing space to be central to male power and to feminist resistance (Hanson and Pratt 1995; Frye 1983; Blunt and Rose 1994). Its importance to power is emphasized more generally in Massey's (1994: 81) argument that '[s]pace is a complex web of relations of domination and subordination, of solidarity and co-operation... a metaphor as well as a set of material relations'. As such, space is a vital variable in my analysis.

The doors of the large (1,100sq m) gym open directly into the reception area. Just inside the doors, there are seats and tables arranged around a 32-inch television.

Hot and cold drinks are provided, along with a free newspaper and videos and DVDs for hire – all of which emphasize the 'leisure' experience of the vicinity and provide a friendly atmosphere. At the reception desk, an attractive young person (usually female) greets the customers, swipes their membership cards and welcomes them through the electronic gates which mark the entry into the main gym. In front and to the right is the cardiovascular (CV) section. The purpose of the CV equipment is to improve general fitness (stamina, heart and lung capacity, etc.) and, most commonly, to 'lose weight' and 'burn calories'. Machines such as treadmills, rowers and cross trainers are laid out in neat rows, reminiscent of a factory production line. Most pieces of equipment have their own TV, with a choice of channels, to help prevent boredom and monotony. The scales are also located in this area. Whilst this space is utilized by diverse clientele, the predominant sex of the users tends to be female.

On the left-hand side of the gym is the hairdresser, beauty rooms and offices. The ladies' changing rooms are located adjacent to them (the men's changing facilities are situated at the far end of the gym, opposite the weights area). The changing room plays an important part in the preparation and transition of the participant. As Sassatelli (1999: 3.2) explains:

> The changing room helps clients to enter the spirit of training, sustaining its specificity and suspending other relevances, stripping individuals of their external identities, equalising their bodies in the moulding object of a serial and yet personalising training.

As it is also a place where people dress/undress, bodily exposure is carefully managed and negotiated through the social interaction order, to prevent embarrassment and retain privacy and modesty.[2] Furthermore, the changing rooms act as a meeting place where gossip and verbal exchange can take place, either before or after the workout (see Crossley 2006b). Attached to the basic but adequately equipped changing rooms, toilets and shower facilities, is the luxurious joint/unisex 'spa relaxation area', consisting of a sauna, steam room and jacuzzi – a place frequented after a 'hard' workout, where gym-goers can relax and reward themselves for their endeavours. It perhaps should be noted from my research observations that compared to ordinary gym members, female bodybuilders spent very little time in the changing rooms, preferring to get changed at home. Likewise, during the study I never saw a female bodybuilder in the spa relaxation areas.

Outside the ladies' changing room, in the main gym, there are stairs that lead up to the aerobics hall, spinning room, stretching area and resistance machines. This stairway 'allows' women to completely avoid the heavy weights area, which is located on the ground floor at the back of the gym, beyond the cardiovascular machines. Upstairs, resistance machines make up the next exercise space, a place frequently used to 'tone' specific muscle groups. Inspirational posters of fit men (muscular) and women (slender) are placed along the walls, next to advertisements for motivating personal trainers and weight-loss supplements. Mirrors are also strategically placed around the gym (particularly in the resistance machine weights area, free-weights area and aerobics hall), inviting participants to scrutinize their training bodies in order to check and rectify technique. This self-surveillance can be a daunting and distressing task for some, and especially for the new and uninitiated gym-goer (Sassatelli 1999).

Back on the ground floor, situated at the back of the gym is an extensive free-weights section designated for the 'building of muscle'. With rare exceptions, the gym users in this area are male. The space consists of free weights, including dumbbells, barbells, benches, squat racks, various bars and more 'heavy-duty' old-style machines such as the hack-squat. Despite notices requesting that users put their weights away, the 'heavy weights area' is usually comparatively untidy. For example, plates are left on equipment, chalk and liquid stains (from knocked-over drinks) are embedded in the floor and dumbbells are left out of numerical order.

Against this depiction of the gym, it can be seen that the specific organization of space impacts directly on corporeal bodies. Put simply, bodies are slimmed, stretched, sculpted or built in the gym. Thus, as Johnston (1996: 328) points out, 'bodies become constructed and inscribed by the environment' in which they move and work. Furthermore, as areas of the gym are highly gendered, providing 'socio-political spaces which confirm feminine and masculine stereotypes', these also help to contribute to the construction of masculine and feminine bodies (ibid.). Women are expected and inducted to use the cardiovascular machines and encouraged to use light 'toning' exercisers that are deemed appropriate for their sex.[3] This point is illustrated by Samantha (a bodybuilder of three years) who recalls the first time she entered a gym and requested the male gym instructor to set her an exercise programme to build strength and muscle. After being told that 'muscle doesn't look right on a female', she was given a meagre high-repetition, light-resistance weight programme, concentrating on women's 'problem' areas of 'legs, tums and bums'.

Whilst there are no longer rules forbidding women from entering the free-weights section and 'hardcore' gyms, there remains a clear gender division of space within the gym.[4] There are two main reasons for this divide. First, many women fear that by training with weights, they will put on muscle too easily and appear bulky and unattractive to heterosexual men. This is illustrated by one potential customer (female, gym 4:1), who commented to a member of the sales team as she was shown around the gym, in response to seeing a female bodybuilder train: 'I wouldn't want to look like her... I don't want to train with weights and get all muscly'. The second reason why women avoid the weights area is the intimidation that they often feel. As one female gym member (female, gym 1:1) explained, 'I don't want to train over there [men's weight area]... There's testosterone flying all around the place...'. The weights section is still deemed a hypermasculine space that is unfriendly and uninviting to women. The ways in which this male domain is protected through noise space, body space and interactions shall now be examined.

Gendered noise/sound

The weights room

Metallic and bodily sounds emanate from the weights area. Clips, chimes, clanks and twangs are audible as iron plates are moved on and off equipment (barbells, dumbbell racks, machines, squat racks etc.) – like the clink of metallic crockery. *Clang* – a weight is heaved with some force back on to the rack. The whirl of the smith machine – ZssZZZ… ZssZZZ – up and down, up and down – can be heard. *BANG.* Loud bangs and thuds reverberate around the room as heavy weights are dropped and thrown to the floor. The crashes, twangs and clonks remain in the eardrum long after the initial noise occurrence.

The sounds of this machinery orchestra are occasionally punctuated by a discordant Clonk. Clatter. The noise doesn't sound 'quite right'; everyone turns around to stare at the 'out-of-place' sound and the person who hasn't been using their equipment properly.

Human sounds of talking, laughing, coaxing, sniffing, sighing and heavy breathing come secondary to the guttural sounds of exertion. For the uninitiated, the intense visceral noises of grunts and groans can be shocking. *Errrrrhaaaaarh!* The strain of lifting heavy weights resembles a volcanic eruption emanating from deep within the person. *Aaaaaarrrh!* The pain escapes through the gasp of the participant. Other sounds of exertion can be equally as violent/expressive: *Arhhhh! Aweeeeeee! Urghh! Grhh. Ooeeffff.*

(extracts from field notes, 15 March 2008)

Goffman's (1971: 33–4, 46, 51) work *Relations in Public* explores how sound is a variable in people's command of public space, and can be usefully applied to analysis of the gym. Goffman argues that one of the 'modalities of violation' when discussing 'personal space' is that of 'sound interference': 'noisy people violate other people's territory of the self by appropriating "sound space"'. Furthermore, Bailey (1996: 64) argues: '[Noise] is an expressive and communicative resource that registers collective and individual identities… it is a form of social energy with the power to appropriate, reconfigure or transgress boundaries; it converts space into territory'. The noises of the weights area can intimidate women and stop them from entering the male domain, thus protecting male supremacy. The dropping of heavy weights, the clanking and crashing of iron, the grunts and groans of the participants and the shouts from training partners all contribute to a cacophony of masculine patriarchal sound.[5] Saltman (2003: 52) draws parallels between the masculine realm of the military and the noises made by male bodybuilders in the gym:

The militarized body of the bodybuilder makes the sounds of war. Under the yoke of heavy iron there are screams, rebel yells, grunts, wails, karate-like Keoghs designed to focus the power of the body into the muscles being taxed. As in boot camp, in the gym taunts are hurled between lifting partners, inspirational clichés slung, boasts belted out, slogans, slogans, slogans: 'no guts, no glory', 'no pain, no gain', 'bigger's better'.

Men often train in pairs or groups of three, encouraging each other to 'work to the max', frequently through bullying comments and assertions of masculinity. For example, I overheard the following on the gym floor: 'Come on, come on big boy, you can do it – you're the man… do you want to get big? Do you want to get muscles? Then work at it fat boy!' (male, gym 5:1). Noise in this context can be seen as a sign of masculinity, virility, aggression, animalism, domination and territory. Such loudness draws similarities with Ackerman's (1990: 186–7) depiction of erotically excited 'sophomore boys', who 'are all decibels and testosterone'. At the same time, these sounds could be interpreted as representing freedom, release, expression, lack of inhibition and tribalism. One female gym user articulates her frustrations in the following comment:

> Men always make so much noise. I don't mean just chatting like some of the women do. But grunts and groans. To me, it sounds so overdone and unnecessary as if they are trying to show off or something. Maybe they just want to get attention, like in the wild – calling attention to the fittest and strongest.
>
> (female, gym 1:2)

Regardless of the interpretation, many women feel threatened by the sounds emanating from the weights area. This is illustrated by another female gym user's comment:

> It's intimidating enough just trying to work out how to use the machines, let alone all the noise the guys make. It just doesn't help your confidence at all.
>
> (female, gym 6:1)

As one aerobics instructor commented to me, even within mixed-gender classes such as 'Body Pump' sessions (a high-rep choreographed workout using light barbells), women are more likely to keep quiet during their exertions, compared to their male counterparts.

Against this backdrop, it might be thought that women's space is violated by the noises made by men within the gym environment. However, before we can reach this conclusion it is important to recognize the complexities of this analysis. I have tended to gloss over the differences between male gym users and bracket them all within the same category. That is to say, I have depicted all men as gatekeepers of the weights arena and as embodying and enacting traits of dominance and power. Men, like women, are not a homogenous group. Indeed, within the heavy weights area, there is almost a 'hierarchy of supremacy' that orders and stratifies the men within this space according to such variables as the age of participants, their experience, muscular size and so on. For example, male newcomers to weight training, particularly teenagers and those bordering on the upper limits of middle age or older, may also feel intimidated. Likewise, there is a tendency (though this is made more complicated by class and sport-specific aims, etc.) to exalt the more mesomorphic, muscular males. Consequently, in the same way that women might feel intimidated or threatened within the weights area, it can also be argued that there are also struggles of power and dominance between men within this ultimately masculine domain. Connell's (1989) work on 'masculinities' is of particular relevance here. He explains that 'hegemonic masculinity' should not be understood as the male role but rather as a *particular variety* of masculinity to which women and others (e.g. young men, as well as effeminate and homosexual men) are subordinated. Nevertheless, despite the actual intentions of different men, the majority of women do feel intimidated by the noises emanating from the weights room, and this contributes to their avoidance of this space.

The penalties paid for crossing into male territory

The minority of women who are undeterred from entering the weights area still have to contend with men dominating the physical space of the gym. Thus, most female bodybuilders who use public gyms train during times when the presence of 'ordinary' male gym members (those outside the subculture of bodybuilding, who are less committed and appreciative of the commitment to the development and display of muscularity as a goal in itself) is least evident. In the words of Barbara (a bodybuilder of seven years):

> I don't want to train when it's busy and there is some clown touching the barbell or something – ruins my focus… some people comment on my physique and there's people that don't really work out but just stand there and stare and it really winds me up – I'm in the zone of lifting weights – so any interruptions get me annoyed.

Many male bodybuilders also seek out training times and spaces in which they will be unhindered by 'clowns', but female bodybuilders may be more vulnerable to such interference, especially from men who 'feel they have a right to look and get in our way just because we are women' (Pauline, bodybuilder of six months). As Monica (a bodybuilder of two years) confirmed, 'men definitely dominate the space… a lot of their mentality is that girls are just playing at it, but they are serious'. This domination of space translates as not only the 'hogging' of the weights, benches, machines and other equipment, but the physical inhabitation of the space around them – using their size and strength to their full/maximum capacity.

Interestingly, not all females who accessed the male domain claimed to have negative responses from male gym users. Several more 'feminine' female weight-trainers (who were not as muscular as some of the other female bodybuilders and made more effort to maintain a 'heterosexual' appearance) claimed that 'men rarely dominate[d] the equipment' (Rachel, bodybuilder of two years). Indeed, Danielle (a bodybuilder of five years) stated that 'men always act chivalrously and never hog the equipment: in fact quite the opposite, most jump off and spot'. In these cases, men would also automatically take the weight plates off the machines or bars in order to 'help' and frequently gave training tips and advice to these women. Goffman (1979: 9) would interpret this chivalry as maintaining gender differences, where even the most straightforward acts of civility are not only symbolic but actually constitutive of gender inequalities. Glick and Fiske (2000) expand this perspective further, arguing that even if the male benevolence is sincere, and in some cases is accepted (or even expected) by the female, chivalry still 'remains patronizing towards woman and provides a powerful ideological justification for traditional gender roles and patriarchy' (ibid.: 367). According to this view, then, chivalrous acts in the gym encourage intimate dyadic dependencies between the genders which inform compulsory heterosexuality and retain the sex segregation of labour by reinforcing the belief that 'women are less competent and are indeed the weaker sex' (ibid.: 390).

Another method often employed to protect the male space of the gym is the use of negative labelling to enforce compulsory heterosexuality. Sharp (1997: 45–6) argues that the stigma of lesbianism is used to control patriarchal gender identities. She claims that problems arise when women do not conform to the appearance and behaviour expected of them in 'ordinary' public space and that women must avoid 'specific male-dominated environments', continuing: 'women who dress, behave, do jobs, or go to places associated with men run the risk of being labelled "butch" and hence "male hating lesbians"' (ibid.). As female bodybuilders disrupt hegemonic norms by not only training in the male sphere, but also wearing the muscular body, they are particularly vulnerable to these accusations. This is demonstrated in comments made to Laura (a bodybuilder of ten months) by several friends at the gym who were commenting on how big her biceps had become: 'show him your bicep'; 'you big lesbian you'. Indeed, female bodybuilders sometimes judge *each other* on the basis of heterosexual femininity. For example, Alice (a bodybuilder of 18 months) referred to another female bodybuilder as 'butch' and suggested: 'she doesn't help herself, she wears vests to train in. It's like she's trying to compete with the men'. More generally, despite these women's determination to 'be different' and 'look different', it is common for female bodybuilders to feminize their appearance in various ways; however, only one of the women in this study worked out in an ostentatiously feminine combination of hot pants and crop top lycra set. Thus, these women frequently navigate the masculine space of the gym by conforming to the gender interaction order of either 'chivalry' or the 'feminine apologetic' (Felshin 1974). To disobey these rules is to risk the stigma of being labelled a lesbian.

Bodies on display: looks and comments act as censorship for spatial transgressions

In addition to the stigma of lesbianism, there are other ways in which the gendered foundations of the wider interaction order appear to impinge on these women's actions and identities. It is possible for the flow of the workout to be interrupted by looks and comments that ask these women to reflect back on themselves, and on what they are doing, in the gendered terms of the interaction order, and to experience as internally divided their subjective sense of self and the reflected portrayal of that self as it is classified by wider society (Goffman 1983: 12; Mead 1962 [1934]). Hence, these stares and comments result in uncomfortable epiphanic moments which remind the women that they 'shouldn't be there' – that the weights arena is men's space and belongs in the male domain.

The fact that these women's bodies are 'on display' forms an important part of the context in which the interaction order has the potential to intrude on female bodybuilders even during their workout. The gym is a space in which body visibility is heightened in relation to its normal position in daily life. Bodies are being worked on, body parts are being toned and shaped and inter-corporeal comparisons are being made all of the time, often by casual users in relation to idealized, normative visions of masculinity and femininity. Hardcore gyms might provide some degree of insulation from these comparisons, although even then, female bodybuilders are not protected completely from gendered norms and unwanted comments about being 'too muscular' for a woman. Several of those using hardcore gyms in this study reported having to deal with 'incidents' regarding comments and stares from male bodybuilders. None of these was as disturbing as Marcia Ian's (1995: 89) story of how a huge male bodybuilder who was working out close by turned to her and said casually, 'One of these days I'm gonna knock you on the floor and fuck your brains out'. Nevertheless, the comments and stares still interrupted the flow of the workout. Elsewhere, in the milieu of ordinary gyms, casual exercisers sometimes looked, stared, commented and pointed at the bodies of muscular women in the free-weights area, and this sometimes filtered through into the experiences of female bodybuilders. The following reflect the experiences of female bodybuilders in ordinary gyms:

> I've had strangers come right up to me in the gym and just say 'You're a woman, women shouldn't be muscular. Female bodybuilders look disgusting', 'She looks like a man', and 'If you carry on training like that you'll look like a man in four months'.
>
> (Gemma, bodybuilder of six months)

> Guys have put down their weights and left when I'm training. People tend to be quite horrified to see a small woman lifting heavy weights.
>
> (Lucie, bodybuilder of eight years)

The strong, direct movements employed by female bodybuilders, such as rowing, benching, squatting and dead-lifting, and the associated gym activities of loading a bar with heavy plates, grasping iron with calloused, chalky hands and shifting weights around, are not body techniques associated with femininity. This is evident in the following comments made by casual male gym users:

Why is she lifting heavy weights like that? Why does she want to look like a man?... She should be doing aerobic and toning exercises not trying to build and bulk herself up... no man finds that attractive.

(male, gym 1:1)

It's not right, women lifting that amount.

(male, gym 1:2)

All of the above comments demonstrate the typical types of verbal censure that female bodybuilders receive for transgressing feminine conventions. As Lorber (1994) points out, women who show physical strength are deemed unattractive to heterosexual men and labelled unfeminine. The feminine ideal in Western society is to be beautiful, small, thin and *weak*, compared to the male ideal, which possesses physical power, presence, strength, size and aggression. Subsequently, 'doing masculinity builds strength, whereas doing femininity builds weakness' (Roth and Basow 2004: 247). In this context it is perhaps unsurprising that the gender deviations of female bodybuilders cause such an outcry. The bodies of female bodybuilders are not just symbolic of societal notions of power, but literally embody them.

Against this backdrop it would be easy to perceive the gym as a patriarchal institution that has a detrimental impact on the identity of the female bodybuilder. This would however be an inaccurate portrayal of how the women themselves navigate, interpret and indeed embrace the gym environment or the 'womb' of the weights area. It is worth looking briefly now at ways in which female bodybuilders manage these negative interactions, before exploring how these women actually find sanctuary away from the outside world and indeed find empowerment through transgressing this gendered territory. Female bodybuilders, aware of the controversy raised by their bodies and actions, generally try to work out at a time when few casual weight-trainers will be around. When faced with adverse reactions, they do their best to block out the comments and stares, and try not to let them infringe on their activities and experiences. This is clearly illustrated by the following comments:

I don't particularly notice other people's comments. Sometimes they piss me off, but most of the time I don't really care.

(Michelle, bodybuilder of five years)

I love the gym. All of it. Apart from the twats... silly little boys with their sideways looks and stares... though I don't notice it as much as my partner does.

(Barbara, bodybuilder of seven years)

The guys who make comments are usually really puny and insecure, with a fragile ego – I don't care what they think.

(Anna, bodybuilder of five years)

The 'ignorant' casual gym users who make negative comments are dismissed as 'insecure', pathetic and unimportant. The sole focus for these women is their training and the pursuit of their muscular endeavour.

The hospitable back region of the gym

Despite the negative reactions from 'casual' gym users and the occasional male bodybuilder, most female bodybuilders still perceived the gym as a supportive environment. In contrast to the hostility that these women can experience outside the gym in the daily interaction order, the distinctive character of collective encounters inside the gym is indicated by the frequency of comments describing the existence of 'camaraderie among all bodybuilders' (Jacqui, bodybuilder of 11 years). As Jacqui continues, this camaraderie is based on mutual recognition of the efforts they make in relation to 'intense training and dieting' and the appreciation of the 'hard work, pain and dedication' it takes to be a competitive bodybuilder. This solidarity also emanates from the pursuit of the same aesthetic goal. Consequently, the identity of the female bodybuilder is affirmed through the shared language, tastes and collective experiences that form part of their 'social capital' (Coleman 1988). This is reflected in the first instance by the arrangements these women often make to train with a partner in a reciprocal arrangement involving spotting and encouragement, thus forming an intimate space in which comments, gestures and actions are directed to the task at hand. More generally, in this activity space of the workout, serious weight-trainers are 'supportive' and frequently 'offer to spot' for those without a partner and 'share training tips' (Katy, bodybuilder of four years). People may ask for advice and it is not unusual for female bodybuilders to receive compliments on their physiques from admiring others (those whom Goffman (1983) would call 'their own'). In this milieu (in contrast to the outside world), the social meanings inscribed on their bodies act as a form of physical capital that translates into a high status (Bridges 2009: 97).

Body in space

Bartky (1988: 67) suggests that 'women are more restricted than men in their manner of movement and in their spatiality'. Similarly, Castelnuovo and Guthrie (1998) argue that Westernised concepts of female beauty are not only symbolic of vulnerability, weakness and invisibility, but actually constitute a form of spatially saturated bodily oppression. For instance, embodied actions, gestures and postures not only encourage women to take up as little space as possible but also severely constrict movement. Connell (1983: 19) postulates that 'to be an adult male is distinctly to occupy space, to have a physical presence in the world'. Male bodies are judged on their 'action and an active orientation towards the world' particularly by exhibiting 'strength and power', and consequentially throw their whole bodies into movement. In contrast, female bodies are evaluated upon their 'aesthetic value', which suppresses their functioning (Uhlmann and Uhlmann 2005: 93–103). Correspondingly, women are 'less likely to reach, stretch, bend, lean, or stride to the full limits of their physical capacities' (Young 1990: 148). Instead, according to this perspective, their bodies are seen as burdens to be carried around with them and looked after.

Against this background, feminist analysts of sport conceive that 'the development of the physical, athletic body and the cultivation of a sense of physical power and competence, can be vital components of women's full equality' (Farkas 2007: 1). Roth and Basow (2004: 19) believe that encouraging women to participate in empowering sports and physical activities opens up possibilities for a true form of physical feminist liberation – one which they believe 'would increase women's confidence, power, respect, wealth, enjoyment of physicality, and escape from rape and the fear of rape', on the basis that it would help their command of and movement within physical space. According to Farkas (2007), women's historical oppression essentially emanates from men's embodiment of physical power, which translates into the threat of violence and rape. Sport, then, according to Castelnuovo and Guthrie (1998: 13), creates the 'potential for reducing physical power imbalances on which patriarchy is founded and reified'. As female bodybuilders not only increase their strength, but embody the physical appearance of power, these women hold the possibility of emancipation more than those involved in any other sport. As Charlie articulates, her new-found trust in her body's capabilities gives her the confidence to overcome the fear of rape and attack:

> I'm less afraid of things now. I used to get really nervous walking home by myself after work in the dark… but I guess I feel I'm more able to handle myself now… put up a good fight.
>
> (Charlie, bodybuilder of four years)

For other female bodybuilders, it was the desire to obtain these 'physical powers' (as a form of self-defence/protection) that motivated them to become bodybuilders in the first place. This is illustrated in the example of Michelle (a bodybuilder of five years) who recalls a horrendous period of her life when she felt 'fearful', 'vulnerable' and 'helpless' against the physical abuse of her father. She remembers:

> Living in constant fear and terror of my father – not just for myself but for my brother and mum… I felt useless not being able to protect them, and I guess I thought that by being physically more powerful than my father would maybe stop his violence – that physical size would somehow be my protection for us.

Evidence from other studies suggests that there are many other benefits for females who participate in sport. Active women, for instance, are more likely to perceive themselves as being better at leading, motivating, sharing, competing and reaching goals, in comparison to their inactive counterparts (Nelson 1994). In her study of women who participated in strenuous sports, Lawler (2002: 43) argues that women 'gain [both] confidence and enjoyment'. One of her interviewees claimed that only through active involvement in sport had she learnt to 'stop apologizing for the space [she] take[s] up in the world'. Similar to McCaughey's (1997) research findings in her investigation into women and self-defence, female bodybuilders gained a 'greater sense of self-efficacy' and overall competence from their training. This is articulated in the following quote from Lucie (a bodybuilder of eight years): 'Since serious weight training I've learnt to realise that I am capable of doing things. I feel more independent and self-sufficient'. When women enter spaces that are traditionally used by men and participate in 'forceful space occupying activities' (Shogun 2002: 16), some analysts believe not only do they challenge the myth of the fragile female body (Castelnuovo and Guthrie, 1998), but '[during the] process they are also awakened to their own bodily potential' (Wearing 1998: 110). Heavy weight training thus allows women to restore their faith in their bodies and capabilities and appreciate what they can actually achieve (rather than focusing on aesthetics). This positivity is shown through the words of Mary and Michelle:

> Workouts are empowering in themselves...They allow you to see how far your body can be pushed with no restrictions.
>
> (Mary, bodybuilder of 12 years)

> [Bodybuilding] gives you the ability to push your body to its limits.
>
> (Michelle, bodybuilder of five years)

The satisfaction and elation that accompanies the achievement of doing something that was previously not believed possible, is demonstrated by Michelle, who, after completing a 100 kg bench press set for the first time, declared: 'I have been wanting to do that for five years!... right now I feel I could do anything'. According to Heywood (1997, 1998), these new-found abilities have the potential to trickle down into these women's lives and act as a form of 'third-wave' feminism (see Chapter 4). Heywood (1998: 60) continues by observing that as women begin to seriously weight train, they become 'less bound by limits they've internalised from years of absorbing cultural mythologies that impose drastic limits on women's strength and potential'. As their strength and muscles grow, so too does their confidence. Using the 'body in space' (expanding, moving, enlarging, growing and strengthening) can act as a form of empowerment for women – emotionally as well as physically. Heywood (1998: 60) claims that their bodies demand they are taken seriously, commanding respect from people and making women more assertive at work.

Postures

According to Sassatelli (1999:6), 'body demeanour in training spaces is obviously divergent from everyday life expectations. Participants need to commit themselves to postures and movements which would be considered inappropriate, and even embarrassing in most situations'. This applies particularly to women who, by accessing leisure spaces traditionally occupied by males, learn to use and experience their bodies in non-conventional ways (Wearing 1998). In the gym environment women wear clothes that allow them to move freely and effectively (such as trainers and tracksuit bottoms, unlike the typically restrictive skirts, tight jeans, high heels and boots frequently worn in the outside world), enabling women to stride through space in an unprecedented manner. The safety of the weights area provides a space where they can perform activities and positions that would normally be deemed unfeminine (for example legs wide open, a position considered 'natural' for men). As female bodybuilders' muscles become swollen and engorged with blood, so too do their postures change. They stand with their heads held high, backbone straight and feet firmly on the floor, thus taking up space (Heywood 1998).

These unorthodox female postures, however, do not pass unchallenged. For example, Charlie (a bodybuilder of four years) is fully aware of the controversy caused by presenting her body (via demeanour and carriage) in a non-feminine manner. She notes: 'Occasionally when I have trained my upper body, I'll be pumped up and have to stop myself walking like a man. You know, take my hair down'. In muscle and fitness magazines' photo shoots, these potentially threatening masculine mannerisms are contained by eroticizing and sexualizing the images of exercises by women in the gym. For example, the gaze will focus on women's glutes, as they bend over to perform straight-leg dead-lifts, or on women's legs invitingly spread wide apart, like a pose from a soft-porn magazine. Whilst a few of the female bodybuilders in my study felt some concern about performing compromising exercises (particularly 'glute exercises' and 'donkey calf raises', where one female sits on the other's back), the majority didn't care in the slightest: 'You can't worry about stuff like that, you've just gotta do what you've gotta do' (Michelle, bodybuilder of five years). Despite these drawbacks, the gym provides an area in which female bodybuilders can move more freely through space and perform actions and postures which would normally be constrained.

Conclusion

Despite violating the gendered space conventions of the gym environment, female bodybuilders negotiate and establish a space of their own. The gym acts as a partial refuge and retreat from the malevolence of the outside world. In this milieu, female bodybuilders can move about in the gym without having to be concerned about the responses their 'unfeminine' physiques, postures and movements may provoke on the street. The gym also provides a zone that helps to re-establish and repair any damage that might have been caused to their self-identity. This occurs not only through positive social interactions with 'like-minded others', but also through these women's total concentration on their proficiency and the skill involved in their weight-training activities, rather than focusing on any perceived aesthetic deficiencies.

Sports feminists argue that dynamic activities such as heavy weight training can teach women to trust their bodies and to enjoy their physical competence and capabilities. Women can potentially take ownership of this new-found power and use it for their own advancement. However, Grimshaw (1999: 108) introduces a note of caution to the female-centred orientation of this discussion. She notes that although the female body has been inhibited in terms of movements, this should not be placed in opposition to an 'unrepressed' male body. Rather than men having unrestricted freedom, much is dependent on the gender coding of activities: for example, men often feel clumsy, isolated and unwelcome in aerobics classes. Grimshaw also makes the valid point that 'in certain circumstances, moving in ways that reach the limits of one's physical capacities can oppress or terrorise others' (ibid.). Subsequently, women re-enacting male behaviour in the gym by occupying as much space as possible (such as dominating equipment, dropping weights, making loud noises) would not necessarily be a positive phenomenon. Cultural, essentialist and radical feminists take this argument one step further, insisting that for women to take on masculine pursuits and activities would be for them to take on the same traits of violence, aggression, oppression and dominance as men.

In order to investigate this debate further, it is valuable to move beyond the spatial elements of inquiry and explore the actual processes, bodily sensations, emotions and feelings of the female bodybuilder as the body is built in the gym. In the next chapter, I turn to the phenomenological experiences of these women, comparing their reality against the aggressive and domineering discourse associated with male bodybuilding.

Figure 7.1 Sarah Lewis and Marina Cornwall. Courtesy of Karla Tizard

Figure 7.2 Sarah Lewis and Marina Cornwall. Courtesy of Karla Tizard

8   Ripped, shredded and cut

Reworking notions of 'pain and violence' in female bodybuilding

The bottom line is the desire and the need to push the limits – to be bigger and stronger, to go heavier and longer than Mother Nature ever intended… When you're pounding the weights like this, you subject your body to a tremendous amount of punishment that can lead to wear and tear and injury.

You don't talk smack. You don't bullshit when you're in the gym. You don't chase ass. You just lift. Plain and simple. There is something so peaceful about it, yet something so violent. To get motivated, you dig deep… Deep into yourself. You imagine a little man looking back at you in the mirror. So you take your anger out on the weights. You punish them. Yeah, this is what you call motivation. This is what drives you.

(www.animalpak.co.uk)[1]

In the previous chapter I argued that female bodybuilders were stigmatized for transgressing gendered space, but managed to turn this aberrance to their advantage. They carve out a space of their own within the masculine territory of the heavy weights area, creating an area where they can move in a (comparatively) unrestricted manner whilst also feeling protected against the harsh ostracism of the outside world. However, as pointed out in the conclusion to that chapter, critical commentators of female bodybuilding believe that women who enter this male bastion and embody masculine traits are not developing a new form of female liberation, but are simply re-enacting oppressive male characteristics of aggression, domination and self-destruction. To investigate this allegation further, this chapter focuses on the phenomenological experiences of female bodybuilders – looking at how the women's subjectivities are expressed, lived and created through their bodies within the weights arena. The chapter begins by depicting the bodybuilder's 'culture of pain' and how this is interpreted by critical feminists and others as being part of a detrimental hypermasculine force that subjects the body to more self-hatred, pain and violence. The chapter then turns to the voices and experiences of the women themselves, to assess whether there are alternative readings to pathology.

Pain and violence in bodybuilding

White *et al.* (1995) suggest that the subculture of bodybuilding punishes the body beyond what is involved in any other sport, and indeed, actually welcomes pain. At the very heart of bodybuilding lies the process of muscle destruction that takes place in the gym. In order for the desired muscle hypertrophy to occur, muscles must first be broken down by strenuously exercising the body against resistance weights until muscle exhaustion is reached. During the bodybuilding process, microtrauma occurs, causing pain due to the tearing of muscle fibres. The soreness, discomfort, stiffness and temporary disability felt after the workout is a result of damaged muscle cells. Only by adequate rest outside the gym environment is the body able to begin its healing process, responding to the trauma by producing thicker muscle fibres, thereby increasing the size and appearance of the muscles. Consequently, the bodybuilding subculture welcomes this pain as an indication of achievement and muscle growth. Embracing the masculine cosmology so exemplified in Fussell's work (1991), the body is portrayed as an obstacle to be overcome – a battle to be won using violent language, analogies and metaphors (Heywood 1998; Mansfield and McGinn 1993). Typical bodybuilding magazine articles depict the body as an object in the gym that needs to be destroyed, controlled and dominated. This is clearly illustrated in the following titles (which act as both inspirational tool and workout manual for readers): 'In the Trenches – Time To Get Personal'; 'Taking Up Arms'; 'Conquering the Die-Hard Chest'; 'Texas Toast' (subtitled: 'That's what your legs will feel like after you try this fried-to-a-crisp thigh trash'); 'Back Bombardment'; 'Screaming Supersets'; 'Intense Triceps Trash'; 'Bloody Thursday' (with the subtitle: 'The guts and gore flow freely in this shoulder session from hell'); 'Killer Instinct' (subtitled: 'A gym potato obeys his instincts, a bodybuilder dominates his'); 'Armageddon'; 'Love And Kisses From Mr. Hate-And-Pain'; 'Slice and Burn' (Locks 2003: 243–8).

As Heywood (1998: 69) summarizes, 'the language of bodybuilding is the language of violence, and the object of that violence is one's own body'. These hypermasculine metaphors and imagery are used and alluded to throughout the subculture, and are readily found in magazines, websites, advertising and marketing (e.g. clothing logos, products), forums and everyday gym discourse. These frequently include militaristic and warrior analogies representing bravery, battles and fighting.[2] In Fussell's (1991) autobiographical account, in Foucauldian style, he compares the bodybuilding subculture to that of the military organization in terms of rank, attention to order, regulation and discipline. The bodybuilder's role in this way parallels that of the soldier. Saltman (2003) explores this analogy further, citing the following three comparisons. First of all, both are bodies made for war: 'from the disciplined routines in the gym and kitchen, to the posturing and posing regimes on stage and street, to the martial slogans, metaphors and boot camp sergeant's screams, to the battle in the body itself' (ibid.: 2). Second, in order to elicit big sacrifices from recruits, both soldiers and bodybuilders are promised the reward of transforming their bodies into human weapons (to be tough, hard and superhuman). Third, detailed attention must be given to the body's surface: the body must be smooth and shaven, hair must be cut short and be tidy. The bodies belonging to both organizations must be stripped of their individuality and wear identical uniforms. For the bodybuilder, whose uniform is their very flesh, this entails creating a perfectly symmetrically proportioned physique. Similarly, the 'bodybuilder is permanently in a state of military attention' (ibid.: 51). Fussell (1991: 82) recites the muscle 'roll call' he would repeatedly do on his own body:

> Every few hours, no matter where I was, I found myself running through my muscle inventory, checking to make sure I was still there. From head to toe, I'd squeeze and flex every body part: traps? check; deltoids? check; pecs? check; lat wings? check; bi's and tri's? check; quads? check; calves? check. All present and accounted for.

Linked to this military comparison, Fussell depicts bodybuilding as a form of protection and defence against the world:

> What were these great chunks of tanned, taut muscle but modern-day armour? Here were breast plates, greaves, and pauldrons aplenty, and all made from human flesh. He had taken stock of his own situation and used the weight room as his smithy. A human fortress – a perfect defence to keep the enemy host at bay.
>
> (Fussell 1991: 24)

The extreme masculine ethos of the bodybuilder is also captured by Animal's successful and prominent advertising campaign for its bodybuilder supplements and products. The 'Animal' evokes caveman-like imagery that implies survival of the fittest:

> This is a game for warriors. The iron sport is gruelling, painful and arduous. Whether it's in the gym or with your diet, being an Animal is about consistency and giving everything you got 24/7, 365 days a year… It's back-breaking labor, day in and day out. You move the heavy weight in the gym and eat the right calories to pack on muscle because you know it's what's required. It's not just what you want to do – it's what you gotta do.
>
> (www.animalpak.co.uk)

For Grint and Case (1998) the bodybuilding discourse, depicting hypermasculine traits of toughness, strength and the ability to give and take violence, are representative of a desire to return to a time when 'men were men'. Likewise, other sociologists have explained the growth in bodybuilding's popularity in terms of a 'postmodern crisis of masculinity' (Klein 1993; Heywood 1998).

These hypermasculine characteristics are encouraged through bodybuilding magazines, advertisements and websites. Furthermore, as Stulberg (1996/7: 93) points out, media space is used to actively construct sexual identity and regulate sexual power, creating further disparity between the sexes. As bodybuilding is usually perceived as a 'man's sport', magazines are marketed at the male consumer. Features are usually about men and for men. On the rare occasions that women's photographs are included, the softer, curvier hyperfeminine look is preferred, appealing to the male gaze and amplifying by sheer contrast the muscularity, size and masculine appearance of the male bodybuilder (see Heywood 1998; Frueh 2001; Mansfield and McGinn 1993; St Martin and Gavey 1996). Furthermore, far from the 'warrior' and 'animal' depictions, women are photographed training with light weights, in sexualized and non-aggressive poses, smiling, with full make-up and styled hair. The models do not grimace or show signs of sweat, pain or hard work. Likewise, the commentary accompanying the images contains no swearing or harsh dialogue (compared to articles on their male counterparts) and women's 'feminine' qualities and achievements are emphasized (for example, being attractive or juggling training with motherhood).

Injuries: being hard enough

In the same way that pain is glorified within the bodybuilding subculture, injuries are often perceived as something to be to be fought through, overcome and not 'given in' to. White *et al.* (1995: 176) explain that this attitude is part of the 'machismo and fatalism of athletic culture', although the 'character-building' qualities of toughness, endurance of pain and discipline can equally be applied to the army or other types of male-dominated institutions. Bodybuilding magazines and documentaries frequently include narratives whereby male bodybuilders conquer their injuries and go on to compete, refusing to submit or admit defeat despite their suffering. As Locks (2003) notes, however, there are no equivalent magazine narratives of women training and overcoming injury.

Klein's (1995: 105) ethnographic study in California illustrates the seemingly masochistic relationship between injuries and bodybuilding: in one gym, Klein (1995: 105) observed 'a bodybuilder suffer a nosebleed whilst lifting weights; it was triumphantly explained that the man in question was a true bodybuilder, paying dues, training in earnest and willing to both risk and endure injury for his calling'. In another instance he saw a bodybuilder 'doubled over in pain from what would later be diagnosed as a symptom of hepatic tumours on the liver and whose obviously unwell condition was again interpreted by the behemoths in the gym as testimony to his commitment to the subculture' (ibid.: 105). Alongside the pain caused by injuries and the pain created by working to one's maximum ability during training, there are also the 'everyday' surface wounds and marks that accompany workouts. These include callouses and skin abrasions from the friction caused by gripping iron weights, bruises and shin grazes from exercises such as dead-lifts and so-called 'blood marks' on the back from exercises such as pec flies on the bench. Even the sheer weight digging into the flesh can cause muscle soreness and bruises (e.g. on the traps during squats). These are, however, daily warrior markings and are nothing compared to the injuries that some bodybuilders contend with due to repetitive heavy weight training, poor technique or poor biomechanics. For instance, during my ethnographic study, I encountered bodybuilders who suffered from hernias, numerous shoulder injuries, torn muscles and torn ligaments.

Reading and interpreting the bodybuilder's pain

Critical feminists (including cultural, essentialist and radical feminists) make three related points regarding the ethos of bodybuilding and its relationship with violence and pain. First, they condemn the tantalizing promise to new recruits that they too can embody masculine traits of power, in terms of 'growth, penetration and dominance' (Saltman 2003: 59). Feminists such as Jaggar (1983) argue that women are naturally less violent than their male counterparts due to their superior innate caring, mothering and nurturing characteristics. Therefore for women to participate in more violent practices would be for them to take on inferior male characteristics. Whilst not all critical feminists take such a radical stance, many still believe that as physical force has been used to create and maintain patriarchy, to utilize this power would be to continue oppression based on violence and domination – thus women must not use violence for their own ends (see Lorde 1997).

Second, these critics claim that the culture of bodybuilding re-enacts the historical dualism between mind and body. This binary is argued to create objectification and hatred of the body, alienation and estrangement. This is nicely illustrated in the following extract from Fussell's autobiography, when he shaves his whole body in order to display his muscle more clearly:

> And when I rose from the bath tub and looked at my naked form, I was amazed. It wasn't my body – it was the blood. I looked as if I'd run a marathon through briars. I waited for the shock of pain, but it didn't come. I didn't feel a thing. I was no longer connected to my own body. It had become simply an abstract concept, a shell to be polished and plucked with regularity.
>
> (Fussell 1991: 84)

He no longer feels pain; instead, he feels nothing. He has become desensitized to both his bodily sensations and his emotions. Saltman (2003: 63) postulates that at its core, 'bodybuilding is about *destroying* the body over and over to become Something Else', a point which resonates with essentialist and cultural feminists' argument that the body 'is never good enough as it is' (Bordo 1988; Chapters 4 and 5). Finally, feminists critical of female bodybuilding are quick to point out that the violent language of the bodybuilder – 'ripped', 'shredded', 'tearing', 'breaking down', 'cutting' and so on – parallels the destructive discourse surrounding other female body modification practices in contemporary society (see Jeffreys 2005). According to this approach, women who take up bodybuilding are simply practising another form of self-destruction and yet another way of enduring pain and injury, which is carved out upon the body (Fournier 2002). This concurs with Scarry's (1985) view that pain, in all its guises, is a powerful and destructive force that is damaging to both the self and the world.

Whilst there are differences in the above feminist perspectives, they are all extremely critical of the liberatory potential of female bodybuilding. I will now turn my attention to, and briefly critique, the three main assumptions on which their analysis is based. First, as I have remarked in earlier chapters, I am deeply sceptical about essentialist notions of men and women; notions which claim that the 'sexes' are inherently biologically and psychologically different. Not all women are caring and nurturing; similarly, not all men are violent, oppressive and dominant. Furthermore, as McCaughey (1997) claims, regardless of whether women are innately non-violent/non-aggressive or have a choice in the matter, this is only a discussion that can be held by the privileged. Female non-violence and 'purity' has only been an option for white middle and upper-class women. For all other women, especially those who are poor, non-white and living in less developed countries, physical assertiveness has been a necessary form of survival (Roth and Basow 2004). I am more sympathetic with the second critical point, which comes from a cultural feminist perspective rather than a radical one. Nevertheless, this approach ironically ends by reiterating the very binary of mind/ body (and related ones of male/female, culture/nature) that it seeks to 'transcend'. It still claims that there can be a harmonious relationship between the mind and body, but fails to depict what this state might be and furthermore fails to explain the mind/body connection – i.e. where the body ends and the mind begins, and vice versa.

In connection to the third point on female bodybuilding, I am particularly interested in the relationship between gender and 'destructive' physical practices. If indeed bodybuilding is self-destructive and masochistic, why is no concern given to the men who take up this practice? Is it only women who become victims of it? Surely if bodybuilding is an inherently detrimental practice, then men too become victims of oppression as a result of the influence of a hypermasculine model of what it is to be a man. Whilst the 'self-hatred' that can follow such a norm could provide evidence to support the view that bodybuilding is pathological and that individual participants suffer from insecurity and body dysmorphia, it might also give weight to the argument that both genders suffer under dominant hegemonic constructions of femininity and masculinity.

So far, bodybuilding has been portrayed as a pathological and hypermasculine power which embraces and encourages pain and violence to the body and can in no way provide any form of empowerment for women. However, the work of other sociologists can be used here to provide an alternative and more positive reading to this fatalistic interpretation. Monaghan (2001: 45) admits that 'anaerobic exercise can be extremely painful'. Similarly, Crossley (2004: 39–40), in his study of circuit trainers, claims that 'experiences of pain, exhaustion and breathlessness are often deemed unpleasant'. However, instead of translating this embrace of pain as a destructive compulsive obsession, Crossley explains how the exerciser's pain is 'reframed' through symbolic and emotional interaction with others, and by experience becomes satisfying and pleasurable. For example, first-time drug users (e.g. marijuana users in Becker's studies of 1963 and 1967) find the experience to be unpleasant, nauseating and frightening; through perseverance, however, agents 'acquire the taste, learn the techniques, and learn to frame the experience in such a way as to render it positive' (Crossley 2004: 40). In this way, rather than simply translating the bodybuilder's desire for pain as determining a masochistic attitude and self-hatred of the body, it can be seen that bodybuilders learn to re-interpret these 'painful' physical sensations as enjoyable (Monaghan 2001: 345). Crossley and Monaghan both point out, however – in complete opposition to the work of White *et al.* (1995) and Klein (1993/1995) – that there is a significant difference between 'good pain' and 'bad pain'. The bodybuilder learns to distinguish between the right forms of pain, 'bad pain' being comprehended when exercises are performed with improper technique or exacerbate injuries.

In summary, critical feminists and sports social psychologists view this 'socialisation to voluntary pain' as simply an emblem of masculine identity that suppresses emotions (Sabo 1989: 159). Furthermore, Scarry (1985: 54–5) argues that pain is not an abstract, passive phenomena, but is *real* – it hurts and is literally carved out and into a fleshy, sentient body. Pain is 'unshareable [and] inexpressible'; regardless of which 'perspective pain is approached [from], its totality is again and again faced'. In addition, critics argue that bodybuilding propagates gender roles, even more than other sports – reinforcing the hierarchical ideology of masculinity and the subordination of women. However, these views contrast sharply with the theory of 'physical liberation' (Roth and Basow 2004) proposed by sports feminists and discussed in the previous chapter. Furthermore, Crossley (2004) and Monaghan (2001) convincingly argue that there is a possible alternative reading to that of pathology, as 'pain is re-interpreted' and reworked to become pleasurable within the bodybuilder's interactions and 'culture of pain' (Monaghan 2001: 345). This point is made more generally by Shilling and Mellor's (2010) analysis of how various cultures have historically employed the infliction and endurance of pain as a positive resource in developing people's self-identities.

At this point it is vital to turn to the lived experiences of the female bodybuilders themselves – to see how these women interpret the 'pain' of the bodybuilding process. How does the reality of their training compare to the violent discourse of bodybuilding? Do they find empowerment in re-enacting male-defined behaviour? What does training actually feel like – what are their bodily sensations and emotional responses? Are they just another manifestation of self-hatred against the body, or are there alternative explanations? In order to try to answer these questions, I next turn to the voices of the women themselves, comparing the reality of female bodybuilders' training to this portrayal of violence and pain.

Female bodybuilders' phenomenological experiences

The bodybuilder's 'culture of pain' encompasses different physical sensations depending on the individual's interpretation and the sequence of events within the bodybuilding process. The sequence of 'pain' can be loosely divided into four periods: during the workout 'rep', directly after the rep/set, after the workout and the Delayed Onset Muscle Soreness (DOMS) that usually occurs 1–2 days later. During the actual anaerobic exercise when the weight is lifted, exertion is felt through the muscles, joints and chest, causing a sensation of tightness and shortness of breath. However, the bodybuilder anticipates that these unpleasant feelings will soon appear to subside in light of another more favourable sensation – 'the pump':

> The pump… It is the holy grail of bodybuilding. It is that most addictive of sensations… It is euphoric and invigorating, an intense swelling of the muscle caused by a training-induced cascade of blood… It is a rebirth experienced on each worthwhile trip to the gym. The pump is instant gratification… An automatic reward for all of the blood, sweat and tears you spill on the gym floor.
>
> (www.animalpak.co.uk)

This feeling has been cited by other sociologists and bodybuilders as a strong incentive and a driving force for training (Gaines and Butler 1983; Mansfield and McGinn 1993; Wacquant 1995). Likewise, in my study, Debbie (a bodybuilder of seven and a half years) describes 'the pump' in terms of the 'amazing feeling' that accompanies the sense that 'your muscles are bursting out of your skin'. In a more descriptive manner, Samantha (a bodybuilder of three years) reflects on her experiences after training her biceps:

> The finishing exercises, consisting of relatively higher reps… allow that blissful engorgement of blood to swell the muscles. Veins become sketched out on the body like a road map, and the intensity feels like a burning sensation throughout the designated muscle group.

Whilst 'the pump' may be the most coveted sensation, it is not a guaranteed physical state and rarely accompanies the heavier and lower reps and sets. However, even without this feeling, female bodybuilders expressed pleasure and satisfaction in the process. This is articulated again by Samantha in the following quote, given after she had completed a two-rep max of squats (in order to improve her strength):

> The heavy, low reps – feel like a battle of wills between body and metal, as the mind and body are forced to work in harmony in full concentration. There can be no doubt, no hesitation nor any negative distraction… You are grounded in the moment. For that second, time feels like it has stopped. The world takes on a surreal quality… Only you really exist, you and the force to be conquered.

Similar to the 'runner's high', the bodybuilder's 'pump' is believed to trigger a whole range of hormonal responses causing the release of enkephalins and endorphins into the bloodstream, which act as natural painkillers. Like Monaghan's (2001: 347) male bodybuilders, my participants also identified the feeling of euphoria and the adrenaline rush as comparable to taking pharmaceutical stimulants: 'the endorphin high – it's like a drug' (Michelle, bodybuilder of five years).

Experiences deemed unpleasant, such as the tightness and shortness of breath and weights digging into flesh, fade into the background during the execution of the weight. Enraptured in the 'positive moment of bodybuilding' (Monaghan 2001: 331), pain and discomfort become reconfigured into a sensual experience. Female bodybuilders thereby associate these changes with a *heightened sense of being alive*; a sense that manifests itself in an emboldening and a merging of the senses. This is clearly illustrated in the comments made by Samantha, who explains how the bodybuilding high involves pain but also something 'beyond pain', including an 'adrenaline buzz, the satisfaction of working to the max. I feel like I'm flying, buzzing. I feel so alive and enthusiastic about life'. Sharon (a bodybuilder of 12 years) aptly quotes from the film 'GI Jane' (1997): 'Pain is your friend – it lets you know you're not dead'. This intense desire to feel 'alive' can be read against the backdrop of an increasingly computerized, rationalized and sanitized society – a place Weber describes as the 'iron-cage' of modernity (Weber 1991 [1904–5]).

Furthermore, the bodies of female bodybuilders undergo changes in the gym that initiate a *metamorphosis* in their sensory experience of themselves and their environment. This is captured in the following excerpt:

> [The gym is] a place of incarnations where our bodies inflate and we shuffle off our out-of-gym bodies like discarded skins and walk about transformed. We begin to grow, to change… we pick up our shoulders, elevating our chins, shaking ugliness from our torsos with a series of strokes, the glistening dumbbells, listening to the blood's rush… Our breathing is quick, our skin is flushed, our hearts are pounding thickly.
>
> (Heywood 1997: 3)

This transformation is demonstrated clearly by Christine (a bodybuilder of five years) who felt considerably 'better' and energized after she had trained:

> I had a really crap day at work today… before I started to train I was feeling tired and pissed off. But surprisingly, I had a really good session… got an amazing pump in my delts [shoulders], normally do shoulder press [dumb-bells] with 20 kg, but today I did to 24 kg [in each hand] – so really chuffed with that.

These 'incarnations' occur through an *undivided* focus on the body. As Rachel (a bodybuilder of two years) comments: 'training time is me time. I can just forget about my worries… focus on my body and how it moves'. Similarly, for Debbie (a bodybuilder of seven and a half years) bodybuilding 'releases a lot of stress and tension and stuff, it makes me feel more relaxed… a place to release my emotions… it's my world for an hour or two'. Hence, immersion in the process of lifting allows these women to escape from everyday life. Furthermore, it provides a cathartic action, enabling these women to 'unleash any internal anguish, stress, anger and numbness. Thoughts and worries that overwhelm me are pushed aside… I live and breathe for the moment' (Anna, bodybuilder of five years; see also Kaye

2005: 8). After the endorphin high, my participants articulated a sense of cathartic peace and liberation as a result of letting go of negative feelings and excess energy (Crossley 2006b: 39). In this way the workout not only enables a transformation of bodily sensation, but transfigures emotions.

Immediately after a hardcore training session (such as 'legs'), the body-builder experiences temporary partial disability in the worked muscle groups. When I asked Rachel to explain how she felt after completing her workout, she replied:

> Physically my legs feel heavy, swollen and grounded. It's difficult to walk. Every step feels like I'm walking through a bog. My calves feel really tight… My body's crying out for rest, yet I'm perversely looking forward to tomorrow's workout already… I feel a bit nauseous and yet peaceful, invigorated yet exhausted.

Samantha (a bodybuilder of three years) provides a similar narrative: 'Post workout… my body feels strange, almost sick, but at the same time everything appears heightened, I feel euphoric'. Mary (a bodybuilder of 12 years) also sees these sensations as things to be enjoyed and embraced, even when they leave her so tired and stiff that she is 'unable to walk down the gym stairs'. There is also a puritanical satisfaction in being able to overcome the pain and push the body beyond what is considered possible. This is captured in the comments made by Corina and Michelle:

> There's some part of me that enjoys it [the pain]. The pain makes me feel as though I've achieved something, pushed my body to the next level.
>
> (Corina, bodybuilder of four years)

> Great session! Totally trashed legs, two hours before they stopped shaking.
>
> (mobile phone text message received from Michelle, bodybuilder of five years)

Post-workout DOMS is welcomed by female bodybuilders as an instrumental pain, signifying a 'good workout', which has successfully torn and broken down muscle fibres. After an intense weights session, the targeted muscles will start to feel sore between 12 and 48 hours after the workout; the pain can last between 24 hours and one week, depending on the severity of the muscle damage. Feelings such as tightness, heaviness and tenderness make everyday exercises such as bending down, getting up and walking downstairs temporarily difficult. Due to the swelling and soreness in them, muscles feel 'worked' and 'larger' than they actually are, again creating a sense of satisfaction. As Emma (a bodybuilder of 19 years) explains, pleasure is found for these women in being 'able to conquer the pain, to feel invincible' and to feel in control of their bodies and lives. Carol, a female weight-trainer who participated in Tate's (1999: 38) research, illustrates these findings more ecstatically:

Yeah it's like the dips. I do love them. Oh I used to hate them. I used to hate them because of the pain. They just killed my triceps and pecs. But oh, it's beautiful, absolutely beautiful.

In this way the hurt and discomfort of working to 'muscle exhaustion', 'muscle failure' or to 'the max' is seen by female bodybuilders as 'beautiful, pleasurable and satisfying' (Tate 1999: 38). The pain that comes with pushing their body to its limits is perceived by these women as 'perversely' enjoyable. Female bodybuilders consequently seek out and engage with discomfort and fatigue as a way of transforming it into an experience to be welcomed (see also Crossley 2004: 55). Male bodybuilders are not radically different from their female counterparts in this respect or, indeed, in some of the phenomenological changes they undergo in the gym (Paris 1997; Monaghan 2001). The contrast for women is arguably far greater, however, given the social ostracism they risk in the wider interaction order as a result of their more radical transgression of gender norms and the distance between their experiences and conventional modes of feminine being (Young 1990).

Erotics of the gym: new bodies, new pleasures?

The 'erotics of the gym' have been documented in some detail by sociologists such as Klein (1993), Mansfield and McGinn (1993), Wacquant (1995), Monaghan (2001) and Crossley (2006b). In Klein's first visit to a hardcore gym, he describes the erotic charge that seems to emanate throughout the place:

> The whole place seemed caught up in one large orgasm, and in the first encounter I did not want to be the dreaded interruption of this erotic scene, between humans, mirrors and metal.
>
> (Klein 1993: 21)

The weights section has been portrayed as an area of hypermasculinity: as a mass of heaving male bodies, an orgy of engorged muscles, throbbing veins, constricted breathing, exposed flesh and physical interaction (through spotting, correction and so on). 'The pump' has been also famously been equated with sexual pleasure:

> It's as satisfying for me as coming is, you know, as having sex with a woman and coming. So can you believe how much I am in heaven?'
>
> (Arnold Schwarzenegger, cited in Wacquant 1995: 176).

Muscles, synonymous with the male, are imbued with sexual metaphors: hard, penetrating, erect, swollen and phallic (see Lingis 1988).

Interestingly, despite – or because of – the pornographic representation of female bodybuilders, very little has been written about the erotic experiences of women in the gym. However, for some female bodybuilders, such as Joanna Frueh (2001) and her friends, the euphoria resulting from the 'bodybuilding high' extends to a feeling of erotic potency, as illustrated by the following comments: 'I catch myself swaggering to the drinking fountain, radiating sex' and 'I feel horniest when I'm working out' (Frueh, 2001: 71). Likewise Natalie Gassel (1997: 4), in her autobiographical writings, explicitly describes the personal connection she makes between muscle and eroticism:

> With a dumbbell in each hand, I flex my arms, alternating, so that my balls of muscle burst out, harder, more congested. My blood rises. My strength asserts its power. My fingers tighten around the cold metal of the weight. My muscles become rigid, never losing the oily fluidity which I want to feel gushing into my muscles. I strain to lift once more. More swelling, capacity, bulk. My skin tightens. My power bursts. An orgy of sensations. I am in ecstasy. Radiance, a mass of fleshy, strong muscle tissue.

Whilst only one of the interviewees confessed that she was close to orgasm whilst performing leg extensions, several 'knew of someone else' who 'got off on weight training'. Another female bodybuilder admitted that she found both herself and others more attractive when she trained. The intimate dyadic relationship and bond between two people as they train can lead to a form of 'primary intensity' (Rich 1980). As Michelle (a bodybuilder of five years) explains, it can be an erotic experience due to 'the very physical nature of what you are doing – paying close attention to another person's body whilst they are sweating and breathing hard'. Irrespective of whether female bodybuilders used sexual terminology to describe their erotic relationships or experiences, all participants expressed a deep pleasure in and stimulation from the sensual act of corporeal transformation.

It can be seen, then, that 'the gym has been and continues to be a pleasure zone that provides challenge [and] sensual transformation' (Frueh 2001: 81) – descriptors that resonate strongly with Monaghan's (2001) comments on the sensuality and eroticism of the gym, but provide an interesting contrast to Crossley's (2006b: 38) identification of sexual motivations for gym use. Whilst, as Crossley claims, some gym users' motivation may be to meet attractive others, the sensuality discussed here can generally be seen as a form of auto-eroticism in which female bodybuilders are revelling in the experience of their *own* flesh. In a society in which women's breasts and legs are fetishized by men (Saul 2003), female bodybuilders subvert heterosexual norms by choosing to eroticize and take pleasure in the creation and physical sensations of *their own muscles*. This self-inscription, like other body modifiers, might therefore lead to a 're-mapping and extension of the body's "erotogenic sensitivity"' (Grosz 1994: 139). This allows these women to explore their bodies and sexuality by 'taking on a pleasure of a different order… [to] reclaim, re-use, and re-intensify, body parts, zones, and functions that have been phallically disinvested' (Grosz 1994: 201). In this way, female bodybuilders potentially transgress hegenomic notions of sexuality and challenge the 'phallic economy of desire' (Sweetman 1999b: 201).

Furthermore, for feminists such as Lorde (1984), Cixous (1991a, b) and Frueh (2001), erotic experiences such as those described by female bodybuilders are of vital importance to women's liberation. As Lorde (1984: 282) explains: 'Recognising the power of the erotic within our lives can give us the energy to pursue genuine change within our world'. From a more essentialist feminist perspective, Lorde perceives the erotic as spiritual; 'as an assertion of the life-force of women; of that creative energy empowered...'. She believes that eroticism, in its truest form, is about 'power', 'honour', 'self-respect', 'satisfaction' and 'completion' (ibid.: 278–9). In this way Lorde's work ironically provides the possibility of creating a 'true form' of *female* bodybuilding by rewriting the erotic, by challenging the very core of bodybuilding, which relies upon a masculine identity and way of being. Although Lorde's theory is not explicitly linked to activities such as bodybuilding, her work (albeit from a radical/essentialist feminist perspective) provides us with an alternative interpretation that bears similarities to the third-wave activism of bodybuilding that Heywood convincingly advocates (see Chapter 4). As Lorde (1984: 281) expresses:

> In touch with the erotic, I become less willing to accept powerlessness, or those other supplied states of being which are not native to me, such as resignation, despair, self-effacement, depression, self-denial.

It is this focus on self-love, joy and sensuality that is captured in the following quote by Monica (a bodybuilder of two years) as she tries to articulate her feelings immediately following a bicep workout:

> My biceps are normally 13.5 inches, but when I flex and train them – by getting a pump in my biceps, they swell to just over 15 inches... as I was contracting my biceps the veins were visible. My arms looked strong – I felt strong and I felt good... It felt like I was doing something purely for my own pleasure... enjoying the sensation of the blood flowing through my arms. Feeling alive, feeling empowered, enriched... with all the positive endorphins flooding through my nervous system... and I felt almost – not attracted to myself exactly but just appreciating my body for what it is, just being... fascinated by it I guess ... what it can do.

Frueh (2001: 24–5) perceives the 'erotic' as a positive and pleasurable connection which takes individuals beyond themselves in a sensuous, intimate and emotional experience of unique meaning. For Frueh, this definition stands in stark contrast to the 'body of pain' and 'erotics of pain' which she claims to be prevalent in society. She believes that the 'beauty idol' is one example of that body and suffering, one which causes a 'strange erotics, an erotics estrangement from the pleasure of increase and expansion'. In this context, Frueh argues that the phenomenological delights that take place in the gym can revitalise the passions and release 'an exuberance of life' (Bataille 2006 [1957]: 179) that has been suppressed in patriarchal capitalist society. Within this interpretation, the eroticism experienced by these women in the gym translates as 'an embodied creative power' that not only provides them with a 'flight from rationalized society', but also provides 'a key to meaningful existence' (Shilling and Mellor 2010: 2, 9). The 'erotics of the gym' can, at least in part, help to explain the motivations and identity of female bodybuilders, allowing these women to find meaning by experiencing their lives as invested with the force of strong, existentially significant, overwhelming emotion (ibid.).

Conclusion

My findings suggest that whilst many female bodybuilders did indeed embrace both the hypermasculine attitude towards pain and the satisfaction of being able to conquer it, there are alternative interpretations of these actions to those put forward by critical feminist and sports psychologists who see them simply as a pathological manifestation of self-hatred and inferiority. Instead, as Monaghan (2001) and Crossley (2006b) suggest (in their comparative studies on male body-builders and circuit trainers), traditional understandings of pain exist within, yet are also subverted by, the centre of the subculture itself. Thus female bodybuilders *reworked* the meanings and physical sensations of 'pain', so that they became pleasurable, enjoyable and desirable. The women cited feelings of 'heightened awareness', 'euphoria', 'flow', 'release', 'erotic intensity' and gratification. In this context it is hardly surprising that female bodybuilders wish to dwell in the gym for as long as possible, in order to savour and relish these sensations. Furthermore, it is the actual experiences, feelings, emotions and intimate accounts of the bodybuilding process articulated by the female bodybuilders themselves which help to explain their commitment to a muscular order. The ethnographic findings in this research oppose the argument made by critical feminists such as Bordo (1988: 98) that bodybuilding is an ascetic act lacking sensuality: 'pre-occupied with the body and deriving narcissistic enjoyment from its appear-ance... [with] little pleasure in the experience of embodiment'. Indeed, the pain 'of the actual process of bodybuilding' and its 'subjective and corporeal effects are central rather than peripheral to the experiences and motivations of many contemporary body modifiers' (Sweetman 1999c: 205). This substantiates the importance of focusing on the 'lived reality' of such practices, rather than simply the text or outer appearance (Featherstone 1991: 171; Radley 1991: 112–3).

So far in this book, I have investigated the daily lifestyle of the female bodybuilder, exploring her interactions and experiences both outside (Chapters 5 and 6) and inside the gym (Chapters 7 and 8). The present situation, in terms of bodybuilding's potential to 'empower' women, appears complex. However, a final assessment cannot be made until the most extreme and important moment in the bodybuilding calendar is explored – competition time.

9   Competitions

A heroic journey

I'VE DEDICATED MY ENTIRE LIFE TO BUILDING UP MY BODY THROUGH HARD WORK, PAIN, HUNGER AND DESIRE. EVERY SINGLE DAY REQUIRES *SACRIFICE*. The moment of truth… The time has arrived… Your heart is racing. Your veins are throbbing with carb-loaded blood. The hot lights are blinding you and all you can hear is one voice barking out orders as if you were in a prison line-up. 'Quarter turn to the right, quarter turn to the right, quarter turn to the right, face the front'… All the diet, cardio, and busting your ass on the iron for weeks on end. All for that brief window of time to show what you've got on stage. You might ask yourself, "Is it all worth it?" If you have to ask, it just might not be. *This is bodybuilding. This is our world, our stage, our time to shine, and our moment of truth.* This is what makes a bodybuilder – the stage, diet, cardio, the selfishness of body over life. Any gym rat can hit the weights hard and get big with eating and skipping the 4:00 am cardio sessions. But it takes *a true bodybuilder* to cut down and step into the light.

(http://my.opera.com/mbodybuilding/blog, accessed 4 August 2009 [italics added])

Previous chapters have explored the daily lifestyle and experiences of female bodybuilders, both inside and outside the gym. This exploration has revealed the ways in which female bodybuilders manage to develop and maintain a viable sense of self, despite being stigmatized by the gendered foundations of the 'interaction order' (Goffman 1983). In this chapter, I turn to the most important part of all in the life of the female bodybuilder – the competition, an event that deals with the culmination of their ambitions and 'sets the seal' on these women's identities. Critical feminists have argued that competitions are the most detrimental aspect of female bodybuilding. This chapter questions this stance by following the lived experiences of Michelle (a bodybuilder of five years) as she journeys from the start of her preparation to competition, to that moment of climax.[1]

The competition as the 'holy grail' of bodybuilding

The competition is the most important day in the bodybuilding calendar. It is perceived as the pinnacle of bodybuilding, where the profane daily struggle of hard work, dedication and sacrifice (both inside and outside the gym) culminates in a unique sacred moment. It is a time to be recognized, a time to stand out from the ordinary; to 'be above the masses, different, a star' (Heywood 1998: 171). This is supported by Amy (a bodybuilder of four years) in the following quote:

> It's a time to prove to myself and to others that I can do it... it's a time to prove to all those other people who said I couldn't... I don't want to be known as just 'Amy', if you know what I mean.

Due to the ostracism female bodybuilders experience in their daily lives, the competition appears to be of particular importance to them, compared to their male counterparts. It seems to act as a consecration of these women's identities – elevating them from the status of just a woman who trains hard to that of a female bodybuilder.[2] This distinction is elucidated by Michelle in the following interview extract:

• What advice would you give a female who wanted to become a bodybuilder?

> I would say, do they really understand what it takes to be a bodybuilder and do they really know what is that difference between training and bodybuilding? The difference is the diet to get ready for competition... Many, many people can train and many people can eat well and eat healthily. But not many people can do that strict, hideous, gruelling, soul crushing diet to get to the end – or go on stage.

The competition then appears to act as a 'rite of passage', whereby female bodybuilders pass from being simply females who weight train in the gym to actually becoming female bodybuilders. Given the travails that have been charted throughout the course of this book, it should be clear by now that this is no straightforward, automatic process. Success would be a major achievement given all we have learnt about people's prejudices about female bodybuilders and the stigmatization these women face, especially outside the gym, in their daily lives. Indeed, there appears to be an element of heroism here (Weber 1991 [1915b]). As these women reject the gendered 'interaction order' (Goffman 1983) on which ordinary life is based in favour of an extraordinary life – which not only threatens the possibility of them ever being able to reintegrate back into society, but also 'entails the deliberate risking of life itself' – they seem to qualify for Featherstone's (1995a: 58) notion of the 'heroic life'. In this context, the women's lifestyle of dedication, sacrifice and commitment to the muscular order bears similarities with heroic characters such as warriors, who battle against the odds on a 'quest for virtue, glory and fame, which contrasts with the lesser everyday pursuit of wealth, property and earthly love' (Featherstone 1995a: 59). Other relevant heroic descriptors identified by Featherstone include masculine traits of 'sacrifice, distinction, discipline, dignity, self-denial, self-restraint and commitment to a cause' (ibid.: 66). Another similarity between Featherstone's depiction of the 'hero' and the female bodybuilder is their sense of fate. For heroes 'to achieve great deeds requires both luck' and a 'sense of destiny' (ibid.: 59). This belief is expounded by Michelle:

> I guess I feel very lucky that I'm doing what I was born to do…It's like on some level I've just always known this is what I was going to do – I knew it was what I've got to do.

Furthermore, the 'gruelling' and 'soul-crushing' pre-competition diet (which requires participants to reduce their body fat to abnormally low levels, whilst at the same time retaining their muscularity) requires almost 'superhuman' extraordinary traits of courage, endurance and sacrifice. In his lecture 'Politics as a Vocation', Weber (1991 [1915b]) claims:

> There is the 'heroic' ethic, which imposes on men demands of principle to which they are generally not able to do justice, except at high points in their lives, but which serve as signposts pointing the way for man's endless striving.

The heroic personality thereby sacrifices all and lives a life immersed in suffering, in order to achieve their ultimate goals and values. As Rubin (1994: 141–6) explains, the moral, life-governing aspirations of the heroic ethic impose 'a tyranny of demand on everyday living', but provide meaning and purpose in an increasingly rationalized world. In a similar manner, female bodybuilders endure their mental and physical hardships, trials and tribulations with the reward of living life according to their own beliefs and principles: a life which may be challenging and difficult, but one that provides them with direction, focus, fulfilment and desire.

Feminist perspectives on the competition

Bolin (1992: 184) claims that competitions promote 'androgyny' and possibilities for women's 'empowerment', and perceives 'dieting and the pre-competition preparation as a liminal phase embodying contestation and anti-structure'. Bolin argues that as women reach their 'peak physique' on competition day, they achieve a moment of 'bodily nirvana and physical transcendence' (ibid.: 195) – 'a moment in and out of time' (Turner 1969: 96). Furthermore, she argues that the bodybuilding competition process allows a form of gender blending, whereby the strict gender dichotomies of masculine and feminine begin to dissolve. Whilst male bodybuilders do diet – an activity firmly associated with the feminine – female bodybuilders diet to display their muscularity and 'hardness', considered masculine attributes.

More critical feminists, however, argue that competitions are detrimental for muscular women. For example, Ian (2001: 82) claims that as the female bodybuilder relies upon the Other – the gaze of the judges and fans – to validate whether or not she has fleetingly achieved 'thingification', she is unable to transcend ideology:

> She can only see herself as reflected by fans and judges, in their appraisals of her flesh... In other words, the pinnacle of the bodybuilder's training cycle is the moment when she offers this body, which she has disciplined with religious intensity as if preparing it for sacrifice, to the reigning social ideology of gender, masked as an impersonal aesthetic ideal with which she has nearly killed herself to merge.

Likewise, Brace-Govan (2002: 418) argues that until females focus on their body-work instrumentally (in other words, use their bodies as vehicles that enable them to act in the world in an assertive and empowering manner) rather than on its appearance, under the 'centrality of voyeurism' they will never 'transcend the status of being an object'.

Thus far, most academic work has presented female bodybuilder competitions as providing, in a pessimistic Foucauldian manner, an intensification of discipline, regulation and restriction (Mansfield and McGinn 1993; St Martin and Gavey 1996; Lowe 1998; Patton 2001; Bordo 1988; Guthrie and Castelnuovo 1992). From this perspective, competitions are regimes of truth or disciplinary mechanisms bounded and informed by patriarchal views of what an acceptable 'feminine' shape should be. These critiques argue that these women have to conform to a 'feminine imperative' characterized by the need to 'perform femininity during contests' (St. Martin and Gavey 1996: 53). Indeed, there has been much evidence to support this view, such as the directives given in 2005 for muscularity to be reduced by 20 per cent (refer to Chapters 3 and 4 for more detail on criticism of competitions). Thus, according to these writings, competitions simply reproduce stereotypical views of what it is to be feminine and police the desires of those who seek to transgress these and make incursions into the field of masculinity.

Whilst critical commentators have focused on the ways in which women are controlled by men in the sport, there has been a tendency to ignore the ways by which female bodybuilders actually 'resist' these restrictive powers. For example, despite all the directives from the sport's authorities, they have failed to stop female bodybuilders (and now even Figure competitors) from going further and evolving in terms of size, hardness and cuts. Similarly, whilst competing women are pressurized to achieve a subjective form of 'femininity', it would be wrong to present this as a completely determining pressure: two of the women who reached the British finals in 2008, for example, exhibited facial hair and wore no make-up. Thus, female bodybuilders have continued to develop themselves and their identities despite the limitations placed on them by bodybuilding authorities.

The start of the journey

In seeking to probe the validity of these alternative perspectives on female body-building competitions (the ideas that they can be liminal or that they are simply still informed by conventional gender norms) my account begins 16 weeks before the event itself. This is when the daily lifestyle and mundane training phase are left behind as the female bodybuilder prepares to compete. It is at this point that the real breaking down of any vestiges of the non-female bodybuilder persona occurs (in terms of the separation from any activities and identities not directly associated with their status as a competitive female bodybuilder). In Turner's (1992) phrasing, it is the deconstruction of past identity in preparation for a new identity. In my narrative, I follow Michelle's pilgrimage on a chronological basis, from the beginning of her competition preparation through to that 'height of recognition'. Here, echoing notions of the heroic as portrayed by Weber, the journey can be seen as a kind of adventure (Simmel 1971 [1908a]). Simmel suggests that within the adventure, time flows in a different way to normal everyday life. The adventurer seizes the moment, takes risks and has a disregard for ordinary concerns of consequence, yet simultaneously creates an alternative order based upon a system imbued with meaning and logical coherence. Against the backdrop of a modern life which organizes itself ever more around consumer culture and immediate gratification, leaving people fragmented and with a 'lack of something definite at the centre of the soul' (Simmel 1990 [1907]: 467), the life of the adventurer might enable an individual to transcend this fate by creating a 'personality' and a unique sense of self. These 'adventurers of the spirit' thus form their actions around a central and unifying purpose, providing the individual with life-affirming significance and meaning (Simmel 1971 [1908b], 1997 [1912]).

As the female bodybuilder begins to embark on her 'adventure' there is a sense of excitement, anticipation and restlessness. As Michelle explains:

> I just can't wait to get started now... I feel a bit in limbo at the moment... I can't wait until the day... yes, I love getting on stage – it's the best day of the year.

As the journey commences there is seen a clear separation from those 'others' who may train hard but do not go through this sacred process. There is a satisfaction gained from being different and standing out from the rest of them by enduring what only a true bodybuilder can: 'going through what I go through and knowing other people can't do that' (Michelle).

There is often a ritual celebration that marks the start of the pre-competition diet (as well as, infamously, a post-competition 'blow-out' or 'binge', where competitors have been known to eat excessive quantities: see Bolin 1992; Lowe 1998). Michelle and her close friends and family, who are supportive of her endeavour, meet up at her house for a 'last supper' before the competition, which consists of the indulgent and forbidden foods of pizza, chocolate and wine. After this event, Michelle will start to purify herself from the 'bad' foods and drink that pollute and contaminate her body. Apart from the 'cheat' meal which many body-builders allow themselves once a week in the first few months of preparing to compete, processed foods and foods containing salt and sugar are now eliminated from the diet. This includes dressings and flavourings, meaning food becomes extremely bland and repetitive.

Bodybuilders may also aid this process of detoxification by using colonic irrigation to rid themselves of impurities (faecal waste and unidentified toxins from the colon and intestinal tract). The cleansing of the body marks a new transitional phase whereby the female bodybuilder begins to depart from her old physical self. At this point, Michelle's weight is 92 kg, and her calorie intake will drop from 5,000 to 3,000 per day over the next week. The diet plan will become more rigid and will intensify as the weeks go on. The aim is to shed the unwanted fat cells and uncover the muscles, so that they can be displayed in their full glory. The difficulty lies in burning away the destructive fat whilst at the same time pro-tecting that all-important muscle (female bodybuilders aim to get their body fat percentage to below 9 per cent and sometimes as low as 4 per cent, compared to the 'ideal' of 20–5 per cent for women). Protein is therefore an essential ally here, and is eaten at regular intervals throughout the day (in the form of e.g. protein drinks, poultry and fish). Whilst essential fatty acids are encouraged, along with vegetables and a few pieces of fruit, saturated fats are to be avoided and carbohy-drates severely reduced. 'Allowed' carbohydrates in limited portions include oats, brown rice and sweet potatoes. Michelle's supplement regime is also dramatically changed and increased in order to burn fat and maintain muscularity. Likewise, to speed up the metabolism and lose fat, cardiovascular training is incorporated into the daily training routine. Besides her routine hour of weight-training, Michelle now adds 30 minutes of 'fat-burning exercise' (low-impact exercises that keep her heart rate under 150 bpm, such as cycling, using a cross-trainer and walking uphill on a treadmill) before she goes to work. She goes back to the gym in the evening to do another 30 minutes, as well as fitting in a walk in her lunch break. All spare time is now dedicated directly to her goal. Fisher (1997: 141) estimates that on average, professional female bodybuilders dedicate six hours per day to their training and competition preparation, including weights and cardiovascular exercises, posing, tanning, food preparation and mental strategies.

On the day of the competition, Michelle will get one opportunity to impress the judges. She will have just one chance to show off her hard-earned muscular body by enacting seven prescribed poses and performing a short (60–90 seconds) choreographed routine to music. Her physique will then be evaluated by a panel of judges on its aesthetics of muscular size, symmetry and condition (e.g. vascularity, low body fat). Practising these poses and the routine is therefore an extremely important component of the 'pre-comp' preparation. It has been suggested by some that there is a tendency for female bodybuild-ers to take these stage performances more seriously than their male counterparts (Lowe 1998). Furthermore, the muscular presentations themselves have been cri-tiqued for being clearly gendered:

Females are more likely to perform fluid, balletic movements and poses on stage; they are also more likely to select popular dance tunes or sentimental love songs... some women incorporate seductive poses, glances and lyric in their routines as well... male bodybuilders are more likely to strike muscular poses in a hard, distinct, and fast manner... they are more likely to grimace, growl and at times, even yell during the presentation round. Moreover, their musical selections differ markedly from those of female bodybuilders in that they are more likely to pose to loud and thunderous rock music.

(Lowe 1998: 122–3)

Despite the fact that these displays may be gendered in comparison with hegemonic norms of femininity, the poses conducted by female bodybuilders appear masculine, defiant and strong, and in no way resemble comparative 'feminine' body displays such as bikini contests, catwalk modelling, lap dancing and so on.

Michelle is all too aware of the importance of posing in order to present her physique to its full advantage in front of the judges. Indeed, by making just the slightest bodily adjustment to her arm, leg or torso, Michelle knows she can accentuate a strong point or hide a weakness. Every day in the studio she goes through her compulsory poses and rehearses her routine, becoming increasingly frustrated when she does not perform these to her satisfaction. Far from being an easy action, 'posing' requires a great deal of mind and body connection. In the same way that a belly-dancer learns to utilize her individual abdominal muscles, so too must Michelle learn body skills and techniques specific to bodybuilding. The compulsory poses (front double bicep, side chest pose, rear double bicep, rear lateral spread, side tricep, abdominal and thigh pose) are initially practised in front of a mirror until they are done 'correctly'. Once the poses have been refined, they are then rehearsed without a mirror in order to replicate the situation on the competition stage (bodybuilders often have friends/coaches who give them feedback on their posing). The bodybuilder must learn to biomechanically 'feel' each pose. As one bodybuilder articulately describes the process:

It can be a sensual experience, being able to focus all your attention on just one movement – onto even just one muscle, and for that moment, just feel that one specific motion with all of your being. It teaches you a lot about how your body works and feels... [it is a] very intimate kind of connection to your own body and how it moves.

Michelle begins by holding each pose for 15 seconds, increasing the time to 30 seconds as the weeks go on (she doesn't know precisely how long the judges will ask her and the other competitors to hold the pose, so she needs to be prepared for all eventualities). Posing is a surprisingly strenuous activity that requires tension throughout the whole body, not just in the anatomical area that is being scrutinized. As the muscles begin to tire, they begin to shake, making it hard to maintain balance and posture.

On top of this, female bodybuilders must also demonstrate 'femininity' through 'graceful movements' of the body. 'Femininity' is expressed through the pointing of toes and 'elegant' hand and finger gestures (which also highlight perfectly polished nails). Poses are tweaked to create the illusion of small waists, and other body adjustments are made, such as one leg being placed in front of the other, to create the appearance of curves. Each pose must flow fluidly into the next one, appear light-footed and be accompanied at all times by a smile. Everyday Michelle runs through these poses so that they become 'drilled into her', in preparation for the sacred day of the ritual.

The hard times

It is now only one month before the contest, and the physical hardship and psychological stress caused by ten weeks of strict dieting and intense training are taking their toll (cf. Turner 1969: 93–111). As the diet and supplement regime intensifies, so too does the debilitating tiredness, aches and pains (including headaches, muscle cramps, shakes, sleeplessness, nausea and mood swings). Michelle articulates her feelings as she suffers from these effects:

> … all sports can require a phenomenal amount of training by the athlete, people train every day for several hours – so it's not that the human body can't cope with the training – but the diet, that's the special thing – it effects your emotions, your food, your sleep, how you're training, your energy – everything. It really does!

The past few weeks have been exceptionally difficult for both Michelle and her partner, Jo. Michelle has decided to leave her job. Whilst at first her employers appeared sympathetic to her competing endeavour, they will no longer let her take a week off before she competes (as had previously been agreed). She says that they seem to have no comprehension of how poorly she will be functioning just before the competition (she knows she will be desperate by then, hardly functioning and constantly 'needing to pee', as her body will be flooded with water). Furthermore, they claim that 'the diet is changing her – she is no longer herself, but is tired and grumpy and no longer sociable or enthusiastic'. Michelle admits this herself. She doesn't want to socialize anymore, but disconnects herself from others in order to preserve her energy:

> When I'm having a bad day, it takes all my energy to just get by, so I go very inside myself, I don't want to talk to people, I don't want people to hassle me about anything or ask me about food… all my energy goes into getting through my workout and to getting my food and to going to work. I think people sometimes think I'm being rude or arrogant, or moody, or whatever. They don't understand that the very little energy I have, I need to keep.

In the gym her partner acts as a 'gatekeeper' and prevents people from interrupting Michelle during and even after her training. Her partner Jo fends off casual gym trainers and gym friends, preventing them from asking annoying questions or making stupid comments. Jo tells me that the most frustrating thing of all is that people seem to treat Michelle as though she is sick or has something 'wrong' with her, such as an eating disorder:

> One thing that pisses both me and Michelle off, is that people treat her as though she is ill... um people 'Oh, are you OK? Oh dear oh, you do look like you are suffering! How long have you got to go through that for? What are you eating?' And they treat her as though she is ill – it's patronizing. Yes, Michelle will feel tired and have less energy to talk and to be bouncy as she is normally... she walks slower, her memory is affected, concentration is affected, there's lots of things that aren't positive but are just simply by-products of the sport and just something that you have to accept with the sport – therefore it's not something that people should feel sorry for her about, because she has chosen this very, very tough sport, but she has chosen it for herself.

Michelle echoes this emphasis on choice, by stating that during the dark times 'I have to remind myself [at times] that I chose to do this, it's my choice...it's a personal challenge... I wouldn't know what to do if I didn't do bodybuilding, I wouldn't feel me – it feels totally "right"'. There is definitely a sense of heroism here, inasmuch as it takes a special kind of person to complete this quest. This is further demonstrated by the following extract written by Teagan Clive, which captures the ethos of the pre-competition diet for the female bodybuilder:

> In every sport there is more than one game, and the most gut-wrenching events in bodybuilding take place in the kitchen, where athletes come to terms with their long *lonely* diets. Now I don't mean to scare you, but although strict dietary control is an essential and exciting *ritual* for competitive bodybuilders, not everyone should ruthlessly restrict his or her food intake... If trying to eat 'like a real bodybuilder' is going to snuff your sense of liberty and pursuit of happiness, don't do it... If you think that dieting is self-abuse, if it's painful for you, if it's a task and not an *adventure*... don't waste your time trying to eat less... It's your life, and your body. You are what you eat, and your physical identity will be shaped by what you swallow. You alone are responsible for your appearance.
>
> (quoted from Bolin 1992: 198, my italics).

Foucauldian feminists, however, would argue that this so called empowering 'choice' is an illusion, and that far from being liberating, the 'pre-comp' diet acts as a 'praxis of social control'. For example, at first glance it does seem that there are parallels here between anorexia and the 'pre-comp' diet, as in both cases bodies are pushed to the extremes and both are seeking to control their bodies as a way of controlling their lives. Unlike the anorexic who diets to 'disappear' from view, however, as the female bodybuilder sheds her fat she appears larger, more defined and more muscular – making her more visible. Thus, in contrast to the anorexic's shrinking body, the hypermuscular female body cannot be ignored.

At this point, the journey to compete appears particularly challenging and arduous. The female bodybuilder is ultimately a lone ranger, fighting a battle that no one else seems to appreciate or understand:

> It sometimes feels lonely when you have a bad day and people don't real-ise the effects of the diet on your body – there's no understanding... yes on the bad days it does feel lonely because when I'm feeling really crap and exhausted and can't even stand up between sets, then I hate it, absolutely hate it, 'cause my body won't do what I want it to... and even Jo doesn't know how I'm feeling and what I'm going through.

> It's a difficult place – I'm tired, I'm exhausted and I'm not very responsive. I know that I can just sit in my vegetative state just listening, but it can come across that I just don't care. I'm just not very enthusiastic – just plodding along. Sometimes I feel like I'm cold, shut off and isolated and completely on my own – and everything gets blamed on the diet and sometimes I feel so alone with it.

The pilgrimage to competition is an isolating experience that no one else can truly understand unless they experience it for themselves: 'the big moment in the education of the body is, in fact, the moment of initiation' (Mauss 1973: 80). In the words of Michelle:

> I think that unless you go through the bodybuilding diet yourself, you can never fully understand what it's like... I can't really even start to explain it to you, you still wouldn't get it.

At this stage there seems to be a clear separation from all activities, thoughts, emotions and people not directly related to the sacred space of the competition. Furthermore, this distancing appears to prepare the way for these women to leave behind any other roles they may have and any other vestiges of the outside world that may have impinged upon them, prior to entering the ritual space of the competition.

The final stretch: creating the elusive body

It's now the final stretch, less than two weeks before the day of the competition. There's a certain amount of relief as the end is now finally in sight. Michelle is feeling far more positive again, and sees the dark 'hellish' days as behind her:

> I was finding it really tough, feeling pretty bloody awful and wondering how the hell am I gonna get through to the end of it... like for a while I was really feeling the strain of the extra training and the stricter diet... but now I'm feeling really good, and everyone seems really surprised.

Moreover, Michelle speaks of an 'unexplained energy' that she has had over the past two days – an almost-euphoria and 'manicness' that she herself compares to an anorexic's 'high':

> Anorexics can actually get to a point where they become stronger than they should be – though their body can obviously go past this, but there's a point that although their bodies are absolutely starved, they are inexplicably strong as the body goes into survival mode... I think that's what I have experienced yesterday and today, because I'm not eating enough fuel to do what I'm doing.

Indeed, there seems to be a kind of restlessness and listlessness about her: her face, now drawn by the depletion of fat cells, is animated by her bright, almost translucent blue eyes, with dilated pupils. She describes an 'almost heightened awareness'. These bodily sensations and emotions trigger memories of a previous competition when she recalls being 'hyperactive' backstage. Moreover, this sublime, 'euphoric' feeling manifests itself in an overall feeling of confidence. This is demonstrated in the gym, when, for the first time – one week before the competition – she trains in a vest and tight shorts, rather than her usual baggy t-shirts and tracksuit bottoms. As her body begins to approximate the latent image in her mind's eye, she feels 'happier' and more content with her body and self. Michelle is both excited and fascinated to see how much her body has changed.

However, as the body appears to increase its armour (through its hard, muscular and lacquered surface), the self is further exposed to criticism and reactions from outsiders. Within the gym, Michelle is greeted by hushed whispers, people pointing and shocked stares. Some men even take one look at her and leave the weights area altogether. Instead of her usual reaction of annoyance and frustration as a result of such unwelcome distractions from her training, she now challenges the onlookers in a direct but non-aggressive manner. Far from turning away and avoiding eye contact, in a dignified manner, she poses audaciously in front of the mirror for all to see.

With one week to go, the final preparations are made (to both the outer and 'inner' body). These include physical touches to the body itself by the way of tanning, make-up, hair presentation and manipulation of the body. Bodybuilders are often associated by the public with having a deep orange tan which, despite skin cancer concerns, is still associated with health and beauty in popular culture. At competition time, bodybuilders tan their bodies in order to clearly show the definition and separation between muscle groups, particularly under the harsh lights of the stage. Michelle has been using sunbeds in the run-up to the competition (over the past few weeks), to provide a base to her tan. The day before the show, her partner, Jo, applies three coats of a deep tanning product – far stronger than a normal self-tanning lotion – to Michelle's body. It is a messy and time-consuming job, as the 'coats' need to dry between applications. A final layer will be applied on the morning of the show, before going to the competition; tanning products have been banned from the show itself due to their ability to stain everything (including walls, floors, doors and toilet seats). Michelle needs her tan to be as dark as possible to define and show off her muscularity, but at the same time she needs it to be applied evenly and to provide an aesthetically pleasing colour, as she will be judged on the tone of her skin.

As critical commentators on female bodybuilding competitions have pointed out, women are also judged on other 'feminine' qualities and attributes. Competitions are undoubtedly controlling, but they include some creative and nonconformist elements that may provide some form of 'empowerment' for female bodybuilders, however temporary or partial these victories may be. For Michelle, as the quote below elaborates, the femininity rules are far from simply a restrictive imperative; rather, they are a pleasurable and integral part of the stage performance:

> It's all about putting on a show, like I become a different person on stage – it's an act. I'm not doing it to become 'feminine', as you'll see when you see my hair and make-up it's not like that – but I do want to present myself the best I can. I have to also bear in mind the judges… I want the judges to look at me favourably and there are certain things that I have to do to do that. There is no point fighting it. And you know, it isn't something I do every day, I don't wear make-up… but then I don't wear a bikini and fake tan every day… So for me it's all part of the enjoyment of doing something different. It's exciting for me because it's different.

Through Michelle's journey we can see that, far from female bodybuilders being 'cultural dupes' (Garfinkel 1967) who do not recognize the imperative of the 'mask of femininity' (Tseelon 1995), they are active agents who are aware of the contingencies of winning and losing and negotiate within these rules and regulations. Furthermore, some female bodybuilders also recognize the charade of this gender construction. As Michelle articulates:

> This whole thing about female bodybuilders having to retain their femininity, as if by the sheer fact of them being female bodybuilders they have to make a special effort (hair, make-up, posture etc.)… but when the fuck was it masculine to shave your body, tan it, oil it, tan and oil up other competitors' bodies and to check each other's bodies out? That's not masculine… muscle, it seems to be assumed, can't be feminine – you have to put on this whole charade.

The 'inner' body is also modified during this last week in order to create aesthetic perfection – 'peak physique' – on the day of the show, in the shape of full muscles with no water retention or bloating. Careful pharmaceutical and nutritional knowledge is therefore utilized to manipulate the ratio of water, carbohydrates and sodium. There appears to be no uniform procedure for doing this, as individual bodies appear to react slightly differently, and even when the bodybuilder has found a method that works for them, there is no guarantee that their body will peak at the right time (Bolin 1992). This uncertainty creates anxiety, as illustrated by Michelle's comment:

I suppose I'm apprehensive, because it's like the last week of four months hard work... you get paranoid about cocking it all up at the last minute... you know eating too many carbs and smoothing out, or not having enough and appearing flat on stage.

The 'work' involved in capturing the elusive perfect body makes the 'normal' athletic attempt to ensure peaking at the right time seem ordinary by comparison. It is an intense and critical period: the smallest 'error' (in terms of timing, nutrition and supplements) can ruin the bodily appearance they have sacrificed so much for. With just days to go, supplements such as vitamin C are dramatically increased (vitamin C acts as a mild diuretic and laxative, helping to prevent bloating and constipation as fibre has been eliminated from the diet). Michelle drinks six litres of water to 'flood the body', in order to 'trick' it so that her body does not hold onto any water. This is in preparation for the stage at which she will dramatically stop drinking in order to dehydrate. Despite the inconvenience of 'needing to pee all the time', the tiredness and lack of concentration caused by depriving her body of carbohydrates and the anxiety about 'cocking up', this is still a time of excitement and fascination as she watches her body metamorphosize.

It's now the afternoon of the day before the show. Michelle must no longer drink liquids but must suffer with a deep thirst that cannot be quenched, for the sake of water elimination from her cells (she is only allowed a small sip of water when she feels it is absolutely necessary). This deprivation is offset somewhat by the reintroduction of carbohydrates into her diet (a process called 'carbing up') to create the appearance of full muscles on stage. Although she has been looking forward to this moment for a long time, Michelle cannot appreciate her carrot cake: it just tastes like 'sawdust' in her dry mouth. She hasn't trained in the past two days in order to retain and preserve her energy. She lies around waiting: there is nothing more that she can do now but wait until the long-anticipated day finally arrives.

The day of the competition (the ritual)

It is 10am in the morning. I knock at Michelle's front door and wait for Jo to open it. I am not sure what to expect or indeed what the day will bring. I find Michelle sprawled on the sofa in her lounge with her eyes closed – trying to conserve as much energy as possible at the same time as allowing her dramatic 'Egyptian' eye make-up to dry. Her skin is covered in a dark brown/orange stain – the final application was applied an hour ago. Her hair, unlike that of many other female competitors, is braided, and she wears short black-and-silver nail extensions. Her face looks extremely drawn due to fat depletion. I am slightly apprehensive as I ask her how she is feeling. She replies: 'Surprisingly relaxed and really good considering... I've left nothing to chance and know that whatever the outcome I have given my preparation everything I could'.

At 11am Michelle, myself, Jo and a couple of friends arrive at the Guildhall. Michelle admits to feeling nervous for the first time, although this soon disappears as she sees familiar faces in the crowd and feels that sensation 'of belonging'. We stand in the queue waiting for Michelle's category (over-55 kg women) to be called out in order for her to be weighed in. Some of the competitors are chatting whilst others are completely silent, yet everyone is subtly checking out each other's bodies and making comparisons. Michelle weighs in at 80 kg, meaning that she has put on an incredible 14 kg of muscle over the past year. Once checked in, I go with Michelle and Jo backstage to the female competitors' changing room, in order to avoid the distractions of the venue and to find a quiet spot where Michelle can relax, focus and preserve her energy. Most of her time will be spent eating, sipping water and lying with her legs raised to keep them drained. Unlike the previous year, when four others were competing, it transpires that there is only one other female bodybuilder competing, and she is in the under-55 kg category. Michelle is disappointed by the lack of competition: 'all that training and dieting and £4,000 in costs, and I could have done none of it and still qualified for the British finals'. There is some chatter backstage between the Bodyfitness girls and their mentors, but otherwise the atmosphere is quite subdued. I know that Michelle needs to focus on herself and so I leave her and Jo and return to the show.

Whilst the competition is a very serious event for bodybuilders, it is also a celebration. The atmosphere, with its music booming out, stuffy air and dimmed lights, is reminiscent of a nightclub. There's a constant hum of noise and excitement in the air. The majority of people are seated, but there are also some milling around, talking to 'like-minded' others, paying for autographs from famous bodybuilders, buying supplements and clothes from the stalls or getting food and drink from the bar. In America, these events are called 'Meets' (Lowe 1998) – a place where bodybuilders feel they belong and feel appreciated. It is a unique occasion where bodybuilders can both see and be seen, within an environment that recognizes their bodies as a form of 'social capital' (Coleman 1988). In this milieu, female bodybuilders consider themselves to be protected from the hostility of the outside world by the 'camaraderie' that exists 'among all bodybuilders'. This common consciousness is forged through sharing the same collective encounters in their quest for muscle. In addition, the emotional collective experience of the rite coalesces in a 'collective effervescence' (Durkheim, 1995 [1912]) which unites members of the subculture further, helping to create a collective and sustainable identity that they can hold on to when they return once again to the outside world and to their profane daily activities.

Most, but not all, of the men in the crowd are muscular and are wearing t-shirts and jeans with labels such as 'XXXL' on them. Many of the women in the audience, regardless of whether they are slim or muscular, are 'hyperfeminine' in appearance, with heavy make-up and long hair extensions, displaying full cleavages under their tight clothes. The crowd appears to be mainly from the working and lower-middle classes. There are some lesbian couples watching the show, but no single women by themselves or overtly homosexual male couples. I'm not sure where I 'fit' in this environment, but I feel comfortable and know a number of people amongst the 1,000 spectators. I sit down amongst my friends and turn to the stage, where bodily displays of engorged muscles demand attention.

About two hours later, just 20 minutes before she is due to go on stage, I join Michelle and Jo backstage in the 'pumping room'. This is the place where competitors carry out their final finishing touches and preparation before going on stage, such as engorging their muscles using small dumbbells or Dyna-Bands. I have a visceral reaction to the atmosphere, which hums with tension and excitement. It is warm, and there is a strange musty odour that permeates the air: a mixture of sweat, chemicals, flatulence and tanning products. The room is littered with confectionery wrappers and bottles containing alcohol or whatever the chosen final 'sugar' hit is, taken just before the competitor goes on stage to increase their vascularity and muscle cell fullness. Despite the ban on 'instant' types, the tans have managed to leak and stain everywhere, over the door handles, floor and walls of the backstage theatre. Several male bodybuilders are slumped against the walls of the room, blending in like inanimate objects; their eyes are lifeless and unfocused. In contrast, a couple of the male bodybuilders are list-less and agitated, unable to sit still due to all the adrenaline and stimulants inside them, and pace the rooms like caged animals. One seasoned competitor smiles at me, appearing calm and relaxed as he sits on the floor against the wall.

There are five female Bodyfitness (Figure) competitors lined up in numeri-cal order, waiting nervously to go on stage. A couple of the Bodyfitness girls are flicking or smoothing out their long, thick hair. One is practising her posing, whilst another is performing lateral raises with small dumbbells to improve the look/size of her shoulders. I am struck by how glamorous they look in their full make-up and sparkly bikinis, with their huge, taut breasts, six-pack abs and tiny waists, as they balance on clear high-heeled shoes. I'm suddenly conscious of my own appearance; of my fine, medium-length dark hair, my paler skin and my softer body – or, put simply, my own physical 'flaws'.

As Michelle begins to 'pump up' her muscles, the audience in the hall are encouraging and urging on the Masters (over-50s) male bodybuilders via applause and yelling. The commentator, like a Butlins host, tries to 'work' the audience and urges them to join in. During the compulsory poses, calls are shouted out: 'come on, James', 'legs', 'that's it, show 'em your guns', 'go on Mark, you can do it', 'keep legs tight, Steve!', 'keep it tight', 'don't forget the legs!' The male body-builders come off the stage and the Bodyfitness girls replace them; they are met by a chorus of wolf-whistles. The girls only perform quarter-turns and have no routine, so their time on stage is very brief. I leave the claustrophobic backstage area and once again find my place in the audience.

At last it is time for the female bodybuilders to take the stage for pre-judging. Due to the lack of competitors, both the lightweight and the heavyweight are asked to go onstage at the same time. It is finally Michelle's turn; I watch her as she walks confidently onto the stage and into the light, with a huge smile on her face. At the commentator's command she does her quarter-turns and then goes through the compulsory poses. The hours of practice pay off: for Michelle, this is her 'time to shine'. In front of an audience of more than 1,000 people and the panel of judges, it is now time for Michelle's two minutes of fame. This fleet-ing space of time provides a moment when glory is possible – to be seen, to exist, to be 'sovereign' (Heywood 1998). Against the backdrop of a postmodern consumer culture, saturated and obsessed with visual images (Featherstone 1991: 67), the female bodybuilder, under the gaze of all, becomes the spectacle (Debord 1995 [1979]). Her identity is validated and confirmed through others' acknowledgment of her embodied performance: 'I am seen therefore I am' (cf. Descartes 1960 [1637]).

Before the pre-judging round concludes, Michelle has one final chance to impress the judges (only the winner gets to perform in the evening show) via the finely choreographed routine that she has put so much time, effort and preparation into. She stands in the middle of the stage, poised under the spotlight, waiting for the beat of 'Insomnia' by Faithless to begin. Instead, a contemporary R&B song blares out. A look of disbelief and anger flashes across Michelle's face as the head judge nods for her to continue on regardless. I can see that she is battling with her emotions as she manages to get through the routine, smiling through gritted teeth, and then walks off the stage fuming. Later on she explains how she felt at the time:

> It was a complete disaster! I couldn't believe it when the music came on… now I know these things happen, but the head judge had no consideration for the effort, time and preparation that had gone into my routine and didn't make it clear to the audience there was a problem. He seemed to think that just playing any old music would be fine! I was livid.

Despite Michelle's disappointment, there is some comfort in knowing that she will get a chance to perform again in the evening show due to the lack of competitors. She takes a deep breath and, now that the pressure is off, decides to 'kill time' by leaving the backstage arena for a few hours and 'heading out front'. She is greeted by a few close friends, one of whom has an eight-week-old baby boy. As Michelle holds the baby, I am struck by the contrast and incongruity of her hardness, muscularity and dark skin against his white, soft skin, thus breaking down and confusing the longstanding Western dichotomies between male/female, hard/soft, strong/weak, resilient/vulnerable and unnatural/natural. Supporting the tiny boy's head in her comparatively huge tanned hands and muscular arms, Michelle sits back to try and relax and enjoy the show.

After the 'big boys' (male heavyweight bodybuilders) have been onstage, there is an interval before the evening show. Often 'guest-posers' will do a seminar at this point. At some events there are other forms of entertainment, such as pole dancers, martial-arts displays and children's activities. As it's Easter, today there is an Easter egg competition. Children are called onto the stage and told to make a bicep pose. Around 15 boys and girls, between the ages of 2 and 13, are lined up under the glare of the lights with their fists in the air, trying to make their muscles stand out. Some are smiling and laughing, a couple of the very young children are crying (their parents quickly rush up to stand beside them) and the majority solemnly face the crowd. The audience is clapping and hooting. This is a family affair, a lifestyle, a celebration. The children are each presented with an Easter egg for their exhibition and participation.

The evening show commences at 6pm. The panel of seven judges (two women and five men) are seated at a long table bench in front of the stage. They are dressed very formally in dark suits and matching ties, pens poised, ready to fill in and make amendments to the score sheet completed during the pre-judging round. There is a pause as the audience waits for the first category to be called up. The juniors (under 21s) are called onto the stage to do a group 'pose down'. This is where the competitors get to do 'free posing' to emphasize their muscularity and to compare and show themselves favourably against their opponents, typically, in the men's case, to the ferocious beat of rock or heavy metal music. For the uninitiated, even the male competitors can appear shocking. The dieting process has caused a thinning of the skin, thus creating a form of 'monstrous transparency' (Halberstam 1995: 7). Their faces are skeletal: the skin is stretched over their skulls, emphasizing the hollows of their eye sockets, from which vacant eyes stare out. In contrast, their muscles appear to have taken on a life of their own (see Lingis 1988: 110), seemingly trying to free themselves from the constraints of the skin (Kaye 2005: 195). As bodies jostle against each other in the pose down, flesh against flesh each muscle shouts for attention. A couple of minutes later, the round is over and medals are given out. The group then leaves the stage. For most of the juniors, their 'time' in the spotlight is now over – they have undertaken 14 weeks of dieting and strenuous effort, time and sacrifice for just a couple of minutes on stage. The top three (those with the highest score), however, are called back for final posing comparisons. The announcement of the winner, which is typically controversial, is greeted by a strongly divided reaction from the crowd. Some members of the audience clap and make 'whooping' noises of delight; others make disgruntled noises such as hissing and booing, to project their frustration with the judges' decisions.[3] Trophies consisting of variously sized bronze sculptures designed to look like a male bodybuilder are awarded to the top three. At some shows the trophies are in the shape of shields, swords or other fighting symbols; at other times, trophy cups are awarded. Women, on the other hand, are frequently awarded with a sculpture in the shape of an athletic woman. Photographs are taken to capture the elusive moment – providing a tangible record for days to come (and further affirming and validating the bodybuilders' identities). The lucky winner is then left to perform his 90-second choreographed posing routine to the crowd.

Michelle is finding it increasingly hard to concentrate, yet there is still about an hour and half before she will be called back on stage. With glazed eyes, she turns to me and confesses: 'I'm really tired and finding it hard to keep going... before, the adrenaline kick was keeping me going, but I'm now done in'. She feels dehydrated, exhausted and appears physically shivery and shaky. Michelle tells me: 'everything feels surreal, I feel detached from what's going on around me – I just feel exhausted'. The irony of bodybuilding competitions is that despite giving the appearance of a 'superbeing' on stage, in reality competitors are extremely vulnerable and weak at this point (see Fussell 1991; Klein 1993 for more detail). As Michelle explained after the event:

The constant influx of simple carbs, alcohol, and pumping up, combined with the fusty smell of tan and unwashed bodies, after a while makes for a definite nauseous feeling... although on stage you look amazing, inside you feel like shit... I just wanted a drink of cold water more than anything.

I refrain from asking her any more questions and wish her luck as she heads backstage to find some sanctuary and I retake my place in the audience. The exceptionally long and challenging day for contestants fits in with Turner's theory that an ordeal must be undergone as part of liminality (initiation ceremonies frequently include trials of pain and stamina). Furthermore, Turner (1969: 65) claims that 'liminality is frequently likened to death, to being in the womb, to invisibility, to darkness'. As bodybuilders have been known to die at competitions (usually due to diuretic use), this is far from a simple metaphorical comparison, but is rather an indication of 'the precarious boundary between life and death, self and body, inside and outside, person and thinghood that the bodybuilder tests, in the hope of merging, however briefly, with the ideal image of totality that only the gaze of the judge can ratify' (Ian 2001: 79).

With 20 minutes before she is due to go on stage, Michelle re-enters the purgatory-like area of the 'pumping room'. This space acts as a 'threshold' before the sacrificial rite takes place, stripping bodies of their external identities and equalizing initiates. Costume rules are strict: for instance, bikinis must be made of plain, opaque materials (no patterns, no padding, no shiny colours), must cover three-quarters of the buttocks and must not be too highly cut. No jewellery (with the exception of wedding rings), accessories or body make-up can be worn, and no props (e.g. sunglasses) can be brought onstage. As Michelle begins to 'pump' up for the last time, new life is breathed back into her organs, causing the separation between her muscle groups to become so distinctly visible and her veins so prominent that her body looks like an anatomy chart come to life. Her pumped-up muscles glisten underneath the oil and perspiration. It is finally time for that sacred moment, when she will 'go into the light' to be appraised and evaluated. Everything has been building up to this one moment in time. As she waits for the moment when she will offer up her body to be judged, there is a sense of inevitability, captured in the words of Simmel (1971 [1908a]: 193): the adventurer abandons themselves to the 'powers and accidents of the world, which can delight us, but in the same breath can also destroy us'.

She has made it. After waiting for and anticipating this moment for so long, it is finally 'her time'. Knowing she cannot lose, Michelle walks on to the stage defiantly, trying to grasp the totality of this fleeting event. She poses against her lightweight competitor, dwarfing the other's smaller build. She then goes through her planned routine, this time to the correct music. The sound of applause and cheers echo around the hall as the crowd shouts for her. It is over so quickly. Michelle is presented with her trophy by a well-known female bodybuilder. Posing for the photographer, she looks confident, radiant and proud. As she stands in the middle of the stage, with the lights shining down on her and the audience clapping and cheering from the darkness of the stalls, she finally feels that she has truly become a bodybuilder.

Conclusion

Despite conquering the trials of the competition (pushing the mind and body almost to breaking point), the sacrifices involved have not resulted in a reduction of any of the tribulations and stigmatization that these women encounter in their daily interactions. There appears to be no real status transition, no re-entry into society with any improved position. After the competition, for the majority of the competitors who do not place well, there is a 'comedown', when female bodybuilders must return to their daily lives, with no reduced stigma. As Michelle says:

> No one prepares you for what happens next – for how crap you feel in the weeks after competition. When you've got nothing to aim for… you've got no immediate goals, no daily structure – you kinda feel a bit lost. You look in the mirror and you look pale, fat and bloated… you just feel sad and generally unmotivated.

If the female bodybuilding competitor is lucky she may be left with a trophy, but all are left with high financial and relationship costs. Thus, from the evidence that has been presented and analysed, I propose that there can be *no* full transformation, in that the activities and role associated with female bodybuilding result in no post-liminal realignment of social roles or norms. Moreover, female bodybuilding is not a vocation that can result in a neatly defined career. Indeed, the most influential bodybuilding organization in the world, the International Federation of BodyBuilders, refuses to offer professional status to British women (signified by the 'pro card'), whilst there is no prize money on offer to women in British bodybuilding contests. Whilst it is extremely rare even for male bodybuilders to be fully professional in this respect, it is simply not possible to conclude reasonably that a formal, structurally induced, occupational transformation awaits women who commit themselves to the pursuit of muscle. In fact, female bodybuilders in the UK are unable to support themselves through bodybuilding earnings or sponsorship, relying instead on such activities as personal training, working in shops, managing pubs, office work and muscle worship. Moreover, there is no resolution to the problems and conflicts confronted by female bodybuilders in the gendered domain of interaction. There appears to be no permanent change on offer for these women. They confront the same problems, the same conflicts in society as they did before they embarked on their journey to competition.

However, whilst there is no structured transition to a new role and social status in society, the individual female bodybuilder may feel that her ritual has led to a new self-identity, reflected in recognition by others within the 'tribe' of bodybuilding. Indeed, female bodybuilders feel they *are* gaining positive recognition, which is consistent with the idea that this rite (the journey to competition and the competition itself) does provide a consecration of identity; she now feels that she 'belongs', is accepted and is 'one of them'. Although competitors will have to repeat the ritual, for the successful competitive bodybuilder who places well, there is also some evidence that might be read as a change and elevation of status. As a winner, she is more likely to have access to media space in bodybuilding magazines, such as having photos and articles written about her (although this exposure is usually very limited), and there are also possibilities for partial product endorsement sponsorships. Moreover, she will gain notoriety, respect and even a kind of 'celebrity' status within the subculture. Her new-found status usually lends itself to new responsibilities such as mentoring aspiring female bodybuilders. As a representative of the sport, the successful female bodybuilder may be asked to do 'guest posing' at shows, further validating her identity in her new-found role. Likewise, she may develop a greater fanbase that is supportive, appreciative and encouraging of her endeavours (often expressed via emails/website posts, etc.).

Here, it seems useful to suggest that these women seem to be developing personalities of the Weberian 'heroic' type. They have chosen a body regime which involves all of their effort, which serves to organize and evaluate their life, including their relationships and other goals, on the basis of coherent and singular criteria. For these women, who cannot abide by the gender restrictions of the interaction order, heroism is the *only* alternative (Chesler 1994). They have chosen their path and taken responsibility for their life, their body and their decisions. As Michelle stands on the stage alone, proud, defiant and victorious, her whole persona cries out: 'Here I stand, I can do no other'.[4]

Sarah's story: part II

The future

(Sarah is being interviewed during her pre-competition diet which is the most emotional and difficult time in the bodybuilder's calendar. Refer to Chapter 9.)

I wouldn't want to go back to how I looked before, but if I could do it without the drugs... I don't think anybody would do them – male or female (even the guys have hang-ups about what they are doing)... and I just think – am I going to get eight years down the line (or however long) – am I going to get to a point where I'm no longer in control?

Sometimes I just want to be left to get on with it, but every single day I have to go to work and deal with people who think I'm a guy. Talk to me as if I'm a guy. I go to the supermarket and get spoken to as if I'm a guy. I go to the toilet and get questioned. I can never ever get away with it and sometimes I think, what is the fucking point? Why? I want to do this and I'm not going to stop doing it. I have two choices. I either carry on doing it or I opt out – and that's when I get to the lowest point. I'm never going to fit into normal society ever again but I get sick of people's judgements and comments and looks and the way they are.

I think that's why I don't worry so much about my health. I remember back when I was younger and took recreational drugs, I used to think taking pills – and they make you feel amazing, and I used to think, well at least if I die, I'll die happy – believing that was 'happy' – when it obviously wasn't. I think that's why, when I hear you, [my partner] and my doctor worrying about my health that I think there's a part of me that doesn't worry about it because it makes that choice for me. I don't have to worry about it. If it happens, it happens, if it doesn't, it doesn't, but it takes it out of my hands... The last fortnight has just been the lowest.

This can be the loneliest sport in the world. You are trapped in this body, which you have created, and you want, but no one else will accept – to be able to just walk in anywhere and not have to think about and not have to worry about it...

• *Where do you see your future in bodybuilding going?*

I would love to be in Iris Kyle's position to be the top of the game, and a couple of years ago I thought it was achievable but I've come to realize... I just want to be at the top of the game for me – I know this sounds cheesy – but I want to be the best that I can be, but to stop worrying about pushing everything to the limits all the times. I will always do that, but I want to do it so that it's right for me. Not so that I'm trying to push my body somewhere it's not ready to go yet. I've got my goals... to come in better condition each time.

I have more of a plan now for the future, I have more realism. I want to go to the Brits. My personal goal is to get in the top five this year, top three next year, win it and then defend the title a couple of years before drawing a line under it. But having said that you don't know what doors will get opened. I don't know if I would ever get to the Worlds. It's my goal, because nobody ever does that – defend their title every year. You never know what will happen.

• *What would it mean to you to achieve your goals?*

To just walk around and know you're the best female bodybuilder in the country. Though to be honest it's great just to be on stage (at the Brits) and know that you are part of the elite few... it's about my personal battle.

There's still a part of me that doesn't feel it's possible for me (winning it). There's a part of me – partly because of the politics, particularly because of my genetic limitation and aesthetic limitations – with my abs and stuff. And that's why I want to max my size and condition.

• *Will there ever be a point when you stop bodybuilding?*

No, I don't think I can. I don't think that I could handle my natural hormone profile now. Particularly when I think of what I've already been through. When I was training under [another bodybuilder] heavy course, off, heavy course, off, and I look back now and I can see how destructive that was for mental state and my physical state. I didn't realize at the time about how it affected me emotionally. But nobody tells you – So I've learnt to manage that myself now.

Although, I've had two men ask me to do strongwomen stuff – and I've been told that if you have strength then it's not difficult to learn the technique... I'd love to do it. It would be nice... Something that I can do after bodybuilding.

• *What are your thoughts about the future of the sport?*

I don't think female bodybuilding will ever get back to the days of Lenda Murray and Cory Everson...where Iris Kyle is at her position must be so hard – and to have such little pay-off, that for me is soul destroying. You think you'd love to be one of the pros – but the female side effects – you don't know what is going on in their bodies. Prize money is crap. Female bodybuilding is not marketable. The women are seen as social outcasts – and it's the sport that is causing the divide.

10 Conclusion

The study started from the feminist perspective that meanings and practices surrounding women's bodies play a central role in the social reproduction of gender and gendered relationships. Whilst these bodily meanings and practices can become inscribed onto women's bodies, they can also be potentially resisted through actions and processes that begin to destabilize cultural norms of feminine appearance. Within this context, female bodybuilding has been heralded by some feminists as one such liberating practice; a form of activity that questions, interrogates and even begins to undermine conventional notions of female bodies as frail, limited and governed by their biology. This research has provided a new dimension to this vital debate through its detailed analysis of the lives of UK women involved in this activity. The purpose of the ethnography was to investigate whether female bodybuilding can be seen as an emancipatory and empowering transgression of hegemonic standards of feminine embodiment. In seeking to explore this question, I felt it was necessary to understand what it was like 'to be' a female bodybuilder. As such, my study endeavoured to facilitate a rich portrait of the values, practices, norms and, above all, the *lived experiences* of female bodybuilders. My research approach sought not only to analyse the wider milieu in which female bodybuilding occurred, but also to explore via ethnography, participant observation and interview the interactions and phenomenological experiences associated with this activity.

Throughout this work I have strived to present an honest, open, accurate and fair portrayal of events. Nevertheless, it is important to note that the findings presented in this study are my personal interpretations of the subculture and are derived from my own corporeally situated perspective on what I heard, witnessed and experienced during this research. I am 'responsible for the reconstructing and telling of the field' (Coffey 1999: 160). As such, it is important to acknowledge that I do not seek to present a universal 'female bodybuilder' experience, but rather my own impression that there existed common themes and some shared experiences that drew these women together. Consequently, instead of offering what could be construed as a one-dimensional conclusion here – that makes generalisations as if they applied to all female bodybuilders, at all times and in all places – I seek instead to reveal the contradictory positions and conflicting notions of empowerment and oppression in the lives of these women, providing a more nuanced and sensitive understanding of the topic.

Summary and analysis of my empirical findings

This research explored the life of female bodybuilders, looking at the most important aspects of their 'world' – life outside the gym, life inside the gym and the competition – key themes which were drawn from the interviews and field notes. I will now return to the overriding aim of the research and evaluate each relevant chapter regarding female bodybuilding's 'empowering potential'.

The daily lifestyle and interactions of the female bodybuilder were explored in Chapter 5. This chapter demonstrated the difficulties, sacrifices and penalties paid for transgressing the gender interaction order and the different strategies that female bodybuilders employed to sustain a positive sense of self and identity to counteract this adversity. Whilst bodybuilding holds out the promise for women of developing a different relationship with their bodies, selves and surroundings, it is a double-edged sword, as women become ostracised for being socially deviant (Gilroy 1989). The muscular female body is potentially empowering as it defies the ideologies of conventional femininity. By embodying traits of power and strength (as muscles and size are traditionally symbolic of male power), female bodybuilders challenge the myth of female fragility and delicacy and the cultural assumption of being the 'weaker' sex. Furthermore, they refute women's societal role by putting their needs and themselves first, resisting traditional feminine traits of domesticity, nurturance, gentleness and dependence (Nelson 1994). Thus, on the surface, it appears that the women in my study, by rebelling against normative ideals of feminine behaviour and appearance, 'threaten the system of sexual difference' and consequently of 'male dominance' (Birrell and Theberge 1994).

However, critics focusing on the textual symbolism of female bodybuilders' flesh argue that any liberating potential is undercut by the fact that it is usual for these women to still strive to be physically appealing in terms of the norms of heterosexuality (Heywood 1997; Hargreaves 1994; Mansfield and McGinn 1993; Schulze 1990). Although focusing on the evaluation of Chapter 5 and life outside the gym, in order to assess this critique, I need to briefly refer to my findings in Chapter 9 on competitions. These findings show that heterosexual hegemonic beauty norms are encouraged in part by the rules surrounding female bodybuilding competitions; sites described as submitting to 'the femininity project in terms of the almost hyperfeminine ornamentation, posture and demeanour required for competition' (St Martin and Gavey 1996: 54; see also Guthrie and Castelnuouvo 1992; Daniels 1992). These rules encourage a veneer of femininity to be placed over the project of muscularity: competitions have been viewed as a context in which 'lipstick and blonde locks are as necessary for the woman bodybuilder as they are for the female impersonator' (Mansfield and McGinn 1993: 64). Furthermore, within the subculture of bodybuilding, women are represented in magazines as displaying elements of this contrived femininity, such as bikinis, make-up, painted nails, long hair, breast implants, erotic poses and so on.

However, despite many female bodybuilders incorporating 'markers of feminin-ity' into their body projects, I do not accept that this automatically means that there is a wholesale recuperation of conventional gender ideals. There are several points to make here.

First, if this 'recuperation' had successfully occurred, how could we account for the hostility these women faced time and time again in their daily lives? Second, their appearance could be seen as a 'postmodern' contradiction that embraces both femininity and masculinity and highlights the charade of gender (see Newton 1979). Third, whilst the 'feminine apologetic' does exist to differing degrees amongst female bodybuilders, these are not necessarily the reflections and moti-vations of the women themselves. As I have argued in the Chapter 9, these women are not cultural dupes, but negotiate and work within the constrictions of a male environment. Indeed, the women in my study had their own individual definitions of femininity. In this way, 'make-up' and 'muscles' could be seen as a negotiation conducted by individual women as part of their attempt to piece together different elements of self in order to construct a satisfactory sense of identity.

According to Bordo (1993), as female bodybuilding involves extreme practices of dieting and exercise, it inevitably reproduces normative notions of gender and upholds the dominant patriarchal order. Here, the strict lifestyle regime followed by muscular women is claimed to be far from liberating or empowering, but based instead on oppressive restriction, deprivation and regulation, resulting in self-monitored, subdued, docile bodies (Bordo 1993; Hesse-Biber 1996). However, according to my findings in Chapter 5, the regimented lifestyle of the female bodybuilder was Janus-faced – it had empowering elements to it as well as being constricting at times. Whilst it did restrict their social interactions and place a strain on relationships, most of the time the women found the structure comforting and a means to achieve their goal. Although the women admitted that manipulation of the body using training and food becomes an all-encompassing and obsessive pursuit of perfection, they claimed that they were doing this for *themselves*, to create a body-project to their *own* ideal rather than for the benefit of men or others. In this way, the women make their own decisions and take control of their own lives, rather than being controlled by male standards and institutions. For the women involved, strict self-discipline was associated with direction, control and accomplishment, which – even with the negative constrictions of this lifestyle –meant choosing a life in accordance with their beliefs and feelings of uniqueness and pride, rather than 'lack' and 'insufficiency'. Thus, the interpreta-tions of the women in my study challenged the claim by Bordo that women's bodily discipline acts solely to reassert existing gender configurations (White *et al*. 1995; Willis 1990).

However, although I disagree with Bordo (1993: 179) that any disciplinary action involved to create the perfect body is an 'illusory' power, there are nega-tive consequences associated with investing too much in the body's appearance. My findings reported many incidences of body dissatisfaction and insecurities, which coincides with Bordo's theory that women's bodies are never good enough as they are, and are forever seeking improvement (although I would add here that all bodies are unfinished entities). Although there were indulgent moments when women cited the immense pleasures and enjoyment that they took in their muscularity, my findings could be used to support the conclusion that female body-building does not generally appear to create high self-esteem through body image. Against this backdrop of social stigma and self-criticism, it may seem difficult to comprehend why a woman would choose to become a female bodybuilder. Here we must return to the motivations of these women cited in Chapter 5.

Contemporary *mainstream* body modification practices by women are argu-ably conducted to present an attractive appearance for men and others within the 'rules' set down by what Butler (1990) has referred to as a 'heterosexual matrix'. However, according to my study, female bodybuilders chose to bodybuild as something 'purely' for their *own* benefit. Whilst original motivations to weight train varied – from having sports time for themselves and recovering from a sports injury to more pivotal moments in their lives – none of them directly claimed it was a way to lose weight or to become more attractive to men. Moreover, several of the women insisted that bodybuilding had had a profound and benefi-cial impact on their lives. A few of these women argued that the lifestyle literally 'saved' them from alcoholism and eating disorders, giving them positive control over their bodies and lives as a form of therapeutic healing. Others argued that since they started bodybuilding, they had learnt to appreciate their bodies more. In this manner, the women's lives were transformed, at least in part, by their attempts to reclaim their bodies for themselves and their own desires. Following on from this, it is also possible to argue that as this sense of 'selfhood' emerges, this will inevitably affect social relations and instigate important changes in soci-ety (MacKinnon 1987; Rich 1980; Heywood 1997; Willis 1995). However, in reality, does this actually occur?

In order to make some brief concluding comments on Chapter 5, it is necessary to return to the fundamental notions of empowerment as laid out in the Introduction, and ask some important questions. First of all, is there any form of individual empowerment? The women cited feelings of empowerment in the form of strength, power, self-control, discipline and determination. In terms of increased self-esteem, self-confidence, positive body image and self-awareness (Hall 1990), the situation appears complex and can be interpreted as liberating or oppressive depending on the specific issue scrutinized. Second, do muscular women's bodies change the nature of gendered relationships and social structures for women in society? As these women actively seek to redefine femininity to include muscles, physical size, power and mental strength, they appear, at least symbolically, to reconstruct elements of cultural discourses regarding female attractiveness and behaviour (Spitzack 1990). However, further questions need to be asked. Does female bodybuilding lead to *permanently* changed subjectivities and improved lives? Does it actively empower and affect women's position in *society*? The findings of Chapter 5 appear to raise as many questions about the potential of female bodybuilding to empower women as they seem to answer. To reiterate, the situation appears complex, contradictory and confusing. Depending on the context and the biography of the muscular woman, the practice can be seen both to liberate and to oppress.

Chapter 6 continues the main themes identified in Chapter 5 (e.g. exploring how the women maintained a feminine and positive sense of self, revealing the motivations of female bodybuilders and espousing the complexity of 'empowerment') by examining the most extreme and controversial aspects of the women's lifestyle – muscle worship and steroid use. By focusing on the women's experiences, both 'deviant' practices are argued to be more complex phenomena than they have previously been portrayed as. Throughout this book I have argued that in order to shed light on these extraordinary women, we need to turn to their phenomenological experiences and explore how their subjectivities are negotiated through bodywork (Obel 1996:196). The 'dark side' of female bodybuilding consequently revealed some of the pleasures and affirmative lived experiences of the women. For example, some of the women articulated sensuous satisfaction and enjoyment in holding muscle worship sessions, rather than them being simply a financial transaction. In addition, the phenomenology of drug taking (particularly steroids) was explored, looking at the positive aspects – allowing these women to create a body of their choosing, strength, power, aggression, confidence, sexual pleasure – and not just the negative experiences. In addition to understanding the identity of the female bodybuilder outside the gym, to further understand their motivations we need to explore the key environments of the female bodybuilder: environments which play an important role in shaping these experiences. For these reasons, I now focus on the findings from the two chapters 'inside the gym' – a place where these women feel most at home and experience the 'workout' as the peak phenomenological heightened pleasure in their daily lives.

Chapter 7 provided an ethnography of the gym, focusing on women's empowerment through underexplored narratives of space. For the women in the study, the gym acted as a partial refuge and retreat against the malevolence of the outside world. It was a place where female bodybuilders could move about without having to be so concerned about the responses which their 'unfeminine' physiques, postures and movements may provoke on the street. Not only does the gym provide an arena where they can build their bodies; it also creates a comparatively protected sphere whereby female bodybuilders can rebuild and repair any damage caused by 'attacks' on their identity elsewhere in their lives. This identity restoration happens both through self-affirming interactions with appreciative and 'like-minded' others, and through a complete immersion in their weight-training endeavour.

The female bodybuilders in my study carved out a powerful niche for themselves – of space, and of accomplishment. They articulated a sense of confidence, control, autonomy, bodily expression and strength that was confirmed in observations of their training (manifest through their demeanour, gestures and appearances). This provides evidence for the argument made by sports feminists that dynamic activities, such as heavy weight training, can teach women to trust their bodies and to enjoy their physical competence and capabilities. Furthermore, the women appeared 'unapologetic' with regard to taking up body space not only in terms of size and structure, but also in terms of bodily movement, mobility and actions. Hence, these women remained undeterred that their bodily behaviour and deportment did not conform to hegemonic notions of femininity, such as being 'delicate', 'graceful' and 'passive'.

In this way, despite gendered interactional 'obstacles', the gym might be seen overall as a place of empowerment for the female bodybuilder: a space in which she can use her body in an instrumental, aggressive and authoritative manner and potentially take ownership of this new-found power and use it for her own advancement. Furthermore, bodybuilding could be perceived as liberating women, as it attacks traditional notions of femininity and replaces them with new constructions of women's bodies, behaviours and practices. However, yet again the situation is complex. Cultural, essentialist and radical feminists argue that for women to take on masculine pursuits and activities would be for them to take on the same traits of violence, aggression, oppression, masochism and dominance as men. For example, Grimshaw (1999) points out that dominating space and striving to reach the limits of physical capacities may terrorise or oppress others. Thus on one hand, female bodybuilding can be discerned as empowering, as it enables women to embody male traits such as power, strength and muscularity, thereby challenging cultural constructions of gender and sexual difference (Schulze 1990); on the other, it can be argued that despite these women building new bodies, new femininities and identities for themselves, they ultimately do not act in a sphere of 'bodily empowerment', as they still submit to the dominant masculine cultural structures and ideologies on which bodybuilding is based (Klein 1993). To investigate this debate further, Chapter 8 focused on the phenomenological experiences of these women in the gym, looking at how their subjectivities are expressed, lived and created through their bodies and through the amalgamation of muscle and iron incorporated within their physical selves.

My findings in Chapter 8 suggest that whilst many female bodybuilders did indeed embrace both the hypermasculine attitude towards pain and the satisfaction of being able to conquer it, there are alternative interpretations to those given by critical feminist and sports psychologists, who see it simply as a pathological manifestation of self-hatred and inferiority. As Monaghan (2001) and Crossley (2004) suggest in their comparative studies on male bodybuilders and circuit trainers, traditional understandings of pain exist within, yet are also subverted by, the centre of the subculture itself. Thus female bodybuilders *reworked* the meanings and physical sensations of 'pain', so that they became pleasurable, enjoyable and desirable. The women cited feelings of 'heightened awareness', 'euphoria', 'flow', 'release', 'erotic intensity' and gratification. In this context it is hardly surprising that female bodybuilders wish to dwell in the gym for as long as possible, in order to savour and relish these sensations. Furthermore, it is the actual experiences, feelings, emotions and intimate accounts of the bodybuilding process articulated by the female bodybuilders themselves which help to explain their commitment to a muscular order. The ethnographic findings in this research oppose the argument made by critical feminists such as Bordo (1988: 98) that bodybuilding is an ascetic act lacking sensuality: 'preoccupied with the body and deriving narcissistic enjoyment from its appearance... [with] little pleasure in the experience of embodiment'. Indeed, the 'pain' 'of the actual process of bodybuilding' and 'their subjective and corporeal effects are central rather than peripheral to the experiences and motivations of many contemporary body modifiers' (Sweetman 1999b: 205). This substantiates the importance of focusing on the 'lived reality' of such practices, rather than simply treating them on the basis of their status as a 'text' or 'outer appearance' (Featherstone 1991: 171; Radley 1991: 112–3).

However, in terms of bodybuilding's potential to 'empower' women in society more generally, the situation appears far more complicated. Although the women articulate an increase in confidence and self-esteem that helps them to re-enter the 'outside' world again, they are still confronted with the same discriminations and stigmatization that they experienced before they entered the gym. As they leave the refuge of the weights arena, they seem to face the same difficulties and problems as before. However, a final assessment could not be made until the most extreme and important moment in the bodybuilding calendar was explored: 'the competition', an event that deals with the culmination of their ambitions and 'sets the seal' on these women's identities.

Chapter 9 assessed the 'outcome' of the competition for female bodybuilders by focusing on Michelle's experiences. It concluded that whilst the female bodybuilders perceived the rite of passage as an event that was taking them somewhere – to a new identity and life within the bodybuilding community (associated with elevated status) – there was no liminality in absolute terms. Indeed, despite conquering their 'gruelling' and 'soul-destroying' diet and beating their opponents on stage, there was no full transformation. The activities and roles associated with female bodybuilding result in no post-liminal realignment of social norms and roles. Indeed, there is no vocation awaiting the women within the subculture and, moreover, there is no resolution to the problems, conflicts and ostracism that female bodybuilders contend with in their daily lives. Thus the women's sacrifices and commitment to the muscular order have no impact on the social role they occupy outside the subculture.

In light of the evidence from Chapter 9, it is difficult to comprehend how competitive female bodybuilding can provide *societal* empowerment for women. Whilst there is a re-definition of normative gendered appearances (as discussed earlier in the findings of Chapter 5), under the gaze of the judges, women's bodies are still judged, objectified and found wanting (according to the criteria laid down by male leaders in the sport). Furthermore, there is little to suggest that the competition holds a 'transformatory potential' (Young 1993: 157) that permanently changes women's political and social positions, resulting in a step towards gender equality. This is, however, not to ignore the satisfaction taken individually by the women. For the competitor, there is a huge sense of accomplishment in achieving this fleeting perfection of the body. Feelings of individual uniqueness, self-control, autonomy and self-respect are equated with a sense of individual empowerment. Nevertheless, as socially discredited individuals facing an unaccepting world (Goffman 1983), there exists no place for these stigmatized women in the moral order of society; they are 'cut off' from respectable society, as other subcultural groups have been in the past (e.g. Hall and Jefferson 2006).

For the female bodybuilders in my study, the costs and sacrifices – even the possibility of an early death – are worth it. The satisfaction intrinsic to building muscle outweighs the disadvantages. Their involvement in this muscular order is a sensual and visceral affair that 'eats into' their identities as they pursue physical transformation (Falk 1994). Female bodybuilding is based in restricted leisure space and may appear to be no more than a symbolic threat, or an 'imaginary solution', to gendered norms (Clarke *et al.* 2006). However, I would argue that whilst 'the body cannot even temporarily transcend ideology – it can certainly bother [it]' (Schulze 1997: 29). In any event, female bodybuilders offend the sensibilities of society's stylistic, experiential and physical norms. They affect people's sense of normality and find pleasure and self-affirmation in what is deemed unacceptable. As was concluded in Chapter 9, the women in my study seemed to be developing personalities of the Weberian 'heroic' type by carving out a life of their own choosing, of dignity, lived in accordance with their own values. They have chosen a body regime which involves all of their effort, which serves to organize and evaluate their lives, including their relationships and other goals, on the basis of coherent and singular criteria. The female bodybuilders have been the agents of their own bodily transformation and created a 'life-space' of their own, for which they take full responsibility. They have chosen a 'heroic journey' through life that gives them meaning, purpose, fulfilment and drive. Their lifestyle gives them both pleasure and pain; it frees them and constricts them. For those outside the female bodybuilding subculture, it may be very difficult to comprehend the women's all-encompassing desire for and commitment to muscularity – indeed it seems fair to state that you have to *live* it and *feel* it to really know it.

Research conclusions

My research findings highlighted the contradictions and complexities in the lives of female bodybuilders, demonstrating how these women actively negotiated, resisted and upheld hegemonic notions of femininity. Furthermore, it captured the complex ways in which female bodybuilders create (and continually renew) their identity through everyday practices. These findings illustrated the dialectical processes at work between agency and structure. Indeed, for these women, 'the conscious refusal to be defined as [a] victim provides them with a sense of agency' (Sparkes 1996: 173). Unlike Bordo, who claims that these women are living under a 'false consciousness', as cultural dupes, I have argued it is vital that we take seriously their voices, experiences, desires and intentions as crucial sources of information. This is not to claim that we should take these women's stories of resistance as the complete truth, providing a pure reflection of its effects and outcomes, but rather to say that these women are active agents within constraining contexts.

These empirical discoveries indicate that it is reasonable to conclude that *no* practice can, in absolute terms, emancipate and empower women. 'No body' can stand outside of the society that we inhabit and be heralded as a total and complete empowering practice or icon (Grimshaw 1999). Instead, therefore, it is necessary to research the ways in which women negotiate, accommodate and resist within the given social context. In the same way as Pitts (2003: 81), my study 'highlights the female body as a site of negotiation between power and powerlessness, neither of which are likely to win fully'. Empowerment then can be seen as a shifting, transitory and evolving process full of complexity and contradictions – just as one 'problem' seems to be resolved, others are revealed.

Furthermore, this research has argued that the lived experiences of enfleshed subjects are pivotal to understanding the motivations and identities of the female bodybuilder. This reveals the importance of focusing on the phenomenological experiences of 'actors' – an approach that allows the subjective experiences of women to be expressed, as embodied agents who think, act and know through their bodies. I espouse this position not with the belief that it captures an authentic experience which is 'epistemologically self-sufficient', but rather in the belief that an appreciation of the lived female body is 'epistemologically indispensable' (Alcoff 2000) to understanding women's lives within specific cultural and social positions. As my research findings highlight, it is important that feminist theory takes into account real, fleshy, corporeal bodies – ones which touch, smell, taste and have internal organs – without falling back on the simplicities of biological essentialism.

What does the future hold for these women?

Pitts (2003: 78) argues that in order for extreme body projects to be 'reclaimative' rather than mutilative and 'harmful', they must at some point eventually come to an end. The competition ritual, however, does not seem to act as a full completion of events, as the competitor must then prepare herself for the next competition – to create a 'better' body than before. I am left concerned as to what will happen to these women in the future – in 20 years' time, for example. The birth of new drugs, alongside scientific and technological advances, has meant that the creation and building of what some regard as 'grotesque and monstrous' bodies has been made possible in an unprecedented manner. The long-term effects of these drugs are still not known. Whilst 'side effects' such as arthritic problems and hernias commonly occur, we do not know what the life expectancy is for competitors or 'serious' bodybuilders today – for example, we cannot be sure about their risks of heart, liver and kidney failure. In addition, women who take steroids risk permanent 'gender defects' (i.e. excess facial and body hair, enlarged clitoris, deep, 'broken' voice) that will never allow them to be fully accepted back into the gendered interaction order – the effects on them are real, permanent and irreversible. For the women in my study, it is still too early to know the full consequences of their actions, in terms of their drug taking and hardcore lifestyle. However, they are fully aware of the risks they take and have a fatalistic attitude to the future, as demonstrated by Michelle's comment: 'I would rather live a short life and do what I want to do, rather than a long life of regret'. Indeed, their bodies, identities and lives are so wrapped up in the pursuit of muscle that I find myself wondering if they could ever afford to doubt the life they have chosen. I am reminded here of the negative articulations of an American ex-IFBB professional female bodybuilder (cited in Kwiatkowski 1995: 58) who had retired after becoming disillusioned with the sport. Towards the end of her career (resonating with some parts of Michelle's story), she feels 'trapped within her body' and trapped within her life. Furthermore, she is filled with feelings of remorse, guilt, self-blame and self-hatred. For example, when she is in terrible pain because of her joints, she reminds herself: 'you know, you wouldn't be here if you hadn't done this to yourself' (ibid.: 50). The full extent of her emotional anguish is captured in the following comment:

> You try not to look in the mirror and see what you've become. You don't look like a woman any more. Some of the side effects are permanent, like my voice. I don't like to talk around people… several of the early competitors have killed themselves.
>
> (ibid.: 64)

Although I do not claim this person's experience to be representative, it does highlight yet again the immense costs and consequences for this chosen lifestyle. In order to discover the long-term effects – and, related to this, bodybuilding's empowering potential for these women – a longitudinal study or a life history approach would be needed to explore these women's lives further.

Concluding comments

The research has been a challenging, fascinating and sometimes exhausting experience. Immersing myself in the field required a dramatic lifestyle change. By its very nature, ethnography demands time, commitment, energy and patience. Furthermore, ethnography is full of political, ethical and moral 'minefields' that need to be navigated carefully: for example, feminist ethnographers must justify to their own conscience what intimate 'data' should remain private and what should be exposed to the public academic sphere. Research, from this approach, is a deeply emotional and political affair and is inevitably subjective. In writing up, I have been the medium through which the field has been constructed, represented and analysed. As I elaborated in the methods chapter, my 'fingerprints' are all over the research and the subsequent findings. Despite these limitations, I believe ethnography was the most appropriate method by which to explore the 'lived experiences' of female bodybuilders. As Taylor (1993:17) recognizes, researching the lived body can often be difficult, as 'living' is essentially a practical activity; it is done rather than reflected upon, and not necessarily told as a narrative. Yet it would have been impossible to fully comprehend the meaning and importance of female bodybuilding without attending to the 'intricacies of its lived sensuality' (Katz 1988: 167).

Journey's end

As I emerge from the tumultuous sea of research that was, for over two years, my life, I slowly begin to return to long-forgotten tastes and ways of being. My eyes, however, take a while to adjust; they still see things differently. Likewise, certain bodily practices have remained with me and become ingrained into my soma. Still drenched by the subcultural meanings, I wade back to the shore, although not to the same place from which I commenced my travels.

My journey into the fascinating 'lifeworld' of female bodybuilders has finished, but for the women who choose to dedicate their whole lives to the muscular order, their heroic journey is far from over.

Notes

2 Researching female bodybuilders

1 However, it would be wrong to assume that there is a singular approach to 'feminist ethnography', or even that there is a consensus that this approach is even possible (see Stacey 1988; Stanley and Wise 1990; Visweswaran 1994; Bell 1993; Skeggs 1995; Dauth 2009).

2 This gym possessed an extensive free-weights area (as well as fixed weights and cardiovascular work-out areas) and retained over 4,000 members during the course of the research (see Chapter 7 for a description of the layout). Catering for a wide range of clientele, from female and male bodybuilders to casual aerobic exercisers, the gym marketed itself as a provider of good facilities at a low cost (i.e. aimed at lower income individuals and families).

3 Quotes from gym members are coded according to an allocated gym number (between 1–6, 1 being the main site) and for the sake of clarity given a number in the sequence in which they are used within this book. For example, (male, gym 2:5) translates as a comment made by a male gym user in my second research site, who is the fifth person within this gym to be quoted in this research.

4 The hardcore gyms in this study all had signed pictures or posters of bodybuilders on the wall. In one of the gyms, porn magazines were kept on the reception counter.

5 Hobbs (2001: 214) argues that participant observation allows the researcher to 'learn the language of the host community'. Whilst I was familiar with everyday 'gym lingo', elements of bodybuilding discourse, particularly in association to competitions, were an enigma to me at the start of my research. For example, 'Christmas tree' refers to the pattern of extreme muscle definition located on the base of the lower back that can be seen on competitive bodybuilders.

6 Refer to sexual orientation and the 2011 census: http://www.statistics.gov.uk/about/consultations/downloads/2011Census_sexual_orientation, accessed 10 January 2012.

7 The dress code of female bodybuilders inevitably varied depending on the social context and individuality of the person. At competitions there were several female bodybuilders who dressed in a 'hyperfeminine' style that called for attention (e.g. very short skirts, low tops).

8 In the gym, my one-rep max reached the following: bench: 72.5 kg, leg press: 330 kg, squat: 110 kg and dead-lift: 135 kg.

9 Anabolic steroids (amongst many other drugs that were used by female bodybuilders) are legally classified as a 'Class C' drug within the United Kingdom. Possession or importing steroids with 'intent to supply' (which includes giving them to friends) is against the law, and could possibly lead to up to 14 years in prison with an unlimited fine.

3 The history of female bodybuilding

1 Whilst Bernarr MacFadden held the first female bodybuilding contests over a brief period at the turn of the nineteenth/twentieth centuries, Henry McGhee has been widely credited as the official founder.
2 The Weider brothers, Ben and Joe, co-founded the IFBB in 1946. Whilst there were other amateur bodybuilding associations around the same period, such as the Amateur Athletic Union (AAU), and the Natural Amateur British Bodybuilding Association (NABBA), the IFBB became the main bodybuilding body in 1965, when it offered prize money to male bodybuilders at the 'Mr Olympia' event. For more detail on the history of male bodybuilding please refer to Wayne (1985).
3 'Pumping Iron II: The Women' was heralded by some as the Feminist Film of the Year (Kuhn 1988).
4 The first Ms. International contest was won by Erika Geisen.
5 Murray retained her Ms. Olympia title and won by a controversial one-point margin.
6 Guidelines can be found on the IFBB website, http://www.ifbb.com, accessed 26 February 2013.
7 The quote is taken from a letter addressed to the competitors from Jim Manion (Chairman of the Professional Judges Committee). Capitals in original.
8 This took place following a memo dated 6 December 2004, directed by Jim Manion.
9 The BNBF and the NPA are the only bodybuilding federations to express explicitly that they are drugs tested and 'natural' competitions.
10 Female bodybuilding contestants are often referred to as Physique Competitors.
11 Bodybuilding promoter Terry Shipman, cited in Huxtable (2004: 5).
12 Taken from his blog 'Hard Talk', GeneX website and personal e-mails.

4 Muscle is a feminist issue

1 The terms '"shredded" and "hard" refer to extreme fat and water depletion which vivifies musculature. A bodybuilder in "vascular" condition is so "shredded" that her blood vessels gain anatomy-text-like definition' (Aoki 1996: 60).
2 A term referring to feminists who focus on the variable of human agency within the structural constraints of society.
3 As female bodybuilders strive for low body-fat levels and manipulate their hormones, they inevitably lose their breast tissue. Consequently, the majority of contenders get silicone breast implants, in 'order to balance muscle and sex appeal' (MacNeill 1988: 209).

5 The identity, lifestyle and embodiment of the female bodybuilder

1 This comment was posted on the website http://www.buzzhumor.com/videos/3052/ Women_Bodybuilders (accessed 17 November 2008) and is not an unusual reaction to the bodies of female bodybuilders.
2 Whilst I do not want to pathologize bodybuilding or suggest this is the only reading, during my research I came across both male and female bodybuilders who felt insecure about their bodies and claimed to look small and 'weak', when this was clearly not the case.

6 The 'dark side' of female bodybuilding

1 Male bodybuilders also do muscle worship sessions for male clients. This is often referred to as 'schmozing' or 'hustling' – see Klein (1990) and Kaye (2005).
2 Email correspondence.
3 Interestingly, male bodybuilding has attracted derision due to 'feminine' aspects of the sport such as 'posing' and men looking at male bodies. The male worshippers here are male and gazing at the female body – this is a traditional aspect of the gaze, yet is seen as problematic.

4 A total of seven muscle worshippers were contacted by email, several through a popular blog and then through a snowball sample. Issues of truth and the representation of self through the internet present problems in validity; likewise, the small sample meant that findings are not representative of the target population.

7   Exploring the 'empowerment' of female bodybuilders through concepts of space

1 As opposed to the hardcore gym.
2 This is of course dependent to some degree on the individual's interpretation of 'modesty' and 'privacy'. Some women are far more uncomfortable than others about revealing their bodies in public (depending on their circumstances, e.g. religion, body image, pregnancy etc.). Nevertheless, there are still unwritten rules and norms within the changing rooms, such as not staring.
3 Women are particularly encouraged to participate in aerobics, yoga and other fitness classes. This has been investigated in some detail by the likes of Bordo (1988), Lloyd (1996) and Grimshaw (1999).
4 Sports sociologists have documented the difficulties women faced when trying to access the gym in the past – refer to Klein (1985) and Cheshire and Lewis (1985) for more detail. Interestingly, there are only a small number of 'men-only' gyms in the UK today, compared to the increasing number of 'women-only gyms'.
5 One of the peripheral gyms that I had observed during my research was trying to refurbish and upgrade itself to more of a health and leisure facility. Consequently the hardcore bodybuilders were asked to leave and a new set of gym rules were displayed. These included keeping tops on whilst training, not dropping weights and making sure they were returned to the rack – but far more unusual was the rule 'no loud grunting or groaning'.

8   Ripped, shredded and cut: reworking notions of 'pain and violence' in female bodybuilding

1 'Animal' advertisements are found in many muscle magazines, such as *Muscle and Fitness* and *Flex*. Several of my female bodybuilders used these texts as motivational tools.
2 An obvious example of this is the alternative name for biceps: they are commonly referred to as 'guns'.

9   Competitions: a heroic journey

1 For the benefit of description, on occasions I have integrated and amalgamated my own observations.
2 It is worth noting that not all female bodybuilders in my study agreed that to be a bodybuilder you need to compete. For instance, Laura (a bodybuilder of ten months) argued that 'bodybuilding is a lifestyle... not an act of participating in an organized physique competition'. Nevertheless, most female bodybuilders, unlike their male counterparts, do compete or aspire to compete (Bolin 1992).
3 Judges are volunteers. In order to become a judge you need to register and then sit on the panel and judge for three shows. Scoring is then compared and the individual's suitability is decided upon.
4 Weber (1915b) uses this famous quote in his 'Politics as a Vocation' lecture. The words were spoken by Martin Luther before the 'Diet of Worms', after he had been summoned to retract half of his 95 Theses. Luther claimed that he could not go against his conscience. When using these words, Max Weber suggests that regardless of whether it is the 'right stance', there is admiration to be found in a man of authenticity and integrity who takes responsibility for his life and actions. See Weber (2004 [1917]): xlii–xlv.

References

Ackerman, D. (1990) *A Natural History of the Senses*. New York, NY: Vintage Books.

Alcoff, L. (1997) 'Cultural feminism versus post-structuralism: the identity crisis in feminist theory', in L. Nicholson (Ed.), *The Second Wave: A Reader in Feminist Theory* (pp. 330–55). London: Routledge.

Aptekar, L. (2002) 'The child in the ethnographer: private worlds and the writing of research', *Phenomenology and Pedagogy*, 10, 224–32.

Aoki, D. (1996) 'Sex and muscle: the female bodybuilder meets Lacan', *Body and Society*, 2(4), 59–74.

Arnoldi, K. (2002) *Chemical Pink*. New York, NY: Forge.

Arthurs, J. and Grimshaw, J. (1999) *Women's Bodies: Discipline and Transgression*. London: Cassell.

Bailey, P. (1996) 'Breaking the sound barrier: a historian listens to noise', *Body and Society*, 2(2), 49–66.

Bartky, S. (1988) 'Foucault, femininity and the modernisation of patriarchal power', in I. Diamond and L. Quinby (Eds), *Feminism and Foucault: Reflections on Resistance* (pp. 61–86). Boston, MA: Northeastern University Press.

Bartky, S. (1990) *Femininity and Domination: Studies in the Phenomenology of Oppression*. New York, NY: Routledge.

Bataille, G. (2006 [1957]) *Eroticism*. London: Marion Boyars.

Becker, H. (1967) 'Whose side are we on?', *Social Problems*, 14(Winter), 239–47.

Becker, H. (1997 [1963]) *Outsiders. Studies in Sociology of Deviance*. London: Simon and Schuster.

BEEF: British Muscle in Action. (2007) 'Q and A', 32(October), 39.

Bell, D. (1993) 'Yes, Virginia, there is a feminist ethnography', in D. Bell, P. Caplan and W. Jahan Karim (Eds), *Gendered Fields: Women, Men and Ethnography* (pp. 28–43). London: Routledge.

Bernhard, L. A. (1984) 'Feminist research in nursing research', Poster presentation, The First International Congress on Women's Health Issues, Halifax, Nova Scotia.

Birrell, S. and Theberge, N. (1994) 'The sociological study of women in sport; structural constraints facing women in sport; ideological constraints of women in sport; feminist resistance and transformation in sport', in M. Costa and S. Guthrie (Eds), *Women and Sport: Interdisciplinary Perspectives* (pp. 323–76). Champaign, IL: Human Kinetics Press.

Bloch, R. (1987) 'Medieval misogyny', *Representations*, 20(Autumn), 1–24.

Blunt, A. and Rose, G. (1994) *Writing Women and Space: Colonial and Postcolonial Geographies*. New York, NY: Guildford Press.

Bolin, A. (1992) 'Flex appeal, food and fat: competitive bodybuilding, gender and diet', in P. Moore (Ed.), *Building Bodies* (pp. 104–209). New Brunswick, NJ: Rutgers University Press.

Bolin, A. (2009) 'Embodied ethnography: seeing feeling and knowledge amongst body-builders', in F. Salamone (Ed.), *Global Culture* (pp. 19–30). Cambridge: Cambridge Scholar Publishing.

Bolin, A. (2011) 'Buff bodies and the beast: emphasized femininity, labor and power relations among fitness, figure and women bodybuilding competitors', in N. Richardson and A. Locke (Eds), *Critical Readings in Bodybuilding* (pp. 29–58). London: Routledge.

Bologh, R. (1990) *Max Weber and Masculine Thinking – A Feminist Inquiry*. Boston, MA: Unwin Hyman.

Bordo, S. (1988) 'Anorexia nervosa: psychopathology as the crystallization of culture', in I. Diamond and L. Quinby (Eds), *Feminism and Foucault. Reflections on Resistance* (pp. 87–117). Boston, MA: Northeastern University Press.

Bordo, S. (1990) 'Reading the slender body', in M. Jacobus, E. Fox Keller and S. Shuttleworth (Eds), *Body/Politics* (pp. 83–112). New York, NY: Routledge.

Bordo, S. (1992) 'Postmodern subjects, postmodern bodies' (Review Essay), *Feminist Studies*, 18(1), 159–75.

Bordo, S. (1993) *Unbearable Weight – Feminism, Western Culture and the Body*. London: University of California Press.

Bordo, S. (1997) 'Braveheart, babe and contemporary bodies', in *Twilight Zones: The Hidden Life of Cultural Images From Plato to O.J.* (pp. 27–65). London: University of California Press.

Bordo, S. (2004) *Unbearable Weight – Feminism, Western Culture, and the Body* (10th ed.). Berkeley, CA: University of California Press.

Bouissaic, P. (1976) *Circus and Culture*. Bloomington, IN: Indiana University Press.

Bourdieu, P. (1978) 'Sport and social class', *Social Science Information*, 17, 819–40.

Bourdieu, P. (2000 [1997]) *Pascalian Meditations*. Cambridge: Polity Press.

Brace-Govan, J. (2002) 'Looking at bodywork: women and three physical activities', *Journal of Sport and Social Issues*, 24(40), 404–21.

Brace-Govan, J. (2004) 'Weighty matters: control of women's access to physical strength', *The Sociological Review*, 52, 503–51.

Braidotti, R. (1999) 'Mothers, monsters, and machines', in M. Shildrick and J. Price (Eds), *Feminist Theory and the Body* (pp. 59–79). Edinburgh: Edinburgh University Press.

Brajuha, M. and Hallowell, L (1986) 'Legal intrusion and the politics of fieldwork: the impact of the Brajuha Case', *Urban Life*, 14, 454–78.

Bridges, T. (2009) 'Gender capital and male bodybuilders', *Body and Society*, 15(1), 83–107.

Budgeon, S. (2003) 'Identity as an embodied event', *Body and Society*, 9(1), 35–55.

Butler, J. (1990) 'Bodily inscription, performative subversions', in *Gender Trouble* (pp. 128–41). New York, NY: Routledge,

Butler, J. (1999) *Gender Trouble: Feminism and the Subversion of Identity* (2nd ed.). London: Routledge.

Cabanis, P. (1956) *Oeuvres Philosophiques*, Vols 2. (trans). Paris: Presses Universitaires de France.

Cash, T. (2004) 'Body image: past, present, and future', *Body Image: An International Journal of Research*, 1, 1–5.

Cashmore, E. (1998) 'Between mind and muscle', *Body and Society*, 4(3), 83–90.

Castelnuovo, S., and Guthrie, S. (1998) *Feminism and the Female Body: Liberating the Amazon Within.* London: Lynne Rienner.

Chapkis, W. (1997) *Live Sex Acts: Women Performing Erotic Labor.* New York, NY: Routledge.

Chare, N. (2012) 'Getting hard: female bodybuilders and muscle worship', in N. Richardson and A. Locke (Eds), *Critical Readings in Bodybuilding* (pp. 199–215). London: Routledge.

Chesler, P. (1994) *Patriarchy: Notes of an Expert Witness.* Monroe, ME: Common Courage Press.

Choi, P. (2000) *Femininity and the Physically Active Woman.* London: Routledge.

Cixous, H. (1991a) *'Coming to Writing' and Other Essays.* Cambridge: Harvard University Press.

Cixous, H. (1991b) *Readings.* Minneapolis, MN: University of Minnesota Press.

Clarke, J., Hall, S., Jefferson, T. and Roberts, B. (2006) 'Subcultures, cultures and class', in S. Hall and T. Jefferson (Eds), *Resistance Through Rituals* (2nd ed.) (pp. 1–57). London: Routledge.

Coffey, A. (1999) *The Ethnographic Self: Fieldwork and the Representation of Identity.* London: Sage.

Cohen, A. (1955) *Delinquent Boys: The Culture of the Gang.* New York, NY: Free Press.

Coleman, J. (1988) 'Social capital in the creation of human capital', *American Journal of Sociology*, 94, 95–120.

Coles, F. (1994) 'Feminine charms and outrageous arms', in M. Shildrick and J. Price, (Eds), *Feminist Theory and the Body* (pp. 445–53). Edinburgh: Edinburgh University Press.

Colosi, R. (2010). *Dirty Dancing: An Ethnography of Lap-Dancing.* New York, NY: Willan.

Connan, F. (1998) 'Machismo nervosa: an ominous variant of bulimia nervosa', *European Eating Disorders Review*, 6, 154–9.

Conquergood, D. (1991) 'Rethinking ethnography: towards a critical cultural politics', *Communication Monographs*, 58, 179–94.

Cooley, C. H. (1922 [1902]) *Human Nature and Social Order.* New Brunswick: Transaction Publishers.

Connell, R. W. (1983) *Which Way is Up? Essays on Sex, Class and Culture.* Sydney: Allen and Unwin.

Connell, R. W. (1987) *Gender and Power.* Cambridge: Polity Press.

Connell, R. W. (1989) 'Cool guys, swots and wimps: the interplay of masculinity and education', *Oxford Review of Education*, 15(3), 291–303.

Corliss, R. (1982, August 30) 'The new ideal of beauty', *Time*, 72–3.

Coveney, L., Jackson, M., Jeffreys, S., Kaye, L. and Mahony, P. (1984) *The Sexuality Papers: Male Sexuality and the Social Control of Women.* London: Hutchinson.

Creswell, J. (1998) *Qualitative Inquiry and Research Design.* Thousand Oaks, CA: Sage.

Crick, M. (1992) 'Ali and me: an essay in street-corner anthropology', in J. Okely and H. Callaway (Eds), *Anthropology and Autobiography* (pp. 175–92). London: Routledge.

Crossley, N. (2004) 'The circuit trainer's habitus: reflexive body techniques and the sociality of the workout', *Body & Society*, 10(1), 37–69.

Crossley, N. (2006a) *Reflexive Embodiment in Contemporary Society.* Buckingham: Open University Press.

Crossley, N. (2006b) 'In the gym: motives, meanings and moral careers', *Body & Society*, 12(3), 23–50.

Curry, D. (1993) 'Decorating the body politic', *New Formations*, 19, 69–82.

Daniels, D. (1992) 'Gender (body) verification (building)', *Play & Culture*, 5, 370–7.

Dauth, H. (2009) *Feminist Ethnography*. Chapel Hill, NC: University of North Carolina Press.

Davis, K. (1995) *Reshaping the Female Body; The Dilemma of Cosmetic Surgery.* New York, NY: Routledge.

de Beauvoir, S. (1993 [1949]) *The Second Sex*. London: Everyman.

Debord, G. (1995 [1979]) *The Society of the Spectacle*. New York, NY: Zone Books.

Descartes, R. (1960 [1637]) *Discourse on the Method and Meditations.* Trans. L. Lafleur. New York, NY: The Liberal Arts Press.

Devine, F. and Heath, S. (1999) *Sociological Research Methods in Context*. London: Macmillan Press.

Devor, H. (1989) *Gender Blending: Confronting the Limits of Duality.* Bloomington, IN: Indiana University Press.

Dobbins, B. (1994) *The Women: Photographs of the Top Female Bodybuilders*. New York, NY: Artisan.

Donohoe, M. (2006) 'Beauty and body modification', Medscape, www.medscape.com. viewarticle/529442, accessed 15 June 2007.

Douglas, K. (2009) 'Storying myself: negotiating a relational identity in professional sport', *Qualitative Research in Sport and Exercise*, 1(2), 176–90.

Douglas, M. (1966) *Purity and Danger: An Analysis of the Concepts of Pollution and Taboo*. London: Routledge and Kegan Paul.

Downes, D. and Rock, P. (2007) *Understanding Deviance*: *A Guide to the Sociology of Crime and Rule-Breaking.* Oxford: Oxford University Press.

Durkheim, E. (1995 [1912]) *The Elementary Form of Religious Life*. Trans. K. Fields. New York, NY: Free Press.

Dutton, K. (1995) *The Perfectible Body*. London: Cassell.

Dworkin, A. (1974) *Women Hating.* New York, NY: Dutton.

Eco, U. (1986) *Travels in Hyperreality.* Trans. W. Weaver. New York, NY: Harcourt Brace Jovanovich.

Falk, P. (1994) *The Consuming Body*. London: Sage.

Farkas, C. (2007) 'Bodies at rest, bodies in motion: physical competence, women's fitness, and feminism'. *Feminism: Influence* – Free Online Library Essay, 8327.

Featherstone, M. (1991) *Consumer Culture and Postmodernism*. London: Sage.

Featherstone, M. (1995) 'The heroic life and everyday life', in M. Featherstone (Ed.), *Undoing Culture – Globalization, Postmodernism and Identity* (pp. 54–72). London: Sage.

Felshin, J. (1974) 'The Social View', in E. R. Gerber, J. Felshin, P. Berlin and W. Wyrick (Eds), *The American Woman in Sport* (pp. 179–279). Reading, MA: Addison-Wesley.

Ferguson, H. (1990) *The Science of Pleasure.* London: Routledge.

Ferrell, J. and Sanders, C. (1995) 'Culture, crime and criminology', in J. Ferrell and C. Sanders (Eds), *Cultural Criminology* (pp. 3–21). Boston, MA: Northeastern University Press.

Ferrell, J. and Hamm, M. (1998) *Ethnography on the Edge: Crime, Deviance and Field Research*. Boston, MA: Northeastern University Press.

Fierstein, L. (2000) 'The modern Amazon', in J. Frueh, L. Fierstein and J. Stein (Eds), *Picturing the Modern Amazon* (pp. 34–43). New York, NY: New Museum.

Fisher, L. (1997) 'Building one's self up', in P. Moore (Ed.), *Building Bodies* (pp. 135–64). New Brunswick, NJ: Rutgers University Press.

Forbes, B., Adam-Curtis, L., Holmgren, K. and White, K. (2004) 'Perceptions of the social and personal characteristics of hypermuscular women and of the men who love them', *The Journal of Social Psychology*, 144(5), 487–506.

Foucault, M. (1980) 'Body/power', in C. Gordon (Ed.), *Michael Foucault: Power/Knowledge* (pp. 45–63). Brighton: Harvester.

Foucault, M. (1981) *History of Sexuality. Volume 1: The Will to Knowledge*. London: Penguin.

Fournier, V. (2002) 'Fleshing out gender: crafting gender identity on women's bodies', *Body and Society*, 8(2), 55–77.

Frank, K. (2003) 'Just trying to relax: masculinity, masculinizing practices and strip club regulars', *Journal of Sex Research*, 40, 61–76.

Franks, D. and Gecas, F. (1992) 'Autonomy and conformity in Cooley's self theory', *Symbolic Interaction*, 15(1), 49–68.

Frost, L. (1999) '"Doing looks": women's appearance and mental health', in J. Arthurs and J. Grimshaw (Eds), *Women's Bodies: Discipline and Transgression* (pp. 117–36). London: Cassell.

Frost, L. (2001) *Young Women and the Body*. London: Palgrave.

Frueh, J. (2001) *Monster/Beauty Building a Body of Love.* London: University of California Press.

Frueh, J., Fierstein, L. and Stein, J. (Eds) (2000) *Picturing the Modern Amazon.* New York, NY: New Museum.

Frye, M. (1983) *The Politics of Reality*. Trumansburg, NY: Crossing Press.

Fussell, S. (1991) *Muscle: Confessions of an Unlikely Bodybuilder*. New York, NY: Poseidon Press.

Gaines, C. and Butler, G. (1983) 'Iron sisters', *Psychology Today*, 17, 64–9.

Garfinkel, H. (1967) *Studies in Ethnomethodology*. Englewood Cliffs, NJ: Prentice-Hall.

Gilroy, S. (1989) 'The EmBODY-ment of power: gender and physical activity', *Leisure Studies*, 8, 163–71.

Gilroy, S. (1997) 'Working on the body: links between physical activity and social power', in G. Clarke and B. Humberstone (Eds), *Researching Women and Sport* (pp. 96–112). London: Macmillan Press,.

Glassner, B. (1989) 'Men and muscles', in M. Kimmel and M. Messner (Eds.), *Men's Lives* (pp. 287–97). New York, NY: Macmillan.

Glick, P. and Fiske, S. (2000) 'Beyond prejudice as simple antipathy: hostile and benevolent sexism across cultures', *Personality and Social Psychology*, 79, 763–75.

Goffman, E. (1971) *Relations in Public: Microstudies of the Public Order*. London: Allen Lane.

Goffman, E. (1974) *Frame Analysis*. New York, NY: Harper and Row.

Goffman, E. (1979) *Gender Advertisements*. London: Macmillan.

Goffman, E. (1983) 'The interaction order', *American Sociological Review*, 48, 1–17.

Goffman, E. (1987) 'The arrangement between the sexes', in M. Deegan and M. Hill (Eds), *Interaction* (pp. 51–78). Winchester, MA: Allen and Unwin.

Goffman, E. (1989) 'On fieldwork', *Journal of Contemporary Ethnography*, 18, 123–32.

Gordon, A. (2008 [1997]) *Ghostly Matters: Haunting and the Sociological Imagination*. Minneapolis, MN: University of Minnesota Press.

Gorely, T., Holroyd, R. and Kirk, D. (2007) 'Muscularity, the habitus and the social construction of gender: towards a gender-relevant physical education', *British Journal of Sociology of Education*, 24(4), 429–48.

Graves, R. (1992) *Claudius the God*. Baltimore, MD: Penguin Books.

Greer, G. (2000) *The Whole Woman.* London: Anchor.

Grimes, J. (2003) 'Glutamic acid decarboxylase (GAD65) immunoreactivity in brains of aggressive, adolescent anabolic steroid-treated hamsters', *Hormones and Behavior*, 44(3), 271–80.

Grimshaw, J. (1999) 'Working out with Merleau-Ponty', in J. Arthurs and J. Grimshaw (Eds), *Women's Bodies: Discipline and Transgression* (pp. 120–45). London: Cassell.

Grint, K. and Case, P. (1998) 'The violent rhetoric of re-engineering: management consultancy on the offensive', *Journal of Management Studies*, 35, 557–77.

Grogan, S. (2004) 'Femininity and muscularity: accounts of seven women bodybuilders', *Journal of Gender Studies*, 13(1), 49–61.

Grogan, S., Evans, R., Wright, S. and Hunter, G. (2006) 'Experiences of anabolic steroid use; interviews with men and women steroid users', *Journal of Health Psychology*, 11(6), 845–56.

Grosz, E. (1994) *Volatile Bodies: Towards a Corporeal Feminism.* Bloomington, IN: Indiana University Press.

Gruber, A. and Pope, H. (1999) 'Compulsive weight lifting and anabolic drug abuse among women rape victims', *Comprehensive Psychiatry*, 40(4), 273–7.

Gutherie, S. and Castelnuovo, S. (1992) 'Elite women bodybuilders: models of resistance or compliance?', *Play and Culture*, 5, 401–8.

Halberstam, J. (1995) *Skin Shows: Gothic Horror and the Technology of Monsters.* Durham, NC: Duke University Press.

Hall, A. (1990) 'How should we theorize gender in the context of sport?', in M. Messner and D. Sabo (Eds), *Sport, Men and the Gender Order: Critical Feminist Perspectives* (pp. 223–42). Champaign, IL: Human Kinetics.

Hall, S., and Jefferson, T. (2006) *Resistance Through Rituals* (2nd ed.). London: Routledge.

Hammersley, M. and Atkinson, M. (1983) *Ethnography, Principles and Practice.* London: Tavistock.

Hanson, S. and Pratt, G. (1995) *Gender, Work and Space.* New York, NY: Routledge.

Hargreaves, J. (1986) *Sport, Power and Culture.* Cambridge: Polity Press.

Hargreaves, J. (1994) *Sporting Females: Critical Issues in the History and Sociology of Women's Sport.* London: Routledge.

Hartgens, F. and Kuipers, H. (2004) 'Effects of androgenic-anabolic steroids in athletes', *Sports Medicine*, 34(8), 513–54.

Helmore, E. (2000, 22 May) 'Two fit ladies', *Evening Standard*, 32.

Henig, R. (1996) 'The price of perfection', *Civilization*, May/June, 56–61.

Hesse-Biber, S. (1996) *Am I Thin Enough Yet? The Cult of Thinness and the Commercialization of Identity.* New York, NY: Oxford University Press.

Hewitt, K. (1997) *Mutilating the Body: Identity in Blood and Ink.* Bowling Green, OH: Popular Press.

Heywood, L. (1997) 'Masculinity vanishing: bodybuilding and contemporary culture', in P. Moore (Ed.), *Building Bodies* (pp. 165–83). New Brunswick, NJ: Rutgers University Press.

Heywood, L. (1998) *Bodymakers: A Cultural Anatomy of Women's Bodybuilding.* New Brunswick, NJ: Rutgers University Press.

Hobbs, D. (1988) *Doing the Business.* Oxford: Clarendon.

Hobbs, D. (2001) 'Ethnography and the study of deviance', in P. Atkinson, A. Coffey, S. Delamont, J. Lofland and L. Lofland (Eds), *Handbook of Ethnography* (pp. 204–19). London: Sage.

Hobbs, D. and May, T. (Eds) (1993) *Interpreting the Field: Accounts of Ethnography.* Oxford: Clarendon Press.

Hockey, J. and Allen Collinson, J. (2007) 'Grasping the phenomenology of sporting bodies', *International Review for the Sociology of Sport,* 42(2), 115–31.

Holmlund, C. (1989) 'Visible difference and flex appeal: the body, sex, sexuality, and race in the Pumping Iron films', *Cinema Journal,* 28(4), 38–51.

Homan, R. (1991) *The Ethics of Social Research.* London: Longman.

Husserl, E. (1936 [1970]) *The Crisis of European Sciences and Transcendental Phenomenology.* Evanston, IL: Northwestern University Press.

Huxtable, E. (2004) 'The history of women's bodybuilding', Sports Business Simulations, http://www.sportsbusinesssims.com/history.of.women's.bodybuilding.htm, accessed 14 February 2007.

Ian, M. (1995) 'How do you wear your body?: bodybuilding and the sublimate of drag', in M. Danenkoup and R. Henke (Eds), *Negotiating Lesbian and Gay Subjects* (pp. 71–90). New York, NY: Routledge.

Ian, M. (2001) 'The primitive subject of female bodybuilding: transgression and other postmodern myths', *Differences: A Journal of Feminist Cultural Studies,* 12(3), 69–100.

IFBB Pro Women's Bodybuilding Rankings List, http://www.getbig.com/ranking/prorankw.htm, accessed 25 October 2011.

Inciardi, J. A. (1993) 'Some considerations on the methods, dangers and ethics of crack house research', in J. A. Inciardi, D. Lockwood and A. E. Poffieger (Eds), *Women and Crack Cocaine* (pp. 147–57). New York, NY: Macmillan.

The Independent (2008, 3 May) 'Bodyworks: photographs from the weird world of bodybuilding'.

Jacobs, B. A. (1998) 'Researching crack dealers: dilemmas and contradictions', in J. Ferrell and M. S. Hamms (Eds), *Ethnography at the Edge: Crime, Deviance and Field Research* (pp. 160–203). Boston, MA: Northeastern University Press.

Jaggar, A. (1983) *Feminist Politics and Human Nature.* New York, NY: Rowman and Littlefield.

Jeffreys, S. (2005) *Beauty and Misogyny: Harmful Cultural Practices in the West.* London: Routledge.

Johnson, J. (1975) 'Trust and personal involvements in fieldwork', in R. Emerson (Ed.), *Contemporary Field Research* (pp. 203–15). Prospect Heights, IL: Wavelength Press.

Johnston, L. (1996) 'Flexing femininity: female bodybuilders refiguring "The Body"', *Gender, Place and Culture – A Journal of Feminist Geography,* 3(3), 327–40.

Jordanova, L. (1989) *Sexual Visions: Images of Gender in Science and Medicine Between the Eighteenth and Twentieth Centuries.* New York, NY: Harvester Wheatsheaf.

Kashkin, K. (1992) 'Anabolic steroids', in J. Lowinsohn (Ed.), *Substance Abuse* (pp. 380–95). Baltimore, MD: Williams and Wilkins.

Katz, J. (1988) *Seductions of Crime. Moral and Sensual Attractions in Doing Evil.* New York, NY: Basic Books.

Kaye, K. (2005) *Iron Maidens: The Celebration of the Most Awesome Women in the World.* New York, NY: Thunder's Mouth Press.

Kennedy, S. (2005) 'The birth of figure', *Oxygen,* December, 108–12.

Kerry, D. and Armour, K. (2000) 'Sports sciences and the promise of phenomenology: philosophy, method, and insight', *Quest,* 52(1), 1–17.

Kessler, S. and McKenna, W. (1978) *Gender. An Ethnomethodological Approach.* Chicago, IL: University of Chicago Press.

Kitzinger, C. and Willmott, J. (2002) "'The thief of womanhood": women's experience of polycystic ovarian syndrome', *Social Science and Medicine*, 54, 349–61.

Klein, A. (1985) 'Pumping iron', *Society, Transactions, Social Sciences and Modern*, 22, 68–75.

Klein, A. (1990) 'Little big man: hustling, gender narcissism, and bodybuilding subculture', in M. Messner and D. Sabo (Eds), *Sport, Men and the Gender Order: Critical Feminist Perspectives* (pp. 127–39). Champaign, IL: Human Kinetics.

Klein, A. (1993) *Little Big Men: Bodybuilding Subculture and Gender Construction*. Albany, NY: University of New York Press.

Klein, A. (1995) 'Life's too short to die small', in D. Sabo and D. Gordon (Eds), *Men's Health and Fitness: Gender, Power and the Body* (pp. 105–20). London: Sage.

Klein, D. (1983) *Theories of Women's Studies*. London: Routledge.

Korkia, P. (1994) 'Anabolic steroid use in Britain', *International Journal of Drug Policy*, 5, 6–9.

Krane, V. and Baird, S. (2005) 'Using ethnography in applied psychology', *Journal of Applied Sport Psychology*, 17, 87–107.

Kristeva, J. (1980) *Desire in Language: A Semiotic Approach to Literature and Art*. New York, NY: Columbia University Press.

Kuhn, A. (1988) 'The body and cinema: some problems for feminism', in S. Sheridan (Ed.), *Grafts: Feminist Cultural Criticism* (pp. 11–23). London: Verso.

Kwiatkowski, M. (1995) 'The experience of an elite female bodybuilder's participation in bodybuilding: a dialogic interview presented as narrative'. Masters thesis. University of Tennessee.

Lang, M. (1998) 'Female bodybuilding: exploring muscularity, femininity and bodily empowerment'. Masters thesis. The University of British Columbia.

Lather, P. (1988) 'Feminist perspectives on empowering research methodologies', *Women Studies International Forum*, 11(6), 569–81.

Lawler, J. (2002) *PUNCH! Why Women Participate in Violent Sports*. Terre Haute, IN: Wish.

Lingis, A. (1988) 'Orchids and muscles', in D. Knell and D. Wood (Eds), *Exceedingly Nietzsche: Aspects of Contemporary Nietzsche Interpretation* (pp. 97–115). London: Routledge.

Lloyd, M. (1996) 'Feminism, aerobics and the politics of the body', *Body and Society*, 2(2), 76–98.

Lockford, L. (2004) *Performing Femininity*. Oxford: Altamira Press.

Locks, A. (2003) 'Bodybuilding and the emergence of a post-classicism'. Doctoral thesis. University of Winchester.

Lofland, J. and Lofland, L. H. (1995 [1984]). *Analysing Social Settings: A Guide to Qualitative Observation and Analysis*. Belmont, CA: Wadsworth.

Lorber, J. (1994) *Paradoxes of Gender*. New Haven, CT: Yale University Press.

Lorde, A. (1984) *Sister Outsider: Essays and Speech*. Freedom, CA: Crossing.

Lorde, A. (1997) 'The master's tools will never dismantle the master's house', in L. Richardson, V. Taylor and N. Whittier (Eds), *Feminist Frontiers* (pp. 26–7). New York: McGraw-Hill.

Lowe, R. (1998) *Women of Steel: Female Bodybuilders and the Struggle for Self-Definition*. New York, NY: New York University Press.

McCaughey, M. (1997) *Real Knockout: The Physical Feminism of Women's Self-Defence*. New York, NY: New York University.

McDermott, K., Laschinger, H. and Shamian, J. (1996) 'Work empowerment and organizational commitment', *Nursing Management*, 27(5), 44–7.

MacKinnon, C. (1987) *Feminism Unmodified: Discourses on Life and Law*. Cambridge, MA: Harvard University Press.

McRobbie, A. (1991) *Feminism and Youth Culture: From Jackie to Just Seventeen.* Cambridge, MA: Unwin Hyman.

Malarkey, W., Strauss, R., Leizman, D., Liggett, M. and Demers, L. M. (1991) 'Endocrine effects in female weight lifters who self-administer testosterone and anabolic steroids', *American Journal of Obstetrics and Gynecology*, 165, 1385–90.

Mansfield, A. and McGinn, B. (1993) 'Pumping irony: the muscular and the feminine', in S. Scott and D. Morgahgiun (Eds), *Body Matters* (pp. 49–68). London: Falmer.

Martin, E. (2001) *The Woman in the Body: A Cultural Analysis of Reproduction*. Boston, MA: Beacon Press.

Massey, D. (1994) *Space, Place and Gender.* Minneapolis, MN: University of Minnesota Press.

Mattley, C. (1998) 'Dis-courtesy stigma: field work among phone sex fantasy workers', in J. Ferrell and M. S. Hamm (Eds), *Ethnography at the Edge: Crime, Deviance and Field Research* (pp. 146–58). Boston, MA: Northeastern University Press.

Maume, C. (2005, 15 October) 'Bulked-up Barbie girl waging war on her body', *The Independent*, 59.

Mauss, M. (1973) 'Techniques of the body', *Economy and Society*, 2, 70–88.

Mead, G. (1962 [1934]) *Mind, Self and Society*. Chicago, IL: Chicago University Press.

Merleau-Ponty, M. (1962) *Phenomenology of Perception*. London: Routledge.

Messner, M. and Sabo, D. S. (1990) *Sport, Men and Gender Order: Critical Feminist Perspectives*. Champaign, IL: Human Kinetics Books.

Mies, M. (1983) 'Towards a methodology for feminist research', in D. Klein and D. Bowles (Eds), *Theories of Women's Studies* (pp. 117–38). London: Routledge and Kegan Paul.

Mills, C. (1940) 'Situated actions and vocabularies of motive', *American Sociological Review*, 5, 904–13.

Mills, C. (2000 [1959]) *The Sociological Imagination*. Oxford: Oxford University Press.

Mishler, E. (1986). *Research Interviewing: Context and Narrative*. Cambridge, MA: Harvard University Press.

Monaghan, L. (2001) 'Looking good and feeling good', *Sociology of Health and Illness*, 23(3), 330–56.

Monaghan, L. F. (2002) 'Vocabularies of motive for illicit steroid use among bodybuilders', *Social Science & Medicine*, 55(5), 695–708.

Moore, P. (1997) *Building Bodies*. New Brunswick, NJ: Rutgers University Press.

Mosedale, S. (2005) 'Policy arena. Assessing women's empowerment: towards a conceptual framework', *Journal of International Development*, 17, 243–57.

Murphy, E. and Dingwall, R. (2001) 'The ethics of ethnography', in P. Atkinson, A. Coffey, S. Delamont, J. Lofland and L. Lofland (Eds), *Handbook of Ethnography* (pp. 339–51). London: Sage.

Nelson, M. (1994) *The Stronger Women Get, the More Men Love Football.* New York, NY: Harcourt.

Newman, C. (2000) 'The enigma of beauty', *National Geographic*, January, 94–121.

Newton, E. (1979) *Mother Camp. Female Impersonators in America*. Chicago, IL: Chicago University Press.

Oakley, A. (1972) *Sex, Gender and Society.* London: Temple Smith.

Obel, C. (1996) 'Collapsing gender in competitive bodybuilding: researching contradictions and ambiguity in sport', *International Review for the Sociology of Sport*, 31(2), 187–202.

Oberstein, K. (2011) *The Last Taboo: Women and Body Hair*. Manchester: Manchester University Press.

Olesen, V. L. (2000) 'Feminisms and qualitative research at and into the Millennium', in N. K. Denzin and Y. S. Lincoln (Eds), *Handbook of Qualitative Research* (2nd ed.) (pp. 158–74). London: Sage.

Olivardia, R., Pope, H. and Hudson, J. (2000) 'Muscle dysmorphia in male weightlifters: a case-controlled study', *American Journal of Psychiatry*, 157, 1291–6.

Orbach, S. (1988 [1978]) *Fat is a Feminist Issue*. London: Arrow Books.

Parker, H. (1974) *A View From the Boys: A Sociology of Down Town Adolescents*. Newton Abbot: David and Charles.

Paris, B. (1997) *Gorilla Suit – My Adventures in Bodybuilding*. New York, NY: St Martins Press.

Patrick, J. (1973) *A Glasgow Gang Observed*. London: Eyre Methuen.

Patton, C. (2001) '"Rock hard"' – judging the female physique', *Journal of Sport and Social Issues*, 25(2), 118–140.

Pearson, G. (1994) 'Youth, crime and society', in M. Maguire, R. Morgan and R. Reiner (Eds), *Oxford Handbook of Criminology* (pp. 1161–206). Oxford: Clarendon.

Pitts, V. (2003) *In the Flesh: The Cultural Politics of Body Modification*. New York, NY: Palgrave Macmillan.

Polhemus, T. and Randall, H. (1998) *The Customized Body*. New York, NY: Serpent Tail.

Polsky, N. (1971 [1967]) *Hustlers, Beats and Others*. Harmondsworth: Pelican.

Pope, H., Phillips, K. and Olivardia, R. (2000) *The Adonis Complex: The Secret Crisis of Male Body Obsession*. New York, NY: Free Press Publishing Co.

Plummer, J. (2007) 'An arresting development', *Flex*, October, 196.

Punch, M. (1994) 'Politics and ethics in qualitative research', in N. Denzin and Y. Lincoln (Eds), *Handbook of Qualitative Research* (pp. 83–97). London: Sage.

Radley, A. (1991) *The Body and Social Psychology*. New York, NY: Springer-Verlag.

Reid-Bowen, P. (2008) 'Why women need to be ripped, shredded and sliced: political, philosophical and theological reflections', in M. Althaus-Reid and L. Isherwood (Eds), *Controversies In Body Theology* (pp. 207–26). London: SCM Press.

Reinharz, S. (1983) 'Experiential analysis: a contribution to feminist research', in D. Klein and D. Bowles (Eds), *Theories of Women's Studies* (pp. 162–91). London: Routledge and Kegan Paul.

Ribbens, J. and Edwards, R. (Eds) (1998) *Feminist Dilemmas in Qualitative Research. Public Knowledge and Private Lives*. London: Sage Publications.

Rich, A. (1980) 'Compulsory heterosexuality and lesbian existence', *Signs*, 5(4), 631–60.

Rich, E. (2002) 'Strong words, tough minds, trained bodies'. Doctoral thesis. Loughborough University.

Richardson, N. (2008) 'Flex-rated! Female bodybuilding: feminist resistance or erotic spectacle?', *Journal of Gender Studies*, 17(4), 289–301.

Roach, M. (1998, November 10) 'Female bodybuilders discover curves', *New York Times*, 9.

Roark, J. (1991) 'The Roark Report', *Iron Game History*, March, 41–3.

Robson, C. (2000) *Small-Scale Evaluation: Principles and Practice*. London: Sage.

Rodin J. (1992) *Body Traps*. New York, NY: Morrow.

Rosen, T. (1983) *Strong and Sexy*. New York, NY: Putnam.

Rosenberg, M. and Kaplan, H. (1982) *Social Psychology of the Self-Concept.* Arlington Heights, IL: Harlan Davidson.

Roseneil, S. and Seymour, J. (Eds) (1999) *Practising Identities: Power and Resistance.* London: Macmillan.

Roth, A. and Basow, S. (2004) 'Femininity, sports, and feminism: developing a theory of physical liberation', *Journal of Sport and Social Issues*, 28, 245–65.

Roussel, P. and Griffet, J. (2000) 'The path chosen by female bodybuilders: a tentative interpretation', *Sociology of Sport Journal*, 17, 130–50.

Rubin, G. (1984) 'Thinking sex: notes for a radical theory of the politics of sexuality', in C. Vance (Ed.), *Pleasure and Danger: Exploring Female Sexuality* (pp. 267–319). Boston, MA: Routledge and Kegan Paul.

Rubin, J. (1994) *Religious Melancholy and Protestant Experience in America.* Oxford: Oxford University Press.

Sabo, D. (1989) 'Pigskin, patriarchy, and pain', in M. Kimmel and M. Messner (Eds), *Men's Lives* (pp. 184–6). New York, NY: Macmillan.

Saltman, K. (2003) 'The strong arm of the law', *Body and Society*, 9(4), 49–67.

Sassatelli, R. (1999) 'Interaction order and beyond: a field analysis of body culture within fitness gyms', *Body & Society*, 5(2–3), 227–48.

Saul, J. (2003) *Feminism: Issues and Arguments*. Oxford: Oxford University Press.

Scarry, E. (1985) *The Body in Pain: The Making and Unmaking of the World.* New York, NY: Oxford University Press.

Schaps, E. and Sanders, C. (1970) 'Purpose, patterns, and protection in a campus drug-using community', *Journal of Health and Social Behaviour*, 11, 135–45.

Schulze, L. (1990) 'On the muscle', in P. Moore (Ed.), *Building Bodies* (pp. 9–30). New Brunswick, NJ: Rutgers University Press.

Scott-Dixon, K. (2006) 'Female bodybuilders, fitness competitors and the crisis of representation', http://www.mesomorphosis.com/articles/scott-dixon/crisis.htm, accessed 23 January 2007.

Shahrad, C. (2010, November 15). 'Bikinis and biceps: the world of female bodybuilders', *The Telegraph*. http://www.telegraph.co.uk/health/dietandfitness/8120067/Bikinis-and-biceps-the-world-of-female-bodybuilders.html, accessed 9 August 2012.

Sharp, J. (1997) 'Gendering everyday spaces', in L. McDowell (Ed.), *Space, Gender and Knowledge* (pp. 263–8). London: Arrowsmith.

Shea, B. (2001) 'The paradox of pumping iron: female bodybuilding as resistance and compliance', *Women and Language*, 24, 42–6.

Shildrick, M. and Price, J. (1999) *Feminist Theory and the Body.* Edinburgh: Edinburgh University Press.

Shilling, C. (1993) *The Body and Social Theory.* London: Sage.

Shilling, C. (2003) *The Body and Social Theory* (2nd ed.). London: Sage.

Shilling, C. (2007) 'Sociology and the body: classical traditions and new agendas', in C. Shilling (Ed.), *Embodying Sociology. Retrospect, Progress and Prospects* (pp. 1–18). Oxford: Blackwells.

Shilling, C. (2008a) 'Body pedagogics, society and schooling', in J. Evans, J. Wright, B. Davies and E. Rich (Eds), *Education, Disordered Eating and Obesity Discourse* (pp. ix–xv). London: Falmer.

Shilling, C. (2008b) *Changing Bodies. Habit, Crisis and Creativity*. London: Sage.

Shilling, C. and Mellor, P. (2007) 'Cultures of embodied experience: technology, religion and body pedagogics', *The Sociological Review*, 55(3), 531–49.

Shilling, C. and Mellor, P. (2010) 'Sociology and the problem of eroticism', *Sociology*, 44(3), 435–52.

Shogun, D. (2002) 'Characterizing constraints of leisure: a Foucauldian analysis of leisure constraints', *Leisure Studies*, 21(1), 27–38.

Simmel, G. (1971 [1908a]) 'The adventurer', in D. Levine (Ed.), *Georg Simmel on Individuality and Social Forms* (pp. 178–98). Chicago, IL: Chicago University Press.

Simmel, G. (1971 [1908b]) 'Social forms and inner needs', in D. Levine (Ed.), *George Simmel on Individuality and Social Forms* (pp. 351–2). Chicago, IL: Chicago University Press.

Simmel, G. (1990 [1907]) *The Philosophy of Money*. London: Routledge.

Skeggs, B. (1995) *Theorising, Ethics and Representation in Feminist Ethnography*. London: Manchester University Press.

Smith, D. (1990) *Texts, Facts and Femininity: Exploring the Relations of Ruling*. London: Routledge.

Sparkes, A. (1996) 'Interrupted body projects and the self in teaching: exploring an absent presence', *International Studies in Sociology of Education*, 6, 167–87.

Sparkes, A. (2009) 'Ethnography and the senses: challenges and possibilities', *Qualitative Research in Sport and Exercise*, 1(1), 21–35.

Spelman, E. (1982) 'Woman as body: ancient and contemporary views', *Feminist Studies*, 8(1), 109–31.

Spitzack, C. (1990) *Confessing Excess: Women and the Politics of Body Reduction*. New York, NY: University of New York Press.

St Martin, L. and Gavey, N. (1996) 'Women's bodybuilding: feminist resistance and/or femininity's recuperation?', *Body & Society*, 2(4), 45–57.

Stacey, J. (1988) 'Can there be a feminist ethnography?', *Women's Studies International Forum*, 1(2), 1–27.

Stanley, L. (1990) 'Doing ethnography, writing ethnography: a comment on Hammersley', *Sociology*, 24(2), 617–27.

Stanley, L. and Wise, S. (1983) *Breaking Out: Feminist Consciousness and Feminist Research*. London: Routledge and Kegan Paul.

Steinem, G. (1994) *Moving Beyond Words*. New York, NY: Simon and Schuster.

Steiner-Adair, C. (1990) 'The body politic: normal female adolescent development and the development of eating disorders', in C. Gilligan, N. Lyons and T. Hanmer (Eds.), *Making Connections: Relational Worlds of Adolescent Girls at Emma Willard School* (pp. 162–82). Cambridge, MA: Harvard University Press.

Stulberg, L. (1996/7) 'Getting big and hard: men's fitness magazines and the construction of the sexual self', *Cultural Studies from Birmingham*, 4, 93–111.

Sullivan, D. (2004) *Cosmetic Surgery: The Cutting Edge of Commercial Medicine in America* (2nd ed.). New Brunswick, NJ: Rutgers University Press.

Summers, L. (2001) *Bound to Please: A History of the Victorian Corset*. Oxford: Berg.

Sweetman, P. (1999a) 'Only skin deep? Tattooing, piercing and the transgressive body', in M. Aaron (Ed.), *The Body's Perilous Pleasures* (pp. 165–87). Edinburgh: Edinburgh University Press.

Sweetman, P. (1999b) 'Marking the body identity and identification in contemporary body modification'. Doctoral thesis. University of Southampton.

Sweetman, Paul (1999c) 'Anchoring the (postmodern) self? Body modification, fashion and identity', *Body and Society*, 5(2), 51–76.

Tate, S. (1999) 'Making your body your signature: weight-training and transgressive femininities', in S. Roseneil and J. Seymour (Eds), *Practicing Identities: Power and Resistance* (pp. 33–53). London: Macmillan.

Taylor, C. (1993) 'To follow a rule', in C. Calhoun, E. Lipuma and M. Postone (Eds), *Bourdieu: Critical Perspectives* (pp. 45–60). Cambridge: Polity Press.

Theroux, L. (2000) 'Scary Monsters', *FHM*, October, 147–54.

Todd, J. (2000) 'Bring on the Amazons: an evolutionary history', in J. Frueh., L. Fierstein and J. Stein (Eds), *Picturing the Modern Amazon* (pp. 48–62). New York, NY: New Museum.

Tseelon, E. (1995) *The Mask of Femininity: The Presentation of Women in Everyday Life.* London: Sage.

Turner, V. (1969) *The Ritual Process: Structure and Anti-Structure.* Chicago, IL: Aldine.

Turner, V. (1992) *Blazing the Trail. Way Marks in the Exploration of Symbols.* Tucson, AZ: The University of Arizona Press.

Uhlmann, J. and Uhlmann J. (2005) 'Embodiment below discourse: the internalized domination of the masculine perspective', *Women's Studies International Forum*, 28, 93–103.

Van Maanen, J. (1988) *Tales from the Field.* Chicago, IL: University of Chicago.

Visweswaran, K. (1994) *Fictions of Feminist Ethnography.* Minneapolis, MN: University of Minnesota Press.

Wacquant, L. (1995) 'Review article: why men desire muscles', *Body and Society*, 1(1), 163–79.

Wacquant, L. (2004) *Body and Soul.* Oxford: Oxford University Press.

Walkerdine, V. (1981) 'Sex, power and pedagogy', *Screen Education*, 38, 14–21.

Wearing, B. (1998) *Leisure and Feminist Theory.* Thousand Oaks, CA: Sage.

Webber, C. (2007) 'Background, foreground, foresight: the third dimension of cultural criminology', *Crime, Media and Culture*, 3(2), 139–57.

Weber, M. (1948 [1915a]) 'Religious rejections of the world and their directions', in H. Gerth and C. Mills (Eds), *From Max Weber* (pp. 323–63). London: Routledge.

Weber, M. (1991 [1904–5]) *The Protestant Ethic and the Spirit of Capitalism.* London: HarperCollins.

Weber, M (1991 [1915b]) 'Politics as a vocation', in H. Gerth and C. Wright Mills (Eds), *From Max Weber* (pp. 77–129). London: Routledge.

Weber, M. (2004 [1917]). *The Vocation Lectures: Science As a Vocation, Politics As a Vocation.* Indianapolis, IN: Hackett Publishing Company.

Weitz, R. (2003) *The Politics of Women's Bodies: Sexuality, Appearance, and Behaviour.* Oxford: Oxford University Press.

Weitz, R. (2004) *Rapunzel's Daughters: What Women's Hair Tells Us About Women's Lives.* New York, NY: Farrar, Straus, and Giroux.

Wennerstrom, S. (1984) 'Women's bodybuilding: the beginning, part 1'. *Flex*, 1(10), 74–7.

Wennerstrom, S. (2000) 'A history of women's bodybuilding', in J. Frueh, L. Fierstein and J. Stein (Eds), *Picturing the Modern Amazon* (pp. 65–71). New York, NY: New Museum.

Wertz, F. (2009) 'Phenomenological research methods psychology: a comparison with grounded theory, discourse analysis, narrative research, and intuitive inquiry'. Conference presentation, Interdisciplinary Coalition of North American Phenomenologists (ICNAP), New Jersey.

White, P. and J. Gillett. (1994) 'Reading the muscular body: a critical decoding of advertisements in *Flex* magazine', *Sociology of Sport Journal*, 11(4), 18–39.

White, P., Young, K. and McTeer, W. (1995) 'Sport, masculinity and the injured body', in D. Sabo and D. Gordon (Eds), *Men's Health and Illness: Gender, Power and the Body* (pp. 158–82). London: Sage.

Widdicombe, S. and Wooffitt, R. (1990) '"Being" versus "doing" punk: on achieving authenticity as a member', *Journal of Language and Social Psychology*, 9, 257–77.

Wilkinson, S. (1986) *Feminist Social Psychology: Developing Theory and Practice*. Milton Keynes: Open University Press.

Williams, S. (1998) 'Health as moral performance: ritual transgression and taboo', *Health*, 2(4), 435–57.

Willis, P. (2000) *The Ethnographic Imagination*. Cambridge: Polity Press.

Willis, S. (1990) 'Work(ing) out', *Cultural Studies*, 4(1), 1–18.

Wise, S. (1987) 'A framework for discussing ethical issues in feminist research: a review of the literature', *Writing Feminist Biography*, 2, Studies in Sexual Politics, 19, 47–88.

Wollstonecraft, M. (1796) *A Vindication of the Rights of Woman*. London: J. Johnson.

Women Win Organisation, http://www.womenwin.org/#/mission, accessed 10 August 2009.

Yalom, M. (1999) *A History of the Breast*. New York, NY: Ballantine Books.

Yates, A. (1991) *Compulsive Exercise and the Eating Disorders: Toward an Integrated Theory of Activity*. New York, NY: Brunner/Mazel.

Young, I. (1990) *Throwing Like a Girl and Other Essays in Feminist Philosophy and Social Theory*. Bloomington, IN: Indiana University Press.

Young, I. (2005) *On Female Body Experience: Throwing Like a Girl and Other Essays* (2nd ed.). Oxford: Oxford University Press.

Young, K. (1993) *Planning Development with Women: Making a World of Difference*. London: Macmillan.

Index

Taylor & Francis

eBookstore

www.ebookstore.tandf.co.uk

Over 23,000 eBooks available for
individual purchase in Humanities,
Social Sciences, Behavioural Sciences
and Law from some of the world's
leading imprints.

*"An innovative
way of approaching electronic
books...Recommended."* – *Choice*

ALPSP Award for
BEST eBOOK
PUBLISHER
2009 Finalist
sponsored by

Taylor & Francis eBooks
Taylor & Francis Group

A flexible and dynamic resource for teaching, learning and research.

DATE DUE

MELCAT		
JAN - 2016		
		PRINTED IN U.S.A.

MARK & HELEN OSTERLIN LIBRARY
NORTHWESTERN MICHIGAN C
TRAVERSE CITY, MICHIGAN 49686-3061